REVIVAL

REVIVAL

Southern Writers
in the Modern City

Ted R. Spivey

University Presses of Florida
University of Florida Press / Gainesville

The poetry excerpts from *Collected Poems*, by Conrad Aiken (New York: Oxford University Press, 1953) are quoted with the permission of the publisher.

UNIVERSITY PRESSES OF FLORIDA is the central agency for scholarly publishing of the State of Florida's university system, producing books selected for publication by the faculty editorial committees of Florida's nine public universities: Florida A&M University (Tallahassee), Florida Atlantic University (Boca Raton), Florida International University (Miami), Florida State University (Tallahassee), University of Central Florida (Orlando), University of Florida (Gainesville), University of North Florida (Jacksonville), University of South Florida (Tampa), University of West Florida (Pensacola).

ORDERS for books published by all member presses of University Presses of Florida should be addressed to University Presses of Florida, 15 NW 15th Street, Gainesville, FL 32603.

Library of Congress Cataloging-in-Publication Data

Spivey, Ted Ray, 1927–
   Revival: southern writers in the modern city.

   Includes index.
   1. American literature—Southern States—History and criticism. 2. Cities and towns in literature.
3. Southern States in literature. 4. American literature—20th century—History and criticism.
5. City and town life in literature. I. Title.
PS261.S65   1986   810'.9'975   85-29507
ISBN 0-8130-0741-0 (alk. paper)

Printed in U.S.A. on acid-free paper

To my wife, Julie,
and to my friend Joseph K. Davis

Contents

Introduction

Twice in the recent past, national attention has focused on the South and its culture: after World War II, when industry began a large-scale move to the American South, and in the 1970s, when fuel bills shot up and many Americans found that they could no longer afford to put up with cold weather. Since 1970 the fate of the southern region and its culture has become a central issue not only because so many people are by choice or necessity moving south but also because the country is locked in a great economic struggle between the Sunbelt and the Snowbelt.

Never before, even during the Civil War and its immediate aftermath, has the question of what is happening in the South been so important. In fact, it is possible to say that since the Great Depression of the thirties a second civil war has been under way, and from this economic and social struggle is emerging a far different nation.

Since colonial days there has been a *Kulturkampf* (cultural struggle) between the two sections of the country. Many now presume the culture of the South to be dead, and some believe that the Sunbelt-Snowbelt conflict will fade because the South has already become very much like the North. But the idea of the two cultures becoming one has been shattered. New ways of life have emerged in the past thirty or forty years in the North, the South, and the West—ways of life based on new economic alignments and on the new megalopolitan city, the polyglot metropolis that John Kenneth Galbraith analyzes in *Age of Uncertainty* and that Oswald Spengler earlier made the center of his gloomily prophetic *Decline of the West*. Joel Garreau in *The Nine Nations of North America* deals with the effect of the megalopolis on the South and other American regions; in doing so he takes the view that America contains nine separate nations with the South the "most distinctive nation of all."[1]

The megalopolis of the South, in fact, is growing in ways different from the great cities of the North and West, but it is too early to foresee in which cultural direction each region's cities will move. It is an oversimplification to say that cities in America are becoming like either New York or Los Angeles. Cities in this country—and, for that matter, all over the world—may outwardly resemble these two urban centers, but one all-important factor causes each city to develop distinctively: its cultural heritage. In the late twentieth century cities in all regions of America are seeking means of renewing themselves that are often attempts to incorporate an inherited culture. Even as the forms of earlier culture decline, new cultural patterns emerge that are based in part on the earlier forms.

To speak of the death of southern culture without speaking of this movement toward cultural revival is to have only a superficial view. For example, one view of today's southern culture is that it is produced by TV and other media. Jack Temple Kirby's *Media-Made Dixie* takes this view, and Robert Penn Warren has expressed it in these words: "The rural South, my South, is vanishing. Because it was such an impoverished place, it was particularly vulnerable to having the TV culture superimposed right on top of it."[2]

The fact that many aspects of cultural life have almost disappeared can be seen in the worldwide growth of crime, violence, and institutional disruption. Culture has various definitions, but the most basic one is: a life-style that deals effectively with crime and violence and makes individual achievement possible. Culture allows for order to emerge while it checks violence sufficiently for life to proceed peacefully. The presence of culture curbs the force of boredom, which often inspires violence. In all of the arts, both major and minor, and in the cultural precepts contained in religion, education, government, and economic life, are found values that restrain man's violent impulses. Culture, as I will continue to suggest, is a way of life that, when fully operative, has the power to check the forces of destruction. As Lewis Mumford puts it, the task of culture is "man's supreme task—that of making himself human."[3]

Southerners have suffered from a decline of cultural values probably longer than Americans of any other region. The South's culture was so deeply threatened by the events that occurred before, during, and after the Civil War that southerners have often responded with anger to any critical analysis of their culture. Thus, serious southern writers of this century have often been attacked by fellow southerners for portraying the violence that attends the disintegration of southern culture. Faulkner and Williams have usually had better audiences in Europe than in their native region. Yet the novelist or poet probably knows better than anyone else where the real decay of his culture is located, and is often the first to notice signs of cultural revival. Moreover, the fact that southern literature is widely read throughout the world indicates that the serious southern writer is saying something universal about the decay of cultures. The agony of cultural decay, because it was felt earlier and by more people in the South than in other geographical areas of the United States, is more deeply embedded in southern writing than it is in most other American literature.

The most pervasive problem southerners have faced in their discussions of the southern life-style (see W. J. Cash, Richard Weaver, and W. A. Percy among writers of the earlier part of the century and more recently Robert Penn Warren and Walker Percy) is that the culture of the South has for many years been devalued by other Americans. For instance, a children's version of the *American Heritage of the Civil War* sums up the results of the Civil War as follows: "[The war] had destroyed one of the two American ways of life forever, and it had brought great changes to the other."[4] This view was commonly accepted by many: southern culture ceased to exist after the Civil War because the region was forced to imitate the lifestyle of the industry-centered North. Nevertheless, George Core, literary critic and editor of the *Sewanee Review,* wrote in 1970, "The South stubbornly remains an entity in its own right, even though it has been progressively affected by the modern temper."[5] In 1981 fifteen southern authors joined to produce a book entitled *Why the South Will Survive.* And in 1982 Louis D. Rubin, Jr., wrote in his introduction to *A Gallery of Southerners* that there "will continue to be good southern writing" because the "community identity is still there."[6]

The best art of Western civilization (southern literature included) speaks poignantly of the death of culture. Yet many of these works speak also of cultural rebirth, particularly works by southern writers. There is a danger that as we find ourselves drawn into literary and artistic visions of decay and death we fail to observe those visions of rebirth that signal the coming of new life-styles. The processes of dying and being reborn have often been represented simultaneously both in art and in human experience. In the South we see some cities attempting to find a new cultural basis—for example, Tampa, St. Petersburg, Jacksonville, San Antonio, and Houston, as well as older cultural centers like New Orleans, Charleston, and Savannah. I believe that this search for cultural revival in southern cities parallels the quest for new life by certain southern writers and that the work of these writers should be related to southern urban renewal. I have selected nine writers from the most important period of southern literature—1930 to the present—for this purpose.

The nine "core" writers are Ransom, Tate, Faulkner, Wolfe, Aiken, Williams, Ellison, O'Connor, and Percy. All show in their work a strong sense of the life, death, and rebirth of southern culture. All hold these three concepts in tension and present a vision of life that sees all three as operative in the life of southern culture in the twentieth century. All nine are internationally significant, all have definite links with one or more important southern cities, and all were influenced by the two writers of the modern world whose influence on the literature of civilized cultures has been most significant: James Joyce and T. S. Eliot. What these writers drew either directly or indirectly from Joyce and Eliot is what Eliot, writing about Joyce's *Ulysses,* calls the "mythical method." This method is directly related, as I will show, to the problem of the death and rebirth of culture.

I may seem to neglect three contemporary southerners who have had a growing impact not only on the literature of the region but on the life of the nation: Robert Penn Warren, Eudora Welty, and William Styron. None writes about the revival of culture, though all three write brilliantly about many aspects of southern life. None of the three is closely identified with any major southern city, nor does any have significant literary connections with the "mythical method" of Joyce and Eliot. Warren, though very much aware of the European masters, has nevertheless described himself as a naturalist who does not believe in God; for this reason he seems, as his literary career continues to develop in the eighties, a part of northern culture.[7] Welty, on the other hand, has deeply involved herself in southern rural and small-town life. Her work retains a vision of the richness, humor, and decay of southern life without ever seizing upon the theme of cultural rebirth. Styron, after his first novel, *Lie*

Down in Darkness, became, like Warren, a northern novelist rather than an artistic interpreter of the South.

Certain ideas explored in the chapters that follow will seem strange to many, mainly because for so long we have viewed the South as a rural Anglo-Saxon culture dominated in earlier times by rich planters and now by large economic and political organizations. In its American context and in the context of Western civilization, the South has never been essentially Anglo-Saxon but has always consisted of a mixture of people from the British Isles, France, Spain, and Africa, as well as Native Americans. And above all, the South is not a rural culture because it is a part of Western civilization, and all cultures of this civilization—as of any civilization—are built around urban cultural centers. Because from the beginning the South was, like the North, an urban-centered culture, agribusiness (and not simple agriculture) was the dominant force even in the early life of the region. Then, as now, economic and political institutions were dominant, but these institutions were upheld by values springing from the region's culture.

What follows in this book must be called an essay on culture, the city in its various aspects, and the southern writer. These views have been developed carefully over a long time, but, since they involve a projection into the future of a possible cultural revival, they are at times tentative. How I came to hold these views can be explained partly by my own regional cultural background as a southerner. An autobiographical element, I believe, is inevitably present when one writes about one's own culture. When I first studied at Emory University under Raymond Nixon, who had written the standard biography of Henry W. Grady at that time, I knew that I, like many other southerners, would have to write something someday about the South. After studying under Allen Tate and other southern professors of literature at the University of Minnesota, I still felt I had something to say about the South. I have been a teacher for more than twenty-five years in the heart of Atlanta and have come to feel that this city is an important part of the southern experience but that, with all its cultural and economic importance, it represents only one aspect of the South. My experience in the U.S. Navy carried me to an assortment of southern cities—New Orleans; Pensacola; Orange, Texas; and Bainbridge, Maryland. Everything in my life has conspired to immerse me personally in the South, and I now feel that I am just beginning to learn something about its culture.

After writing about and teaching southern literature for many

years, I began to see that southern culture could not have been centered around a plantation culture alone, in an era of expanding
capitalism; that the mainstream of southern agriculture has always
existed as a continuum with the southern urban center, although
Eugene Genovese maintains the contrary in his book *The Political
Economy of Slavery*. Southerners have had agribusiness at the center
of their lives since King Carter's complicated operations began on
the James River shortly after 1607 and since the Drayton family established itself in Charleston in 1671. I also came to see that a book
I admired, W. J. Cash's *The Mind of the South,* was, in spite of its insights, wrong in depicting the yeoman farmer as the center of the
South. There is never one center of a culture, because culture is
what provides the context for the many elements that make up a
society. This is in fact the chief contemporary definition of culture
that I use in this study. American anthropologist Clifford Geertz
defined *culture* as a "context, something within which they ["events,
behavior, institutions, or processes"] can be intelligibly—that is
thickly—described."[8] Thus, to understand the South as a regional
culture within the larger framework of American culture, I have
sought to observe both the unity of that culture and the breakup of
that unity into the individual values that have gradually been dying.

As I studied the South, I came to see that one cannot learn to
transcend one's own cultural orientation. My view of the unity of
southern culture is based largely on two events: I was born and
spent my early years on the Florida Atlantic coast, and I later moved
to Georgia with my parents and lived near the Georgia coast. Everything I read about the cultural history of the South seemed to come
from a viewpoint other than my own, usually one having to do with
large plantations or fair-sized cities. When I read *Children of Pride*,
Robert Manson Myers's collection of letters written by the Jones
family of Liberty County, Georgia, I was reminded again of the
rural-urban South I had experienced, centered in the commerce of
the sea, with ties to Charleston and Virginia. Knowing about this
South of the Atlantic seaboard seemed to clarify something not explained in other books I had read. As I will suggest in some detail
in the next chapter, I think the chief cornerstones of culture in the
South, even in the upland pioneer areas, were such centers as Baltimore, Williamsburg, Charleston, Savannah, and St. Augustine on
the Atlantic, Mobile and New Orleans on the Gulf of Mexico.

I found in my study of the South that community really does
mean "common unity," and when one element of community con-

siders itself the central and only necessary element the union begins to fall apart. Yet communities have continually declined and
risen again as individuals sought a revival of communal values. The
revival of values presupposes a determined battle with (and triumph over) the malign element that undermines the content of
culture.

The malign element that destroys cultural unity, according to
Arnold Toynbee, is a kind of narcissism that causes certain classes
in a society to "rest on their oars" because they believe they have
reached a peak of performance beyond which they cannot go. "A
fatuous passivity towards the present," Toynbee writes, "springs
from an infatuation with the past, and this infatuation is the sin of
idolatry."[9] Idolizing the past, Toynbee goes on to say, results in a
schism of the body politic and the soul. The possessing classes of
the antebellum South, living off agribusiness, had clearly reached
such a condition on the eve of the Civil War, and many events that
followed in the New South directly resulted from the rise of other
groups who were still able to move into the future, free of the grip
of a narcissistic view of the past. Through the period of American
commercial and industrial expansion that followed the Civil War,
the South, joining in this expansion, maintained a kind of cultural
unity. In fact, the South after World War II moved into a new period of its history that has not been recognized as such until recently. Walker Percy has fully grasped the meaning of this new period; in a 1979 essay in *Harper's*, Percy outlines the major aspects of
this period: the dominance of the sprawling great cities like Atlanta
and Houston as a result of two interdependent events, the agricultural revolution that forced all but a few out of rural areas, and,
with the advent of civil rights legislation, the removal of race as the
major obsession of the region. Journalists have long been proclaim-
ing a series of "New Souths," but only Percy has shown in detail, in
essays and in fiction, what happened after the decline of the historical period first proclaimed as the "New South" by Henry W.
Grady in 1886.

The period after 1945 I distinguish from the New South by the
tentative title of the "restored South," a region restored to the nation as a whole, no longer a region proud of its separateness. This
restoration, which began in the thirties with Roosevelt's New Deal
and the agricultural revolution, followed by racial conflict and the
growth of large cities, is generally regarded positively, and its creative aspects have helped inspire in one way or another all of the

writers I discuss. And yet, being serious writers in the literary tradition of the Western world, these writers are concerned with the agony of cultural decay, which they see as the prime fact of modern
life. This agony for most modern writers springs largely from the
decline of old cultural values and the painful quest for replacement
values in the sprawling new cities, often hidden inside the uncontrollable megalopolis. Some found amid the exploding growth of
New York the remains of an old cultural center that helped to inspire them in their artistic efforts. Others returned to the South
and found in old cities like New Orleans or Savannah the still potent seeds of culture that served to inspire new values. Still others
went to the new university cities to seek possibilities of cultural revival. Finally, some saw in the new cities of the South signs of new
cultural development and were thus prompted in their search for
new life to write about their inherited vision of cultural decay. In
fact, one of the differences between the New South and the restored South is that many literary artists—Reynolds Price at Duke
University or Harry Crews at the University of Florida, for example—find cultural sustenance in southern cities and universities
and do not feel compelled to live in cosmopolitan centers. As I hope
to demonstrate, the response of southern writers to the modern city
is complicated by the variety of types of cities, a variety that is often
obscured by our contemporary obsession with megalopolises.

Encountering the modern city, serious southern writers inevitably seek their own visions of a new cultural unity; their visions,
however, are often unrecognized by those readers and critics who
see only the depiction of cultural decay. Fortunately, contemporary
students of culture accept the views of many disciplines—biology,
anthropology, history, psychology, and now even literature and philosophy. As historian George B. Tindall has suggested, poets have
fared better than historians in expressing the sense of oneness in
the South.[10] In an age when some kind of unity or context for values must be sought, writers' visions of the possibility of cultural
unity in the South are particularly significant. But writers also record their own and others' attempts to breathe new life into those
human values that decline as cultural unity gradually disappears.
To be meaningful, values must be lived out fully. Simply honoring
values by making abstract statements about them is not enough. For
cultural values to function, a cultural context must exist that inspires individuals to realize fully the basic values of a society.

Louis D. Rubin, Jr., has written that "genuine human communities, as opposed to economic societies, are rare commodities in the modern world."[11] Rubin and other writers have continued to call attention to southern communal values while writers like Jack Temple Kirby note that since World War II, "the South has become urbanized, standardized, neonized."[12] Kirby focuses only on the economic and entertainment aspects of modern society; like so many others, he tends to see not the southern community but rather southern economic structures, which since 1945 have come to resemble those of the rest of the nation. The Sunbelt-Snowbelt controversy is of course largely economic, but it also continues a cultural struggle. Although seemingly won by the North in 1865, this struggle was renewed after 1945 as the South gained economic muscle and found a new belief in its own culture.

It remains necessary for southern writers and historians to insist that the South actually has something important to contribute to the nation. Journalists such as John Egerton and Joel Garreau have continued to assert that little of importance remains of southern culture itself, but after 1970 historians like William C. Havard, more careful in their assessments, tell us that "every time the death knell for the distinct South seems about to ring, the hand at the toll ropes is stayed by a resurgence of vital signs."[13] George B. Tindall puts the matter even more succinctly: "It is not the South that has vanished but the mainstream."[14] With the decline of mainstream America after 1960, industrial areas of the nation have begun to offer their own regional values as necessary ingredients for the creation of a new mainstream. Thus it is inevitable that a struggle of rival economies like the Snowbelt (which sometimes calls itself the Brainbelt) and the Sunbelt would also be a struggle between rival value systems. When Rubin spoke of the genuine human community of the South, he was affirming those values that are related to a sense of cooperation and that are still found in the southern region.

Communal cooperation is, I believe, the greatest surviving southern cultural value. Communal values are important not only in what we call life-style but in economic competition as well. For instance, in 1982 the employees of a major airline headquartered in Atlanta took up a collection at a time when profits were declining and bought the company a 747 jetliner. Many observers noted that this would probably not have happened in northern industry, where employees' attitudes toward work are much less collective. Parallels between communal southern industries and Japanese industry were cited at the time. However, I believe it is necessary to be some-what more cautious than Rubin, Charles Roland, Grady McWhiney, and others who have expressed qualified optimism about living southern values. Emphasis should be placed primarily on the con-tinuing need to revive values in order to check the destructiveness attendant upon the inevitable barbarism that fills the vacuum left by a dying culture. Lived cultural values can spring only from genuine community, not from mere social collectives.

With emphasis placed on the central need for cultural revival, the regional cultures of this and other nations will find cooperation much more profitable than struggle. Before the American Revolu-tion the southern and northern colonies struggled with each other as they forged similar but different cultures, yet their cooperation made victory over the British possible and, more importantly, led to a new American culture. The South learned much from the North about values related to education and the concepts of egalitarian-ism and individualism; it passed on to the North values relating to community and hierarchy, particularly in the political arena but also in the communal arts of music, architecture, and cooking. The third great American area—the West—also has its own particular values and its influence on the nation continues to increase.

At this juncture, I believe that certain southern writers have more to offer the nation concerning the problem of cultural revival than any other literary hierarchs of our time. They realize how long and arduous the process of reviving values can be. Inheriting from southern history a sense of defeat and tragedy as well as a belief in man's basic imperfection, they are quick to turn away from the easy solutions that many Americans, caught up in journalistic clichés, have so often sought. The West is the region where the easy solu-tion often prevails, and the North since 1945 has tended to follow the lead of Los Angeles or San Francisco. For instance, the counter-culture movement of the sixties had its true headquarters in Cali-fornia. Its adherents saw that America needed cultural revival but their solutions were often puerile. One of them, Theodore Roszak, wrote in the late sixties: "In an historical emergency of absolutely unprecedented proportions, we are that strange, culture-bound animal whose biological drive for survival expresses itself *genera-tionally*. It is the young, arriving with eyes that can see the obvious, who must remake the lethal culture of their elders and who must remake it in desperate haste."[15] No important southern writer would have proclaimed the young as the cultural saviors of the nation, nor would any have said that culture could ever be remade in haste. And none would ever have referred to the human being as an animal.

Southern writers still have a strong sense of myth and history that is lacking in most modern writers. They are also aware of the continuing power of two forces in southern society—community and hierarchy. Above all, I believe, they have encountered more deeply than many other writers the modern city in its many forms as well as the problems of industrialism and commercialism connected with the modern megalopolis. Southern writers, unlike so many others, have faced the challenge of the great city but have also had the courage to hold on to their southern heritage. They have refused to be rootless and have therefore achieved visions of the possibility of cultural revival. How they achieved them is the subject of the chapters that follow.

1

The City and the Quest for
Cultural Values

Like literary artists throughout Western civilization, many southern writers in the early twentieth century went to large cities to practice their art in order to escape increasing narcissistic and solipsistic tendencies in the provinces. To a greater extent than most other Western cultures the provinces of the South were caught up in an encompassing narcissism, a result of the persistent tendency of southern cultural leaders to look back to the largely imagined glory of the antebellum past. As Arnold Toynbee, Pitirim Sorokin, and other scholar-philosophers have noted, all of Western society after 1800 surrendered to an ever-increasing narcissism. Western culture, Sorokin tells us, became a "sensate" way of life based not so much on fundamental values of culture as on surface images, primarily on the images of imagined collective and individual greatness.[1] One outcome of the growing cultural narcissism was a collision of rival narcissistic cultures that resulted in World War I, the one event that more than any other brought to fruition the modernist movement in the arts.

As early as the mid-nineteenth century serious artists throughout the world had become aware of the decline of values brought about by narcissism and by the attitude that often accompanied such narcissism, puritanism. Narcissism in its extreme form, as analyzed by Christopher Lasch in *Culture of Narcissism* (1979), becomes solip-

sism. Eventually an ever-increasing narcissism threatens that group
cooperation necessary for the life of societies, and a reaction sets in
that takes the form of an enforced moralism, often called puritanism. After 1830 provincial societies even in advanced countries like
France, England, and Germany were dogged by the growing tyranny of a stifling moralism, or Victorianism, as it came to be called
in England. Minor artistic talents often clung to the provincial setting, becoming regional artists; but for most major talents after
1850 the cities beckoned as refuges from a moralism that threatened all new artistic endeavor. Cities offered the artist a freedom to
experiment not found in the provinces. As Gertrude Stein once put
it, what mattered was not so much what Paris gave the artist as what
it did not take away. In great cities like Paris, London, Berlin, and
New York, artists found the freedom to search for a revival of serious artistic values. When such herculean figures as Stravinsky,
Picasso, Rodin, Joyce, Yeats, and Gropius brought forth art forms
that were truly modern, they found that they had in fact challenged
values in many areas other than the arts. Above all, they found that
the integrity of the human being had been challenged by rapid scientific and technological advances. In 1900 Henry Adams maintained that the chief symbol of civilization was the dynamo and not,
as in the past, the more human symbol of the Virgin Mary. Adams,
like other modern philosophers and artists, saw the need for the
revival of those humanistic and cultural values related to the full
development of individuals so that humans would not feel dwarfed
by their technological creations.

Robert Langbaum, in *Mysteries of Identity* (1977), maintains that
the primary task of the great modern writer is "reconstituting" the
twentieth-century self. For Langbaum the loss of human identity is
the great modern problem: "Both Yeats and Lawrence, in their attempts to reconstitute the twentieth-century self, take into account
the two opposite manifestations of lost identity—solipsism and collectivism."[2] Solipsism, as Lasch suggests, results from a pervasive
narcissism that finally isolates individuals from each other, whereas
collectivism, or totalitarianism, as Yeats called it, arises largely from
the demands of a large number of people for a morality given and
enforced by a dictatorship. Hannah Arendt and others have shown
how totalitarianism flourishes in societies where the majority of
people have little or no personal identity. The gradual loss of identity springs from both solipsism and the absence of a sense of the
individual self and its relationship to others. The self, in fact, can-

not believe in its own value without taking into account human relationship, as Langbaum suggests by quoting the psychologist Erik A. Erikson: "Societies create the only conditions under which human growth is possible."[3] The great artist then is called, along with other cultural leaders, to combat what Lasch calls the dominant syndrome of this century—the narcissistic-solipsistic syndrome—because, as Langbaum puts it, "No values or persons seem to the solipsist real or important enough to be worth the sacrifice or even postponement of one's own gratification."[4]

Langbaum's importance lies primarily in his analysis of new cultural forms on which creative societies may be built. Thus he counters the pessimism of Lasch, who sees narcissism as a personal and social cancer whose growth is seemingly impossible to check. Actually, of course, artists and other cultural leaders throughout the nineteenth and twentieth centuries have continually fought narcissism-solipsism and the dissolution of human values it brings about. The results of their efforts can in fact still be observed. I take these efforts to be part of the cultural renewal that Sorokin speaks of when he refutes Oswald Spengler's gloomy followers, saying that the "alleged death agony" of civilization has been but "the birth pangs of a new form of culture, the travail attending the release of new creative form."[5]

Possibly the greatest achievement of Western civilization since 1750 has been the ability of its various societies to discover new values as well as to revive old ones. For this reason, even more than for its science and technology, the West is imitated by all of the major societies of the world. Chinese musicians, for example, risk imprisonment to play Western music, and Japanese readers form groups to study William Faulkner or Thomas Hardy. Certain nations of the West have declined into totalitarianism, but evidence of meaningful Western cultural renewal since 1800 is revealed by the fact that major nations like Britain, France, and America—and many smaller ones also—have avoided totalitarianism and social disintegration (which always go together) by maintaining the spirit of freedom and creativity, by keeping an "open society," as Karl Popper has called such nations. One of the chief reasons for this growth is that the great cities have remained open to artistic experimentation and new ideas and have resisted the rigid puritanism of the provinces. Modern artists and philosophers put aside Victorianism without sinking into moral anarchy; they explored and revived human values and formed a new chapter in the development of cultural values even as much of Western culture was disintegrating. The best modern artists were witnesses to the enormous inhumanity and acts of violence of a century that is now regarded as a major transitional period in human history—transitional, let us hope (and as Sorokin maintains) to a new age of cultural formation.

All I have written thus far about modern artists and their encounter with the great city can be said of the nine significant southern writers I have chosen to examine. But these southerners, all of whom were deeply influenced by modern cities as well as by the great universities connected with them, also turned to the South to examine the culture of their region. In fact, they saw more clearly than many other artists, particularly other American artists, that the great cities exacted an enormous price in loss of cultural values and that the vision of creative freedom they offered was sometimes dimmed by those megalopolitan aspects of great cities about which Spengler writes. Modern literary artists as diverse as Baudelaire and Matthew Arnold, of course, have dealt with the numbing effect of cities like Paris and London, but they seldom have shown any awareness of values other than those of the great city itself. Major southern writers, on the other hand, even when they were most at war with the South, maintained a belief in certain cultural values that they absorbed from their native region. The two chief values they cling to, I suggest, are community-centeredness and hierarchy. Even when, like Wolfe or Ellison, the southern writer does not return to his native heath, he still maintains those values—and his adopted city is in part judged by them. Indeed, in the case of a writer like Wolfe, as Paschal Reeves has pointed out, the experience of extreme individualism in New York brings forth a vision of not only a southern but also an American community awareness. Wolfe was first drawn to Harvard and then to New York because he hoped to find a hierarchal leadership that would enable him to become a literary artist, but when he encountered the extreme individualism of megalopolitan New York he reacted by returning to his deeply held southern values and by bringing forth in his later works visions of communal existence. Wolfe and other southerners found in New York the remnants of an old cultural center that for a time provided hierarchal leadership, but they also found the megalopolitan individualistic spirit of urban sprawl.

Although largely disowned by southern writers of the Agrarian tradition, Thomas Wolfe is in fact typical of most of the better-known southern writers of this century. His sense of hierarchy not only drew him to the cultural values found in great cities like New York, London, and Berlin; it also led him to accept the influence of professors in two universities, North Carolina and Harvard. In fact, the university and its surrounding city have had in this century probably as much influence on southern writers as the great city itself. Universities like Vanderbilt and North Carolina played important roles in freeing many southerners from the grip of southern narcissism and puritanism. Like Wolfe, the Agrarians encountered a small center of culture in a southern university; and many went from Vanderbilt to other American universities as well as some of the great cities of the world. Some, like Wolfe, chose to live in the North, others returned to the South. Most of the Agrarians, like other southern writers, struggled to retain the old southern emphasis on certain cultural values like community-centeredness and to acquire at the same time the values of other regions and countries. Although some, like Warren and Styron, ceased to be southern in their outlook, most of the major writers remained stubbornly southern, often to the point of returning to live in the South and struggling with the problems they found there. They became, in a sense, revivers of culture in the South by reviving certain cultural values within themselves and then, as teachers and writers, helping others to revive these values, particularly in the realm of higher education.

The hierarchal attitude of southerners in regard to higher education meant that their attutude toward culture was largely shaped by the humanistic tradition of letters as handed down by professors who upheld a literary continuum from Shakespeare to Tennyson and Arnold. Southern writers went beyond their professors by accepting as their chief literary hierarchs such moderns as James Joyce and T. S. Eliot; several in their roles as professors and critics helped to bring these and other esteemed modern writers into the canon of Anglo-American letters. In fact, what they had learned about English literature prepared them for the emergence of Joyce and Eliot as literary leaders. After all, these southerners, particularly in the realm of culture and literary criticism, harked back to a tradition that began with Goethe, Wordsworth, and Coleridge, all of whom saw the need to restore cultural values in order to restore true community.

Wordsworth declared in his best poetry that visions of harmony leading to emotions of joy and love were necessary for a true restoration of community; his friend Coleridge, in his influential essays, proclaimed the need for the development of the imagination to allow humans to glimpse the essence underlying matter—essence, according to Coleridge, that was based on harmony and organic form and that gave meaning to all life. Culture was also a matter of personal development for the romantics. According to Arnold, in his famous essay "Sweetness and Light" in *Culture and Anarchy,* "Culture places human perfection in an *internal* condition, in the growth and predominance of our humanity proper, as distinguished from our animality. . . . Faith in machinery [is] our besetting danger."[6] Obsessions with material objects, Arnold says, can keep us from our true cultural activity, the quest for "the peace and satisfaction which are reached as we draw near to complete spiritual perfection, and not merely to moral perfection."[7] Yeats, whose ideas influenced Joyce and Eliot, emphasizes in his criticism the "return to imagination" and to "organic rhythms, which are the embodiment of the imagination."[8] For Yeats, as Richard Ellmann points out, unity of being was the most significant cultural value. In all of these injunctions of the romantic and neoromantic critics there was always an emphasis on moving forward toward a deeper personal life that denied the claims of both narcissism and materialism. This refined personal life was based on spiritual growth, an idea that attacked the puritan belief in the supremacy of morality as the great human good.

Southern writers in their hierarchal conservatism also held to Shakespeare and the Bible, as well as to certain tenets basic to the Judeo-Christian tradition, the chief of which is the primacy of love in the hierarchy of values. Love of God and neighbor have traditionally been for Christians and Jews the chief commandments, and love is considered to be the fulfillment of God's law. I do not mean to suggest that only southerners were aware of the need for love. One of the great themes of both nineteenth- and twentieth-century literature is love in all its various forms. In a wide-ranging study of literature since 1800, *The Romantic Heroic Ideal* (1982), James D. Wilson writes about love and voluntary cooperation: "In America, then, it was possible to see solipsism as antithetical to that kind of voluntary cooperation among citizens demanded by emergent democracies."[9] Wilson goes on to claim that "love can be for the hero a potentially redemptive force, but not if it is narcissistic."[10] Narcissism and puritanism continue into this century, and their presence encourages many writers to demand a principle that will bind people together. Jung wrote, late in his life, "The free society needs a bond of an affective nature, a principle of a kind like *caritas,* the Christian love of your neighbor." He follows this injunction with an even more pointed statement: "Where love stops, power begins, and violence and terror."[11]

Northern writers have been just as aware of the need for *caritas* as southern writers, although southern writers think of love in terms of a particular community, their own, and in terms of a hierarchal tradition of letters, with Shakespeare and the Bible representing the fountainhead of that tradition. Northern writers in this century, like southern writers, have sought the freedom of the great city in order to escape provincial puritanism, but they have often tended to become exiles in megalopolis before moving on to join artistic enclaves. The great southern writers, even when living in the North, have linked themselves to the southern community. Northern writers let go of much of the past, but southern writers at their best have continued to work out of their cultural heritage. A sense of the past as well as an awareness of the need for community drew the best southern writers to Joyce and Eliot. In these two writers they found men who could carry on the Anglo-American literary tradition and at the same time accept new concepts of mythology that grew out of James Frazer's *The Golden Bough.* It was Eliot's mythical method that enabled southern writers to discover their cultural roots.

The struggles of southern writers with the complexities of myth led them to understand the hidden and often misunderstood depths of their own culture. These struggles led them past pseudo-myths like that of the story of the great white mansion, which concentrated on the plantation splendors of the South. They were often able to discern the usefulness as well as the limitations of social myths like those connected with the Old South and the New South. But above all, the mythical method led them to look more deeply at the values of their own culture, to see how many of these values were dying, and to bring forth visions of cultural rebirth that were related to that revival of values necessary for individual and community existence. Through myth they hoped to find again the hidden unity—or context, in the anthropological sense—that lends coherence to a revived culture. With myth they could fight the forces of narcissism, puritanism (in the sense of fanatical moralism), and an ever-growing collectivism. But before I seek to define myth as it was developed in the work of Joyce and Eliot and then passed on to the southern writers, it is necessary to look briefly at that hier-

archal, community-oriented culture which these writers inherited
and which their work, in one sense, was dedicated to reviving.

The South has suffered from stereotyping more than most cultures
of the Western world. The most pervasive stereotypes depict either
a rural paradise or a rural hell. Actually, because of its close connections with Europe the South has been traditionally one of the most
cosmopolitan regions in the nation.

Close examination of a society that is considered to have origi-
nated in a plantation economy reveals that the region's tobacco and
rice plantations served in part as a sieve through which culture
passed from Europe to the people of the early South. These plantations, however, were not part of either paradise or hell but rather
part of an urban-rural continuum that included both New World
and Old World cities and communal towns. They were part of what
we would call today agribusiness. Owners of the first great plantations that became the models for the later upcountry plantations
spent much of their lives in urban communities and traveled as ex-
tensively as their incomes permitted. Carl Bridenbaugh, discussing
the differences between the Chesapeake gentry and the Carolina
gentry, points to money as the central factor in the early development of what we now call the Deep South: "Unlike the illusory
wealth of the Chesapeake gentry, that of the Carolinians was real;
for its time, it was the big money. Upon favored possessors it con-
ferred a precious endowment of abundant leisure and the coveted
privilege of living in the city, at the same time that it sucked dry the
rural low country." Yet, as Bridenbaugh shows, this early foundation of the Deep South was not based on a "grasping materialism"
but instead was "circumscribed by a still powerful aristocratic tradition with a clear-cut standard of taste." What regulated behavior
was "status, accepted as a yardstick." [12] Thus the social hierarchy of
Britain extended into the South from earliest times.

The most important element of southern culture has always been
the urban center. The European settlements in the American South
were urban-based, beginning with the city of St. Augustine in 1565
and continuing in 1607 with Jamestown and later Williamsburg,
Charleston (1670), New Orleans (1718), and Savannah (1733). The
most important characteristic of the southern urban center, as
Bridenbaugh suggests, was that it maintained a lifeline to certain
European metropolises. This fact has continued to be important

and accounts for a sometimes unexpected cosmopolitanism as well as a European-style decadence in the personalities of people who have lived at the center of southern culture. Brownell and Goldfield explain the position of the southern city in the British trade system: "Southern cities in the colonial period were basically creatures of British mercantilism. Their markets were defined by trade laws emanating from London and their very existence was in part the result of British colonial designs. In a 'typical' colonial economy, southern cities functioned as market centers for agricultural products destined for final processing in the mother metropolis." From its beginnings in colonial days the South, as Brownell and Goldfield indicate, was an urban-rural continuum: "The close interdependence with agriculture became a characteristic feature of southern urban growth." [13]

The majority of people who created the northern and western cultures of America thought of themselves as leaving behind the evils of Europe, carrying with them a few old ideas and techniques; but in the South there were always strong ties with the Old World that were never denied—that were, on the contrary, cherished. One of the many evidences of this is that little "isolationism" has ever existed in the South. In World Wars I and II southerners of all classes led the nation in volunteering to fight in Europe.

The second most important fact about the South and the one least understood is its kinship with the French and Spanish cultures in the New World. In his study *Myths and Realities: Societies of the Colonial South,* Bridenbaugh deals only with the Chesapeake and Carolina societies, ignoring the fact that the colonial South also included Florida and Texas of the Spanish colonial empire and Louisiana of the French colonial empire. The South is the least white—Anglo-Saxon—Protestant culture of the three major cultures of the United States. Like the French and the Spanish, southerners—many of whom in fact were French and Spanish—became deeply involved with large African and native American populations. Northerners and westerners, with a few notable exceptions, kept Indians and blacks at a great distance. The English throughout the world have always feared "going native," and this psychic fear was deep both in the Puritan forefathers who stayed at home and in those who went west.

The English element in the South, to be sure, has always been strong; and the southerner shares many attitudes with his northern countrymen. But existing side by side with "Englishness" in the southerner is that Latin element absorbed from the beginning by contacts with the Spanish in Florida and the West Indies and with the French in South Carolina and Louisiana. The "Englishness" of Southerners led them to hide from others and sometimes even from themselves their blood connections with Indians and blacks. These hidden connections are so vital and underestimated that I will return to deal with them at length later; it is impossible, for example, to understand much of William Faulkner's work without taking them into account.

The branding of the South as Protestant—and for many non-southern intellectuals it is indeed a brand—is a mistake, as much so as supposing that the South is basically white and Anglo-Saxon. The North and the West, until recently, were Protestant cultures, but the South began as a Catholic culture, both Roman Catholic and Anglo-Catholic, and, in a general religious sense, remained so, despite the rural Protestant elements. The Spanish and the French—even the Huguenots—brought with them a religious vision that was deeply bound to medieval Catholicism. And the settlers at Jamestown, Charleston, and Savannah brought with them an Anglicanism that had the imprimatur of the liturgical Catholicism of a conservative queen, Elizabeth I. Even Methodism began in America as a society within the Church of England; Francis Asbury, first bishop of the Methodist church, sought to preserve the hierarchal tradition in Anglicanism by keeping the title of bishop. Even the Baptists, and various Pentecostal sects both black and white, preserved in their religious life a lavish and sometimes outlandish communalism that is not found in the individualistic Protestantism of the North and West.

Two terms sum up the southern culture better than any others: community-centeredness and hierarchy. The southern emphasis of the community over the individual has its roots not only in the religiosity of the culture but also in the strong influences of the tribal life of Africans and Indians on the South. In fact, Bridenbaugh has said that in the colonial life of the Chesapeake and Carolina societies the "Negro supplied to each society its common determining human element."[14] As for hierarchy, the fact that the South was in many ways an extension of European society made southerners respect all the trappings of the hierarchal, aristocratic way of life that dominated Europe until the twentieth century. One who persists in thinking of the South as an Anglo-Saxon culture should study how the Irish and the Highland Scots—both groups that were originally

Catholic, communal, and persecuted by the English and the Protestant Scots—found a way of life in the South that held a profound attraction for them. They and the Spanish, the French, the Africans, the Indians, the English Catholics, and the Anglicans finally combined to make a way of life far more complex than that society called to mind by clichés having to do with white mansions and backwoods Protestantism.

Many reasons can be found for the misunderstanding that non-southern Americans have about the South. In fact, southerners often feel they are better understood by Europeans than they are by other Americans—partly because most other Americans broke many of their ties with Europe, whereas those people who lived at the center of southern culture carefully cultivated their European roots. There is an even more important reason for these misunderstandings, one which has to do with several of the major social myths of America. The three great cultures of the United States have each been represented by certain myths. The North early became associated with mechanical inventiveness and self-improvement; it has since become the site of the largest financial-industrial complex in the world. The mythology of the West has dealt with shaping and harnessing natural forces and with containing and eliminating destructive human beings who exploited nature for personal gain—that is, with bringing "law and order" to untamed man and nature. The southern social myth centers around the plantation, which represented the union of the advantages of urban and rural life in order to bring European patterns of hierarchy and community to the New World. But the myth of the plantation has too often taken the form of what I call the story of the great white mansion, which deals with a house located in an idyllic natural setting replete with happy slaves and resplendent lords and ladies. An opposing myth of the South as one large concentration camp was bound to arise in reaction to these magnolia-blossom stories.

The chief social myths of a society by no means sum up all of the life, good and bad, of that society, but they do contain most of its major tasks, or missions, as a society, and therein lies much of their value. A culture that has no mission loses a sense of cohesiveness and dies unless new tasks are found. The failures associated with the southern mission were possibly greater and certainly more obvious than those of the North and West. For example, the failures of plantation life yielded stories of effete "ladies and gentlemen," on one hand, and of slave-driving fanatics on the other.

Pseudo-myth always gathers in clusters around true myth and eventually, according to Gresham's Law, drives it from the intellectual and the cultural marketplace. The Horatio Alger stories of the North, the dime novels of western banditry, and the moonlight-and-magnolia sagas—all pseudo-myths of America—have had great effect on huge audiences. Harmless at best, they become dangerous when taken literally. The southern pseudo-myths, which have a far more ridiculous quality about them than those of the other two regions, have often been taken literally by many Americans who passionately admire or hate southern culture.

The historical background of the southern pseudo-myths shows why they have led to such profound misunderstanding, even animosity, about the South. The aim of the Chesapeake settlers to create something like the English country estates (which were always closely connected with the life of London) and the phenomenon of the plantations of the Deep South (which were also urban-oriented) was never understood by early northern Protestants. This misunderstanding goes back to hostility during and before Reformation and Counter-Reformation wars between northern and southern Europe.

Since the days of Greek and Roman culture, agricultural and urban life-styles have always been more intimately connected in southern Europe than in northern Europe, which was not as strongly influenced by Roman culture. This difference continued into American colonial days, when anything Spanish was considered the devil's handiwork. Later many northerners and westerners looked at the South the way most English colonials looked at Spanish America, seeing only a society of decadent aristocrats tyrannizing a debased slave population—the sort of vision of Latin America we find in Herman Melville's story "Benito Cerino."

Henry Adams, one of America's most perceptive students of culture, found the South like another world. In *The Education of Henry Adams* (1907), he describes his visit to Mount Vernon. His usually acute mind could not square the greatness of George Washington with the place he was seeing, the meaning of which lay beyond his historical imagination and understanding. His mental confusion was representative of how deeply the North and South misunderstood each other in the nineteenth century. A culture is measured in part by those people in it who rise to eminence. This fact Adams could not accept; for him Washington could not be a part of the South. Yet no one who sprang from southern culture represented its eighteenth-century leadership better than George and Martha Washington. Not that they were typical; they simply epitomized a period of southern culture when Virginia led the South, in the way that Louis XIV personified French culture in the late seventeenth century. Stories about Washington, some real and some apocryphal, became an important part of southern as well as American mythology. Washington and his wife had the fine sense of hierarchy typical of the colonial South and also a sense of community not readily understood today, because since their day it has been assumed that the hierarchal patrician is aloof from the demands of community. It was neither Washington's intellect nor his money nor his ability to command soldiers that held together a community of soldiers and later a young nation, but simply his character, as Thomas Jefferson pointed out—the kind of character that made most Americans feel reverence and awe in his presence. Like all people, Washington had more weaknesses than history can properly record, but, like the early Spanish conquerers, the strength of his personality enabled him to do the work the times demanded. Like the Spanish conquerers, Washington was torn between the good life on an estate and the ambition that drove him into worldly affairs. In a 1976 biography of Washington, Noemie Emery describes the father of the nation: "There was no choice ever for the shy and driven half brother for whom fame and service, duty and ambition were inextricably interwoven and set into his bones and blood. His intermittent efforts at 'retirement' . . . were recuperations, repair between exertions, the background for his efforts and the repair for his belief."[15]

The South, as I have already suggested, has been fortunate to possess a literature that is one of the most acclaimed in the twentieth century. What has generally not been understood is that much of this literature is closely connected with the development of the modern urban centers in the South. In fact, the role of the urban center in both southern literature and southern culture has been ignored. The chief reason the southern urban centers have not received the kind of study they deserve is that the only urban center considered to be a true city by many people in the late twentieth century is the megalopolis, what John Kenneth Galbraith has more recently termed the "polyglot metropolis." Only very recently have we seen cities like Atlanta, Memphis, Houston, Dallas, and Miami turning into smaller versions of New York. Faulkner and O'Connor depicted Memphis and Atlanta as cities whose growth was shapeless, thereby signifying at least some of the chaos of megalopolis.

However, cities such as Savannah, Charleston, Richmond, San Antonio, Memphis, and New Orleans are now exploring the possibilities of participating in cultural renewal instead of allowing their inner cities to become museums surrounded by a polyglot metropolitan sprawl; we see more and more in the seventies and eighties a search for the role that inner cities can play in the cultural development of a region. Galbraith has contributed to the study of cities as types in his *Age of Uncertainty*, noting that in addition to the polyglot metropolis there are also the governmental city, the merchant city, the industrial city, and the bedroom city. What is still needed, however, is a contemporary concept of the American cultural city. Studies of the Italian Renaissance, for instance, have for many years dealt with certain European cities as cultural centers, but Americans have never believed in themselves as creators of urban cultural centers. When sophisticated Americans like Franklin, Jefferson, Henry James, or T. S. Eliot have sought urban culture, they have often turned to Europe. The continuing influence of European culture is responsible for causing southerners to seek ways in which the city can be made a center of cultural development.

American individualism and the myth of the frontier have made Americans in many cases forget the meaning of the city as a cultural center. Frederick Jackson Turner and other mythographers of American history would have us believe that the frontier is the dominant fact of American life. The experiences and stories of Americans living on the frontier have of course been an important part of American life; their importance should never be underestimated. But the frontier is not the dominant fact of cultural life in this country. Indeed, the frontier itself loses all meaning (except as the expression of individualism) unless it is seen as a part of the expansion of America to the Pacific coast.

The reason that the frontier has always held such sway over critics of America is that it was the place where two great dramas could be acted out. In fact, the entire New World was thought by many to be made for these dramas. The first is the exploitation of resources, both environmental and human. *Exploitation* sounds harsh to those who prefer the word *development*. But the idea behind this drama, call it what one will, is simply to strike it rich, either quickly (by finding gold or seizing someone else's) or, in a more extended manner, by setting up great estates and factories and marshaling huge labor gangs to create wealth. The other drama that is always present, sometimes as a reaction against the first, is the search for complete freedom from the demands or even the help of others, for the achievement of self-sufficiency as envisioned by Thoreau in *Walden* or by Emerson in "Self-Reliance." Huck Finn's story is a great mythic statement of this drama of the quest for a freedom beyond the demands of society, just as Daniel Boone's is a real-life version of it.

The American quest to develop natural resources and to find room for personal growth is not inherently evil. But when separated from culture, the concepts of development and freedom become absolutes that lead to the opposite of what is desired: absolute freedom, as Socrates once pointed out, leads finally to absolute tyranny. In other words, the myths on which the frontier was based had some creative results as long as they had a cultural basis. The concepts of freedom and development have been explored endlessly in this century, but the exploration of the meaning of culture still awaits our serious attention.

Culture represents the unification of humanity's values at a given time in a given geographical area. Sorokin says that "any great culture, instead of being a mere dumping place of a multitude of diverse cultural phenomena . . . represents a unity."[16] There have been thousands of individual cultures and there will probably be thousands more; like stars in the galaxies, cultures are always burning out and coming into being. The nature of humanity is such that it needs a certain amount of unity and order in its life to maintain a basis for creative activities, but unity and order alone are not enough; there must also be a certain amount of diversity to stimulate creativity so that boredom can be overcome.

The breakup of cultures all over the world has led to two responses that do not work over any length of time. One is to set up a rigid authoritarianism and enforce unity at any price. The other method is to allow complete diversity or "freedom." Extreme individualism, as polities have often shown in their decline, often leads to a demand for order at any price, which brings us back to centralized authority. Only through the development of those human and cultural values that make a true civilization possible can the extremes of totalitarianism on one hand and anarchy on the other be avoided. Culture accommodates freedom and individualism as well as order and responsibility and thus allows for a meaningful civilized existence. All known cultures have flaws that are evinced in the human failings of individual members. But the difference between a people with culture and a people without it is the difference between a certain amount of order, individual happiness, and a widespread distinctiveness on the one hand and political-state tyranny on the other.

Possibly the greatest single theme since 1850 of all the arts, and literature in particular, has been the growing collapse of cultural values in the West. But in the West, as opposed to other cultural areas of the world, there has been in the arts and other areas a strong creative effort to recover the values that undergird civilization. The best of our artists have recorded this effort to give new life to values. Nietzsche in the late nineteenth century saw that Western humanity's greatest need was what he called the transvaluation of all values. Creative writers in particular have sought in their best work to present visions of the possibility of this transvaluation. Historians also have sought to give us insight into basic values that still exist in our disintegrating culture.

As I have suggested, the best southern writers have long emphasized the central values of hierarchy and community even as cultural unity itself has steadily declined. With the decline of this unity there has been a tendency to forget these values and to see the South only in terms of certain pseudo-myths. The pseudo-myth that sees the South in terms of a great white mansion has led some to think of the region as once having been a "sacred community." There are other pseudo-myths, supported by James Baldwin and other writers, that portray the South as nothing but a concentration camp. All cultures are prone to certain delusions and evil practices. If such cultures survive it is because at least some of their members have worked to revive the culture's basic values.

Modern southerners have often doubted that their culture ever contained many important values worth reviving. For instance, one southern journalist, W. J. Cash, writes, with insufficient understanding of his region's culture, that the South has always been "simple in its culture, always inclined to lag, never having had within itself any very fecund principle of intellectual development." [17] Yet southern culture in this century has produced several of the most complex and advanced writers found anywhere in the twentieth century, not to mention colonial America's most influential intellectual, Thomas Jefferson. Obviously Cash never looked at

southern culture as a whole; neither did he consider the role of mythology in southern history. Tindall may well be right when he asks,
"Can it be that the historians have been looking in the wrong places,
that they have failed to seek the key to the enigma where the poets
have so readily found it—in the mythology that has had so much to
do with shaping character, unifying society, developing a sense of
community, of common ideals and shared goals, making the region
conscious of its distinctiveness?" [18]

Yet myths, particularly social myths, often mislead southern writers. The social myths of the Old South and New South, now nearly
worn out, have misled many into thinking there have been only two
historical periods in southern life—one before the Civil War, based
on slavery (when in fact only a relative handful of southerners
owned more than five slaves and the majority never owned slaves at
all), and the other after the Civil War, when the South tried to catch
up with the North in industry and education. Actually there have
been at least four periods of southern culture before 1945: from
1660 to 1763, when religious and commercial expansion were at a
peak; from 1763 to 1819, when southern leaders like Jefferson
helped unify the nation under federalism; from 1820 to 1865,
when the so-called Cotton Kingdom and southern nationalism
were dominant; and from 1877 to 1945, when the South, though
still partly nationalistic, moved toward an acceptance of certain aspects of the dominant commercial-industrial life of the North.

I have already suggested that it is time to recognize that the
South since 1945 has been in a new period which I call the restored
South—restored, that is, to the dominant currents of American
life. This restoration of the South to the American mainstream
came in a period when those who lived in the major regions of the
country, including various ethnic and racial groups—blacks and
Hispanics in particular—were searching for a better understanding of their own ways of life. Southern creative writers and historians have been in the vanguard of this movement. In searching for
values inherent in their own regional culture they have sometimes
achieved visions of the meaning of culture in general and of the
South in particular. Writers like Faulkner, Wolfe, Ellison, and Percy
have even suggested the possibility of a new, unified national
culture.

One reason why millions of readers everywhere in the world
have found southern authors so appealing is that they have been
prompted by an essential conservatism of spirit; the best modern

southern writers have sought to recover memory and history. But they also have made the inner quest for renewal. In their search into history and memory, as well as into their psyches, they have discovered the real meaning of both death and rebirth; namely, that death has meaning only to those who can fully accept it and still desire life. These writers have seen life in the South as having once been communal because it was based on cultural values that united the region's urban centers with farms and plantations in an agribusiness complex. With the decline of southern culture they have perceived and written about the possibility of cultural rebirth taking place in this century.

With the rise to dominance of the megalopolis in the South as well as in the other civilized cultures of the world, many have forgotten the cultural beginnings of the city. Megalopolitan values are often read into the past by good historians and novelists who see nothing but the struggle of isolated individuals trying to grab the world's goods for themselves. But although the spirit of megalopolis had come by 1960 to dominate the cities and even the small towns of the world, surviving fragments of the old culture still existed, and attempts to revive the basic function of the city as a cultural center, rather than seeing it only in terms of the modern megalopolitan sprawl, continued to be made.

One of the best statements about the values underlying southern culture is Robert Manson Myers's *The Children of Pride,* a book of nearly two thousand pages devoted mainly to the letters of the Jones family of Midway, Georgia, in the nineteenth century. This work reveals the nature of the urban-rural continuum of southern culture in general and the role in particular that the city and agribusiness played in the development of the region. Above all, the letters testify to the continuation of culture in a family that began as a communal multi-ethnic group and became one of the great families of the South, with its members eventually playing leading roles both on farms and in cities. This family sums up the meaning of culture at its best in nineteenth-century America. Of the family itself Myers writes:

Throughout the antebellum South the Midway people were justly known for their remarkable way of life. No planting community could boast deeper religious convictions, higher intellectual cultivation, gentler social refinement, or greater material wealth. The church was the very cornerstone of their

being. . . . Education was second only to religion. . . . In a society thus fixed on the things of the mind and the spirit the
people were virtuous and accomplished. If few were extrava-
gantly rich, all were comfortably disposed; equality of rank
and fortune generally prevailed, and social life was leisurely,
gracious, and polite.[19]

Indications of the life of true culture in all aspects of the South
continue to multiply with the growth of scholarly investigation, but
what is now needed are large views of all three of the nation's major
cultures that will show the unity underlying the diverse activities of
different peoples in a region, as well as the elements of disharmony
and chaos—the power of anticulture. The Emery biography of
George Washington has some of this scope. The author begins her
work by establishing the city as the central focus of life in Virginia,
and London as the city that most influenced Virginia's culture; she
quotes Hugh Jones, writing in 1724 in *The Present State of Virginia*:
"The habits, life, customs, computations &c. of the Virginians are
much the same as about London, which they esteem their home."
Emery reveals the obsessive and brooding qualities of Washington,
his coldness toward those on the lower rungs of the social ladder as
well as toward his own mother: "The youthful acolyte at the shrine
of aristocracy would never find much enchantment in the ignorance or antics of the poor." She also shows us Washington's ravenous land hunger, which drove him to acquire a "500-acre tract
on Bullskin Creek in Frederick County, bought with his first saved
cache of his surveying money, when he was slightly more than six-
teen years of age."[20] Yet Emery also depicts Washington as a representative man in a culture directly linked to the very centers of European life, in which the hierarch held sway not only because of
breeding but also because of an innate ability to unite disparate
groups. Thus the biographer who plunges into the heart of Washington's life or that of a lesser person will find the thread of culture
that makes possible the individual's creative acts and restrains those
inevitable forces of entropy that exist at all times in people and societies.

    In the later decades of this century one of the significant chal-
lenges of cultural history has been to perceive what was creative
and destructive in past cultures, so that a cultural hierarch like
Washington is neither idealized as a figure wrought in marble nor
reviled as an absurd, even malevolent figure to be studied only be-

cause he must be debunked. The same may be said of the different
stages of the development of the three American cultures and of
American culture generally.

The cultural historian must also recognize that another challenge facing the modern age, particularly since 1960, has been to
see that life is in many ways the opposite of what it was a hundred
years ago. Then the forces of culture still held in check a growing
personal and social chaos. Now, as the century closes, chaotic forces
have been unleashed; but much good still remains within society
and individuals. Fragments of culture exist, as do visions of cultural
rebirth. For that rebirth to take place there must be a renewal of the
city as cultural center; this renewal will lead in turn to the renewal
of the urban-rural continuum. The question now is: can we prepare ourselves for new life and can we bear the pain of this renewal? The answer, I think, can be seen in the renewal process that
is even now going on in certain southern cities.

Even as some cities have disintegrated from within since 1960, we
have seen others renewing themselves. Charleston has been a prime
example of cultural renewal. Chosen by Gian Carlo Menotti as the
site for the greatest contemporary American art festival—an American Spoleto—Charleston is a living refutation of many pseudo-
myths about the South. It is and has always been a place of struggle
and development where people from many parts of the world have
found a home and where religious and civic freedoms have always
been cherished. Charleston in the 1980s is a living reminder that
individual as well as communal cultural revival is possible.

A study of the culture of early Charleston reveals that instead of
being simply an urban area surrounded by plantations, it was actually a kind of city-state, in effect an urban-agricultural continuum
governed culturally by a city center. The spirit of frontier individualism, together with the New South spirit of individual enterprise,
tended to obscure this early urban and communal development of
southern culture. Historian Blaine Brownell says of two cities that
came into their own in the New South period, "In Memphis and
Birmingham the spirit of the twentieth-century metropolis was
traced back to the adventurous frontiersman rather than to the pa-
triarchal planter."[21] Actually, both frontiersmen and planters played
roles in developing upland cities like Memphis and Birmingham,
but the basic southern culture that underlay these cities first grew
in the Tidewater cities. By the end of the seventies both Memphis
and Birmingham, in the new period of the restored South, were

seeking a kind of urban renewal that would place greater emphasis than ever before on both communal and artistic forms of individual expression. With the growth of black political and economic power in Birmingham, Memphis, and other southern cities there came an even greater emphasis on urban community. Indeed, the southern black community is the most community-centered of all the different groups in the South. Increasing black and Hispanic influences inevitably mean more emphasis on communal activities. The revival, beginning in the sixties, of many southern cities— Savannah, Tampa, San Antonio, New Orleans, and Charleston, for example—was the work of representatives of four traditional southern communities: the gentry, the yeomanry, the Hispanics, and the black community. The urban renewal of San Antonio, for instance, was based in large part on the traditional Hispanic concern for communal life. Urban revival was also greatly aided by northerners newly arrived in the South as well as by Europeans and Latin Americans who were drawn to the South after 1945. Southern urban cultural development in the restored South forms an important chapter in American life of the late twentieth century.

Unless we view both urban revival and the growth of the arts in America as part of a larger cultural development, I believe we will not understand the emergence after 1960 of a long-range attempt to renew the nation's entire culture. If this development is not understood, then we are left only with an awareness of the decline of cultural forms everywhere. The powerful effect of cultural decline was seen in the sixties, when it drove counterculture advocates to try to create a new culture overnight. It has caused others to advocate a totally regulated society in which human emotions are eliminated. Amaury de Riencourt, attacking B. F. Skinner's utopian vision, tells us that "nothing specifically human remains in the Skinnerian world" and cites one of Skinner's most damning quotes: "To man *qua* man I say good riddance." [22]

Are there concrete signs that any kind of rebirth is really taking place amidst what seems to be overwhelming cultural decay? If we look at changes in language, the most basic of all cultural forms, in the South we definitely see new growth. Emory University linguist Lee Pederson states that although one southern speech pattern is passing away, another that is distinctly southern is coming into being: "Atlanta's speech is changing, but it is not changing to Northern speech, but to another version of Southern speech, quite different from Northern urban." [23] A large view of cultural history, as

Sorokin tells us, indicates that cultural death and revival go on side by side. When one way of life dies, no instant vacuum is created into which flows some totally new way of life. For instance, when the urban culture of the Roman Empire died in the West between A.D. 400 and 700, the new rural societies did not totally cease to be Roman; neither were they swamped by the incoming barbarians. (In fact, the barbarians were looking for a new way of life when they invaded the dying Roman Empire.) A way of life that eventually became Western civilization had been emerging for several centuries from the wreckage of Greco-Roman culture. The concept of rebirth must be included in our understanding of culture, which should be seen, as R. W. Collingwood maintains, not as something static but rather as a continual becoming. Collingwood thus refutes Oswald Spengler's concept of culture as a social entity without issue: "There is no static entity called culture, there is only a perpetual development. . . . And this conception of 'turning into', the conception of becoming, is the fundamental idea of all history."[24]

If a new culture is indeed emerging in the revived cities of America, one may well ask what it is that the various groups taking part in urban revival want most. The answer, I think, can be found in the searchings of American writers and other artists in the cultural centers of Europe and America during the early twentieth century. What they sought was a realization of their inner selves and the chance to express themselves as artists in an atmosphere removed from the puritanism and narcissism of the provinces. Their first concern had to be with cultural values connected with their own particular art form, but as they saw the culture of cities like New York and Paris slowly dissolving before the rising megalopolis, they also became concerned in their work with other cultural values— those related to the family, politics, religion, and the male-female relationship, among others. The spirit of megalopolis as defined by Spengler is that of individualistic effort without order, leading to what we now call urban sprawl. Its spirit is everywhere in the civilized world, but increasingly since 1960 provincial cities in America have fought this spirit, seeking to revive the freedom and creativity found in urban America and Europe earlier in the century. Cities like San Francisco, New Orleans, San Antonio, and Baltimore sought after World War II to capture the spirit of the earlier great cities. Spengler noted that the world's supercities devalue the provinces, but the great event in American urban culture in this century has been a movement toward restoring cities to what they always are at their best, cultural centers. Even the greatest of America's cities like New York, Philadelphia, and Chicago had by 1960 joined the attempt to rediscover their cultural roots, long concealed by the disorganization of urban sprawl.

Arnold Toynbee has defined the true city as a place where "the inhabitants of the built-up area are citizens in the non-material sense of having, and being conscious of having, a corporate social life." For Toynbee the true city provides both an order and a sense of freedom that make creativity possible. Out of this creativity comes cultural development, or, to put it the other way, creativity becomes possible because of the living culture of the city. We recognize the cultural quality of a city, Toynbee tells us, by the nature of its soul. Thus he says, of a city that became a megalopolis without first having created its own culture: "Los Angeles may swell physically to the size of a sub-continent, but the tropical luxuriance of its physical growth may never succeed in making a city of it. In order to become a city, it would have to evolve at least the rudiments of a soul. This is the essence of cityhood."[25]

Although we cannot easily define the word *soul*, we can see the effects of the quality of soul in certain cities—Paris, New Orleans, San Francisco. It is a quality existing even in the midst of the urban decay present in every city; it may be called joie de vivre, a sense of communal joy. This joy is possible because of the freedom and creativity related to culture. Artists are gifted at discovering this quality. Literary artists, in particular, plunge into the mythic basis of individual and social creativity that makes possible both culture and the quality of life associated with the intangible quality of soul. Robert Langbaum has written of W. B. Yeats: "All through his career Yeats was concerned with the question of how you get over from the flesh-and-blood creature to the mythical person who puts forth those magical powers from which all value and culture derive."[26] This mythic realm described by Langbaum is similar to what Jung meant by the archetypal realm or what Mircea Eliade means by the realm of the sacred. Culture has been defined as a system of values that helps to refine and develop the manners, taste, mind, and emotions of individuals and to promote creative interaction between groups. If this is so, then the modern writer's search for self-realization is in fact a quest to develop his inner qualities and to bring into being revived cultural values. He seeks, in short, to embody in his work an inner human quality that we associate with the word *soul*.

For Joseph Campbell the essence of myth is for the seeker who ventures into the immaterial realm of myth "to die to the world and to come to birth from within."[27] This inner development consists of an activation of symbols contained within the unconscious mind, symbols that are "inspirational, informative, initiatory, rendering a sense of illumination."[28] One of the great examples of this illuminative quality of a mythic symbol is Joyce's description in *Portrait of the Artist as a Young Man* of Stephen Dedalus's illumination when he sees a young girl walking on the beach. The girl becomes an anima archetype in the same manner that Beatrice became a symbol of love for Dante; she allows Stephen a glimpse into the realm of mythic experience. Deeply influenced by Dante, Joyce records the same sense of life renewal that Dante gives us in *La Vita Nuova*, a revival of life flowing from the illuminated awareness of love flowing from the anima achetype.

Jung, who was also a great influence on Joyce, has described the mythic life as the life of the archetype. A myth, in fact, is a collection of archetypes. For Campbell and Jung the chief archetype is the mandala, a mythic image that represents an essential unity contained within the continuum that makes up the life process. Mircea Eliade has written that the basis of myth is a continuum called life-death-rebirth. This continuum, as he demonstrates in *The Sacred and the Profane*, underlies the birth of culture. The mandala indeed points toward that unity which exists beneath the process of human history. Campbell in *The Mythic Image* demonstrates how the essence that Eliade calls the sacred is symbolized by the mandala in the building of cities that are the cultural centers of communities. For a primitive tribe the cultural center may be no more than a sacred stone or pool, but in a civilization the cultural center consists of buildings often constructed in the design of the mandala. Preserving the meaning associated with the mandala, the cultural center embraces the surrounding countryside, becoming then an urban-rural continuum. The revival in the late twentieth century of the city center as a cultural unit that seeks to embrace the surrounding suburbs is in fact an attempt to fight the megalopolitan concept of total urban sprawl and to proclaim the necessity of an urban-rural continuum to preserve cultural values.

Cultural revival in contemporary American cities does not by itself constitute the rebirth of culture but is, rather, one piece of evidence of the long search necessary for both mythic and cultural renewal. To the definitions of myth by Campbell, Eliade, and Jung, I add that of Alan Watts: myth in effect is a game of hide and seek.[29] Since the early romantic period the West has been searching for those symbols necessary to recover a unified context for new culture as well as such basic values as *caritas,* needed for social cohesiveness and a recognition of the proper balance between men and women, children and parents, leaders and followers.

This search for new cultural contexts is worldwide, as Alexander Solzhenitsyn made clear in a speech at Harvard University in 1978. A literary descendant of Tolstoi and Dostoevski, Solzhenitsyn is himself a member of that branch of existentialists that includes, along with the great Russian novelists, Kierkegaard, Jaspers, Berdyaev, Marcel, Buber, and the southern novelist-philosopher Walker Percy. Unlike such atheist existentialists as Sartre and Camus, who are far better known to the general public, the religious existentialists take into account the destructiveness inevitable in dying cultures, but they place a major emphasis on the continuing quest for those visions necessary for cultural renewal. In his Harvard address, Solzhenitsyn asserted that modern humanity is in a period of history similar to the transitional period between the Middle Ages and the Renaissance. The Russian novelist ended his speech by saying that we have nowhere to go but up, which is a simple statement of the fact that one complex of cultures is dead, though its values still remain, and another is struggling to be born through the revival of dying values.

Marion Montgomery, a southern novelist and critic, has rightly compared certain attitudes of Solzhenitsyn to those of the South. Montgomery even maintains that the Russian novelist bears witness to a "strikingly similar life, grown out of a common ground," to "that of the southern Agrarians."[30] Southern writers, he tells us, have a worldwide appeal, not only because they are linked with leading modern figures like Joyce and Eliot as well as with the Coleridge-Arnold tradition of English-culture criticism, but also because they are so remarkably similar to some European existential writers and philosophers. Their similarity to certain Russians in particular, like Solzhenitsyn, is due primarily to the fact that they accepted their own dying culture with all its imperfections and sought to find new visions and symbols on which cultural renewal could be based.

What is needed to fully explain the work of writers like Solzhenitsyn and the leading southerners is an active critical movement that examines how the quest for self-realization is related to the quest for cultural values. Part of this burgeoning movement are writers like Langbaum, who studies the quest for values and identity; Geoffrey Hartman, who takes into account the realm of the sacred in literature; and James D. Wilson, who examines in his work the relationship of love and solipsism to cultural values. Studies of the search for self-realization in literature have so far dealt primarily with the individualistic aspects of this quest. But now we see emerging—for example, in Langbaum's *Mysteries of Identity*—an attempt to show that much expressive art based on the quest motif, as opposed to mimetic art, is an effort not only to discover the depths of the human psyche but also to bring forth new cultural values. As contemporary authorities on myth like Joseph Campbell and Mircea Eliade have already shown, the mythic quests of individuals are necessary to bring to light those creative human powers needed to establish a living culture. More than most writers in the modern world the southerners were aware of this connection between the individual quest and communal needs; for them the community was always a central concern. The philosophical groundwork for much of what was most mythic and expressive in southern literature after 1920 was laid by a group called the Vanderbilt Agrarians, and it is necessary to look first at their work in relationship to the city before proceeding to better-known writers.

2

Ransom and Tate
Agrarians in Nashville

Two of the most urbane men in modern southern literature—John Crowe Ransom and Allen Tate—were leading spokesmen of a movement called Agrarianism, which advocated a link between the modern commercial city and regional agrarian values. What the movement really accomplished is still debated. A book entitled *A Band of Prophets: The Vanderbilt Agrarians after Fifty Years* (1982) grew out of Vanderbilt University's fiftieth anniversary celebration of the 1930 publication of *I'll Take My Stand,* the group's original manifesto. This book concludes that the twelve participants who wrote the manifesto were not, as once thought, primarily southern diehards but were instead secular prophets. Lewis A. Lawson, in his review of *A Band of Prophets,* writes that "we're just catching up to it [*I'll Take My Stand*]" and that at the anniversary celebration several of the original Agrarians were still looking toward the future: "Lanier, Lytle, and Warren never once looked back, but began to prophesy once again of the need for Barry Commoners, rather than more commoners, of a world hag-ridden by old ideas."[1]

Because the original Agrarians were twelve in number, their views about industry and southern culture were somewhat varied, but all were concerned with reviving certain southern cultural values and the dangers of basing a society on what they called "the industrial drive." The Agrarians believed that the South's values were primarily grounded in the life-styles of the rural areas; yet without Vanderbilt University and Nashville, whose citizens gave support both to the movement and to the university, and without the leadership of that urbane, gentle professor John Crowe Ransom, there would probably never have been an Agrarian movement. Lewis P. Simpson, in his assessment of the movement, emphasizes Allen Tate's statement that he, Tate, had always thought of "the Agrarian group as being rather like the French Encyclopedists."[2] Indeed, what we see in the writing of important Agrarians like Tate is a concern for the propagation of certain ideas in order to bring about cultural change, ideas that since 1700 have been generated primarily in cities and universities rather than in rural environments.

The Agrarians were mainly a group of enthusiastic young men in Nashville during the twenties who had been inspired by Ransom's persuasive teaching. To explain all the complexities of Agrarian thought would be to add yet another book to an already large list on the subject; therefore, my purpose is to examine the leading figures of a literary movement that sprang from a particular city and university and had important literary and cultural consequences for the South. The Agrarian movement revealed that even in the twenties it was possible for a middle-sized city in the South to give birth to a genuine literary movement. In addition, the movement itself made an important contribution to Vanderbilt and to Nashville, as well as other universities and cities, in the realm of cultural development. The activities of the Agrarians and others like them in the South helped to revive the cultural activities of certain cities like Nashville, thus preventing "industrial drive" from overcoming, for example, the arts. One of the minor cultural consequences of Agrarianism for Nashville was that philosophers and artists frequently came to the city to discuss the movement and its leaders.

The major cultural consequences of any movement, nevertheless, are based on the lasting influence of at least some of its members. Agrarianism is known, wherever modern literature is studied seriously, for three major figures—Ransom, Tate, and Robert Penn Warren. As I have mentioned, Warren, who was only twenty-five when *I'll Take My Stand* appeared, had by 1940 moved to the North, where at the University of Minnesota and then at Yale he gradually became dissociated from the southern literary viewpoint. Ransom and Tate, on the other hand, are at the very center of the modern southern experience in literature. In their long-term efforts as professors, critics, essayists, and poets they continued to write about the southern cultural values of community and hierarchy that they believed still existed and had the potential to be revived—even as the old unified culture of the South was disappearing. Long known as fighters for lost causes, they helped prepare the way for a widespread acceptance of literature as an art form rather than as a collection of historical and textual documents. The two leading figures in America of a movement called the New Criticism, Ransom and Tate, together with Warren and Cleanth Brooks, prepared the way for a revolution in the college and university teaching of literature. In *The World's Body* (1938) Ransom issued a call for universities to take up a consideration of literature as art. In the same year appeared *Understanding Poetry*, edited by two of his former students, Brooks and Warren. According to Ransom's biographer, Thomas Daniel Young, this textbook "effected many of the changes that Ransom desired." Young also writes, "To say that it initiated a virtual revolution in the way literature is taught to undergraduates would scarcely be an overstatement."[3]

The chief Agrarians were thus the most successful in their sophisticated defense of this approach to teaching literature, which by 1950 had been largely accepted. By that date Ransom, Tate, and Warren were among the most important literary critics in America. Some were even calling Tate the dean of modern critics. During the thirties Ransom and other followers had, as Young tells us, also engaged in verbal assaults on industrialism to the point of entering debates and writing popular articles, but these efforts by the Agrarians to propagate their ideas failed. Holding up the land as an ideal alternative to increasing industrialization, the Agrarians were unable to find many followers. Ransom's ideas concerning the cultural value of literature did eventually find acceptance in both northern and southern universities. These universities came to play an increasingly significant part in an urban renewal that included a growing number of artists and obscure poets, essayists, and novelists, as the Agrarians themselves had once been.

As the leader of the Vanderbilt Agrarians, Ransom wrote the "Statement of Principles" for *I'll Take My Stand*. A basic principle for the Agrarians, according to the statement, is that "Art depends in general, like religion, on a right attitude to nature."[4] Ransom's views were much more balanced and far less radical than those of some of his younger colleagues; he believed that "an Agrarian so-

ciety is hardly one that has no use at all for industries, for professional vocations, for scholars and artists and for the life of the cities."⁵ Certain other members of the group seemed to look back to
an ideal and imagined past, and some even believed that it was possible to return to that past. Although they denied this aspect of
their essays when they were called neo-Confederates in the minor
uproar created by the book's publication, there are passages that
suggest strong nostalgia. Although Alfred Kazin in *On Native
Grounds*, for instance, quotes Tate, Donald Davidson, and others
out of context, there is some justice in his view that the Agrarians
were backward-looking. However, Ransom never maintained that
the Old South could be brought back, and by the late thirties he was
beginning to accept the facts of modern industrial society. Young in
his biography quotes an editorial Ransom wrote in the *Kenyon Review* in the mid-1940s: "That innocence is irrecoverable Ransom
had argued since the middle twenties . . . but now he moved
considerably beyond that position, Donald Davidson and others
thought, in his insistence that the division of labor of the modern
industrial society is a part of the postscientific world that twentieth-
century man must accept."⁶ The Agrarians, Ransom tells us, did
not return to the land to live; in fact they accepted the modern
world as they found it. But they accepted it with certain protests.

What made Ransom the chief inspirer and leader of the other
Vanderbilt Agrarians, as stated in the "Principles," was his protest
against "the curse of a strictly business or industrial civilization,"
the word *strictly* being the key in this statement. This protest was
common in artistic circles in America and Europe in the early twentieth century. In his various writings on the subject Ransom makes
clear that what he wants is a more balanced modern society, one in
which nature, religion, and the arts are taken into account. Values
associated with the rural and natural world as well as those found
in religion and art are necessary for cultural and civilized existence;
we cannot live by business and industry alone, Ransom maintains.

To understand his viewpoint, we should study, as Louis D. Rubin,
Jr., has done, Ransom's Nashville environment. When Ransom first
came to Vanderbilt from the home of his father, a small-town Ten-
nessee Methodist preacher, Rubin tells us, he encountered the New
South "represented by the busy business community of Nashville
and with the philosophy of Progress as exemplified by such men as
James A. Kirkland and Edwin Mims."⁷ Although Vanderbilt and
Nashville seemed somewhat alien, Ransom found he could never

return to the small Tennessee towns of his youth. In many ways he adapted his life to the new commercial cities, becoming a good golfer and tennis player and even working briefly as a reporter and editorial writer on the *Memphis Evening Scimitar*. Ransom's reactions to the New South were similar to those of W. E. B. Dubois at Atlanta University, who called the official doctrine of the New South (endorsed by Booker T. Washington) that of "work and money." It was an exaltation of the Protestant work ethic with the proof of the value of one's work being large quantities of money. Work and money had become a way of establishing one's identity. For white southerners the New South also represented a view of history that idealized the Old South and that was produced mainly by a general mania for idealized history. Although Edwin Mims as head of Vanderbilt's English Department gave Ransom a job there and continued to praise his work, it was against the kind of literary scholarship Mims stood for that Ransom launched the movement called the New Criticism. Ransom found art and religion—his two chief areas of cultural interest—swallowed up in history, becoming artifacts to be considered in an objective historical light. For him both the Old South of the cotton kingdom and the New South of commercial-industrial expansion tended to ignore the cultural values contained in art and religion.

Ransom's revolt against the New South and the Old South too can best be seen in his poetry. Modernism was in part a revolt against a puritanical Victorianism that set up work, morality, and progress as the only important values. These values, particularly in the South, were propagated with a kind of idealism that the moderns usually found thin and false, and, above all, lacking any logical basis. By 1924, with *Chills and Fever*, Ransom had established himself as an important modern American poet, and as such he was in revolt against both Victorian idealism and the doctrine that material progress should be the central concern of modern culture. His attitude toward southern idealism can be seen in his attack on Sidney Lanier, an attack that annoyed some at Vanderbilt because Lanier was also considered an early southern Agrarian. Lanier, Ransom tells us, was "one of the Platonists, in love with big abstract ideas."[8] Instead of idealism and abstractions, what Ransom wanted was a way of life prevalent in the eighteenth-century South rather than that of the nineteenth century, which was based on cotton production. Leading modern writers like Joyce and Eliot also turned against the nineteenth century, seeking their values in the Middle

Ages and the Renaissance. Ransom turned primarily to eighteenth-century viewpoints for support in writing his modernist verse; his mind was neoclassical in many ways, having been nourished from his earliest schooling through three years as a Rhodes Scholar at Oxford by intensive reading in the Greek and Roman classics.

What Ransom found in southern idealism was vagueness, lack of form, and a sense of individual isolation rather than a full acceptance of the need for community. In both Old and New South idealism he detected narcissism, which for both the individual and the community means an essentially static view of existence. In "Captain Carpenter," a difficult poem that sums up certain aspects of nineteenth-century southern idealism, Ransom presents a man with the eighteenth-century virtues of courtliness and gentility, a man of pistols and horseback riding and chivalry, whose life is caught up in absurd violence. In "Captain Carpenter" and other Ransom poems, Rubin writes, "there is . . . this precarious set-to of violence and order, savagery and courtliness. The urbane diction contrasts with the bloody happenings."[9]

Rubin notes the prevalence of violence in southern literature and suggests that part of the reason for southern violence lies in the shift from traditional values to those of the New South. Yet violence was fundamental to southern life and literature before the Civil War. The chief cause of southern violence, I suggest, lies primarily in both the conscious and the unconscious attempts of southerners to break through the sometimes static condition of a society that held attitudes of idealism and narcissism throughout most of the nineteenth century. Like many French writers in this same century (Poe and Baudelaire are almost literary brothers), cultivated southerners were fascinated with beauty and death. Ransom takes this southern cult of beauty and death into full account in "Captain Carpenter" and other poems, but his approach is exactly opposite that of the southern idealist—Poe or Lanier, for instance. As Rubin says, "With Ransom . . . the violence is masked, made to contrast at all times with resilient irony and gentility. It is never directly and baldly experienced."[10] Ransom's way is that of the classical Greek playwrights, who put violence offstage, and of the eighteenth-century satirists, who saw life with an ironic eye and in the context of a hierarchal society that maintained standards of gentility and reason.

Ransom's satire is never harsh and his wit is seldom acid. In "Blue Girls," one of his most quotable poems, he centers on that symbol of southern opulence, the beautiful girl. These girls (for whom the real-life models were students at Belmont College, observed by the poet from his Vanderbilt office) are caught in a static, narcissistic dream. In their pride of life the world seems timeless. "Practice your beauty, blue girls, before it fail," Ransom tells the southern belles, who "think no more of what will come to pass / Than blue-birds that go walking on the grass / And chattering on the air." The poet, who knows that life and death are a continuum, tells them what they cannot accept in their narcissistic youth: that beauty is what "all our power shall never establish, / It is so frail." He ends with a description of "a lady with a terrible tongue, / Blear eyes fallen from blue" who was once "lovelier than any of you." [11]

Some of Ransom's best poetry thus offers a kind of gentle and urbane criticism of southern life caught in a fading dream. In "Blue Girls" he suggests artistic and educational values necessary for viewing life and death in a human context in which neither is overvalued but each is accepted in its turn. In "Bells for John Whiteside's Daughter" the poet exalts a community that is grounded in traditional forms and rites. The young girl of the poem, unlike the proud beauties of "Blue Girls," is seen as "the little / Lady with rod that made" the geese rise "From their noon apple-dream and scuttle / Goose-fashion under the skies!" Yet the touching fact of the mythic child's death is not the central event of the poem; rather, the bells, which are symbolic of the ordered, ritualized existence of the traditional community, serve as the central image of the poem. Strengthened by the rituals symbolized by the bells, the "we" of the poem are able to accept even the most difficult of deaths. In the last stanza, the people of the community, comforted by the sound of the bells, are able to visit the dead child in her home: "But now go the bells, and we are ready." [12]

For Ransom, a preacher's son, religious and educational values formed the basis of the good community. But unlike traditional Tennessee Protestants, Ransom believed that neither dogma nor religious experience was absolutely basic to communal existence; the only essential was a web of traditional rites. An English critic, Graham Hough, tells us that "to the English reader the sense that Ransom's poetry is rooted in a society is strongly welcome, and on the whole un-American. . . . The feeling of contact with a close-knit world of friends, neighbors, aunts, children, and families is stronger in Ransom's work than in any English poetry that I can recall"; Ransom's poems rest more than anything else on "fairy-tale and folk-tale, from ballads, and the more accessible kinds of romance." [13] Myth and ritual, then, form the basis for both art and traditional community in Ransom's vision.

Ransom's poetry grew out of his return to nature, tradition, myth, and regional community after his three years at Oxford studying philosophy and classics. Early poems show his struggle to accept the southern community from which he sprang, especially its rural and natural aspects. In 1912 Ransom, still at Oxford, announced to his father that he thought he would go into journalism instead of teaching. Returning to America from Oxford, however, he chose to teach at Hotchkiss, a New England preparatory school; he seriously considered living in New York because he believed he could best develop his literary and philosophic abilities there. But after his return from military service in World War I he became ensconced as teacher and poet in Nashville. His poetry records many of his intellectual struggles as well as his acceptance, often with disguised reservations, of southern community. Looking at much of his best poetry, we might even conclude, as Hough suggests, that Ransom became a Tennessee version of Robert Frost. But unlike Frost, Ransom did not see himself as primarily a poet. Like Matthew Arnold, though lacking Arnold's excessive moralism, Ransom took up the task of trying to revive the foundering culture of Western civilization—beginning, as Arnold did, at his own back door. Both were Oxford men, and Oxford pointed them toward religion and literature. Both wrote a handful of poems no complete anthology can do without, and then devoted most of their lives to writing essays on literature, philosophy, religion, and culture and to participating actively in the educational establishments of their country with the practical aim of renewing what they believed were certain basic values.

Ransom was too creative to be a mere follower of Arnold or anyone else. He was a natural hierarch who drew followers in a way Arnold could not. In fact, the development of his theories of literature led him to refute many of Arnold's ideas, and in continuing Arnold's work but departing from many of his ideas Ransom is similar to T. S. Eliot, whose influence on him was also strong. Of Eliot, Ransom wrote to his friend Robert Graves in 1925 that "he confirms many of my own ideas . . . or beats me to them." [14] When *I'll Take My Stand* was published in 1930 Eliot gave his complete approval, though for him Tate was the major Agrarian: "It is a sound and right reaction which impelled Mr. Allen Tate and his eleven

Southerners to write their book." [15] Ransom actually resembles Eliot
more than either Arnold or Frost because of his intense concern
with modernism and its meaning. Despite an eighteenth-century
sense of form and wit in his poetry and a deep awareness of myth
and tradition in both his essays and his poems, Ransom was chiefly
concerned with facing the challenge of living in an urbanized world
in which the activities of the conscious mind, particularly scientific
activities, dominate life.

When Ransom and younger poets and critics like Tate, Warren,
and Donald Davidson collaborated in 1922 to publish a journal, *The
Fugitive,* they were already in exile, as the name that they chose suggests. Donald Davidson remained in exile for all his life as a professor at Vanderbilt. Simpson suggests that Davidson "was led back
toward the ancient community of clan and pagan pietas," [16] though
Davidson is far more modern and urbane than is often thought.
There was from the beginning a right-wing group in the Agrarians, but although Ransom was personally close to Davidson he
never really belonged with the ultraconservatives. In 1924 Ransom
wrote an essay for *The Fugitive,* Young tells us, "in which he admits
that poetry must face up to modernism, a difficult assignment indeed because no one seems to know what modernism is." [17] In the
twenties Ransom asserted in poetry and essays that modernism in
serious literature was partly a revolt against vague idealism, excessive moralism with its tendency to "improve" and "uplift," and Victorianism's penchant for platonic abstractions. But in the *Fugitive*
essay Ransom was really asking where modernism was headed; toward what values it was tending; what would replace Victorianism
in literature. After intense thought and discussion in Nashville in
the twenties came one of the great modern apologias for poetry,
summed up by Young: poetry is "not an instrument through which
one can 'improve' or 'idealize' the world." Rather it must be seen as
"a means through which one can know that which he can know in
no other way." [18]

That which can be experienced in no other way than through poetry, for Ransom, was a quality that is basically mythic; for, as he
and most of the Agrarians saw, mythic understanding informs true
poetry. The modern mind, Ransom believed, put far too much emphasis on abstractions and not nearly enough on the kind of par-
ticularity, individuality, and intimate communal responsibility that
form the subject matter of myth and poetry. The result, in the
words of Simpson, was that Ransom and his Agrarian followers

would "encourage mind to reverse its status, to become as it once had been: the consciousness of the webbed order of myth and tradition, always submissive to ritual, manners, and customs." [19] Yet Ransom, for all his efforts on behalf of poetry in the twenties and thirties, came to see as some of his followers did not that to return to an old way of life was impossible, that one aspect of modernism was a continuing emphasis on abstractions, necessary because only abstract ideas can fight against an abstract view of life. He always believed that something could be salvaged from modern life, something poetic and mythic that might put human beings in touch with forgotten parts of themselves.

Karl F. Knight asserts that "Ransom seems to be saying that modern man has lost his capacity for total experience" and therefore "has lost his appreciation for poetry." The result of this failure, Knight goes on to say, is that modern individuals are unable "to give adequate expression to their love." [20] No poem in the Ransom canon illustrates this split between head and heart better than "The Equilibrists," a work that shows two people bound to each other but never able to give full expression to their love because of abstract and Victorian concepts like "honor." There were concepts of honor in the eighteenth century and in the Renaissance, but only Victorian honor could interrupt sexual activity. What lies behind an abstract concept like Victorian honor, Ransom suggests in "The Equilibrists," is narcissism. The narcissist looks out in fear from a psychological prison at a partly alien world. The solution to the problem of narcissism then is a unity that ties the individual closer and more lovingly to the world outside. Fifty years after *I'll Take My Stand,* upon Vanderbilt's 1980 anniversary celebration of the volume, Robert Heilman tells us in *A Band of Prophets* that the Agrarians sought an unfragmented world; the collection's concluding essay by Rubin speaks, in Louis A. Lawson's words, of the Agrarians' "creating a complex of images that would evoke the conception of the whole man." [21] Yet it is a paradox that many of the Agrarians and their followers often appear to outsiders to be pitting North against South or even "my little group" against everybody else. A writer like Walter Sullivan, for instance, often seems to pit the past against the present without taking into account the historical continuum that suggests that the problems of the present are usually those of the past that have not yet been solved. Thus, a literary group advocating wholeness sees itself firmly split off from other, rival groups or even rival cultures.

By 1930 Ransom had concluded that for culture to be revived
and civilization to be restored religion must be taken into full account. That year he published *God without Thunder,* in part an attack
on liberal Christianity, not unlike similar attacks found in Flannery
O'Connor and Walker Percy. Yet its description of the deity bears
little resemblance to the God of either Christianity or Judaism.
Ransom avoids the great modern theological problem of transcendence and its relationship to immanence. Ransom's inscrutable and
unknown God, taught him by Kant, is largely cut off from man;
thus, the sacred-secular continuum, in Eliade's sense, is denied.
Neither Hebrew prophets nor Christian saints, in Ransom's view,
can even briefly link transcendence with suffering humanity.

Borrowing the term *New Criticism* from an earlier critic, Joel
Spingarn, who wrote "The New Criticism" in 1911, and applying it
to his own group's activities, Ransom, with the help of Brooks and
Warren's textbook *Understanding Poetry,* made his movement the
dominant one in university circles from 1945 to 1960. Actually, his
critical theory is part of a larger movement in criticism begun by
Yeats, Eliot, and I. A. Richards. The criticism of these three is more
typically holistic than Ransom's because it leans heavily on Coleridge's concepts of imaginative vision and the organic nature of literature. Ransom's views have prevailed in many universities and
colleges. Above all, he urged the recognition of eighteenth-century
artistic virtues like wit and irony, and he insisted that the work of
art be seen as having an integrity of its own. Yet art alone was not
enough for Ransom; only in relationship to basic cultural values
could art do its necessary work. Even as early as 1943, as Young
points out, Ransom was concerned that his followers—Brooks and
Warren by this time being the most outstanding—were putting too
much emphasis on the texture of poetry. Young claims that, according to Ransom, only by first emphasizing "'the positive or prose elements of the poem' [Ransom's own words] can one be fully aware of
the eternal human values contained in a work of art."[22] Like Arnold, Ransom finally prized the basic values necessary for a living
culture even more than the individual art work.

Ransom remained a traditionalist at heart, but he was intelligent
enough to change as the South and the nation changed and become more urbanized. He is often called urban and sophisticated,
and rightly so: after 1940 the term *Agrarian* seemed wrong for a
man who wrote essays on economics and sometimes addressed Ro-
tary clubs. The ultimate paradox of the Fugitive-Agrarian move-

ment is that its founder and leader came at last to resemble anything but a man of the "land" (though he was an expert gardener).
However, he remained loyal all his life to southern views concerning hierarchy and community. After 1920 community for Ransom
would be defined primarily in terms of a city like Nashville and of
the university community that was becoming increasingly important in America.

In the best Yeatsian sense Agrarianism was largely a mask for
Ransom. Like Yeats in his support of the Irish Renaissance, Ransom was totally secure in the role he chose to play between 1930
and 1937 when, in support of Agrarian views, he wrote essays, engaged in public debates, and even considered buying a newspaper.
In 1937, after leaving Vanderbilt for Kenyon College in Gambier,
Ohio, less than forty miles from Columbus, he explained that he
wanted more time for his own work. It was the same reason Yeats
gave when in 1910 he stopped directing the Abbey Theater. At
Kenyon Ransom moved more deeply than ever into the two cultural areas he was most concerned with—education and the arts; as
editor of the *Kenyon Review* he became a major figure in the literary
establishment of the nation.

Ransom at Kenyon remained thoroughly southern while playing
his role as hierarch of American letters. He continued to believe in
the communal approach to creative writing in the sense that, for
him, conversation between writers, including serious discussions of
cultural values, was an important part of the creative process.
Robert Lowell and Randall Jarrell were but two of the young poets
who benefited from Ransom's teaching. Ransom took his role of literary hierarch seriously, but as a teacher he was in certain ways the
opposite of earlier literature professors in the South, such as Edwin
Mims. Ransom often seemed tentative in his teaching, never adopt-
ing the role of a great authority as Mims did, because his method
was mainly to draw out what was most creative in his best students.
In a lecture at Georgia State University in 1972, Allen Tate spoke of
Ransom's many creative students and said that one was never like
another; that is, students never directly bore the stamp of Ransom's
personality but instead found through him their own creative ability. That Ransom related communally to his students can be seen in
a remark he made about Tate, his student, colleague, and friend.
Asked at a 1956 Vanderbilt Fugitive-Agrarian reunion if his poetry
would have been the same if he "had not been at Vanderbilt with
the Fugitives from 1920 to 1925," Ransom (in the words of Young,

his biographer) attributed the "tremendous advance" between his *Poems about God* and the later poetry "almost entirely to his association with this group and, specifically, to Allen Tate's introducing him to modern poetry and criticism, particularly to the works of Eliot."[23] Seldom has such a great poet and teacher given so much credit to a younger man who was his student and follower.

In the period of the Fugitives' greatest activity, between 1920 and 1925, Tate and Robert Penn Warren clearly emerged as the two with the greatest literary ability. For a time both gained greater recognition than Ransom, even while their mentor was establishing himself in the eyes of many critics as the chief southern poet of this century. In the fifties Tate was considered the dean of American literary criticism, whereas in the seventies and eighties Warren became arguably the nation's most highly regarded practicing man of letters. Both Tate and Warren took up a major philosophical problem, the problem of dualism, which Ransom had only partially solved. The solution called for by Ransom involved communal ritual, through which he believed the creative powers necessary for cultural revival could somehow emerge from the arts and religion. Tate and Warren, however, challenged Ransom's formulaic solution by showing in many of their works a declining culture and claiming that traditions and rituals of art and religion had become meaningless to people. Warren's most important novel, *All the King's Men,* presents a vision of the underlying continuum of history, and, like Ransom, he suggests the possibility of overcoming social dualism through communal ritual; but most of his novels and poems point to a continuing decline of society accompanied by the gradual unraveling of culture. Tate, on the other hand, suggests in many of his best works that cultural revival is still possible. In doing so, he follows the lead of another mentor, T. S. Eliot.

In *All the King's Men,* Warren writes about a southern capital, Baton Rouge, but his real subject is not so much this city as the collapse of the southern gentry and the rise of southern "bosses" like Huey Long who believed that through political manipulation they could put society back together again. The book, as Warren has made clear in several statements, is not about Huey Long but, rather, the failure of southern power brokers to create meaningful cultural values and restore some sense of unity to a fragmented society. Above all, it is a book about the reaction of a younger member of the southern gentry, Jack Burden, to southern populism. Burden, himself one of the "King's men," does not know how to cope with the flood of violence unleashed by cultural decline. He finally escapes the wreckage of Willie Stark's political empire and achieves a personal vision that grows directly out of the philosophy of Ransom and the Agrarians. Jack sees that personalities and events interact, are all of a piece; thus past, present, and future are a continuum. "From this truth," Young writes in *The Past in the Present*, "Jack acquires a faith; not only does he know that he is responsible for the results of his actions, whether intended or not, he also comes to believe in a metaphysical reality that justifies the existence of evil in the world."[24] He thus achieves a glimpse of a metaphysical reality whose presence, he suddenly sees, is necessary if individuals are to overcome their moral failure.

Yet, by the end of *All the King's Men* Jack is left with one friend, Ann Stanton, and his final vision of communal collapse. From Warren's first novel, *Night Rider* (1939), on through his fiction and poetry of the fifties, sixties, and seventies, the author's predominant vision is of the overwhelming power of the past to poison the communities of the present. This strong sense of collapsing values, as I have noted, is doubtless what made Warren in the seventies describe himself as a naturalist unable to accept an ultimate metaphysical reality called God.

Lewis P. Simpson has characterized Warren's best work as being about "affirmation of the existential self within the history of the world of human beings, as this is framed by the implacable natural history of the universe."[25] The work of Warren and other writers of the Southern Renaissance, Simpson tells us in *The Dispossessed Garden*, deals in large part with modern gnosticism, based, in Simpson's words, on the belief "that knowledge available to men (gnosis) can be used to change the very construction of being."[26] Willie Stark in *All the King's Men*, for instance, believes that with Machiavellian political knowledge and methods he can build a social substitute for a lost culture. What destroys him is not so much his crude gnosticism but his narcissistic worship of his success as political boss. Jack is drawn to him in the first place because the stagnating narcissism of his own "aristocracy" prevents it from acting to preserve even rudimentary political and economic services. But in moving from his own class to the populist politics of Willie Stark, he only exchanges one form of narcissism for another. Jack and succeeding fictional protagonists in Warren's work are left with what Simpson calls "a struggle between a gnostic society and the existential self."[27] War-

ren's brief vision of continuum fails him, and his protagonists, bereft of any vision of either personal or cultural renewal, are caught
up, in Simpson's words, in "the intensely personal struggle of the
individual to find some meaning to our absurd and undefinable
world." [28]

Warren's existential character struggling in an alien world is a
typical protagonist in modern literature, particularly in much of
French and American literature. Yet many of the protagonists of
major modern writers who remained southern in their outlook
seek ways of continuing community through the revival of at least
some cultural values. They know that though the world may often
seem absurd it is given meaning by the cultural community that
overcomes narcissism and makes personal and social growth possible. Warren's existentialism, which is often despairing, is that of
Sartre and Camus, whereas the existentialism of Tate (who seldom
used the term) is more like that of Kierkegaard, Buber, and Marcel. As I will demonstrate in a later chapter, Walker Percy, like Tate,
is a religious existentialist similar to Kierkegaard. Percy's work
clearly defines the differences between the naturalistic existentialism of Warren and the religious stream of existentialism that first
appeared in Kierkegaard's work.

Tate began his literary career as a precocious teenager, like Warren coming to Nashville from a small Kentucky town. In some ways
he resembled a Warren protagonist struggling in an absurd world.
But the Warren protagonist, after first accepting hierarchal guidance, becomes disenchanted with all leaders and, like Jack Burden,
is left on his own in a world he considers hostile. Tate, on the other
hand, found two mentors early on—Ransom and T. S. Eliot—and
he remained loyal to the teaching of these two men all his life. Bed-
ridden in his last years, Tate, his biographer Robert Buffington
tells us, kept photographs of his two mentors on his wall and liked
to tell visitors, "Those were my two great teachers." [29]

Tate was early drawn to the eighteenth century, no doubt following Ransom, as his poem "Mr. Pope" in his first volume, *Mr. Pope
and Other Poems* (1928), shows clearly. But wit and irony, often
handled quite well by Tate, did not satisfy him, nor did his quest
into southern history. Like Faulkner's famous character Quentin
Compson, Tate left the South for the North. He left Vanderbilt and
the literary community he had found in Nashville to seek a wider
sphere of literary activity. In the late twenties he was in Paris and
New York, an associate of Hemingway's, a close friend to Hart

Crane. But the southern past still held him, and Simpson likens him to the Quentin character, who was "to Faulkner a symbol of the self of the writer as a self who is not only isolated in history but who has willed the isolation of history in himself."[30] But Tate did not, like Quentin, commit suicide. The self isolated in history did not destroy him. Other stronger selves emerged to combat the narcissism that had led him toward an isolation and solipsism that eventually threatened him with psychic and even physical death. Tate knew the meaning of his struggles with the southern past. They were the struggles of the southern gentry who had often lost themselves in a past of their own imagining when the Civil War seemed to destroy everything. At the point where suicide might have beckoned to Tate, his course resembled that of another literary character, Walker Percy's Will Barrett. In *The Last Gentleman*, Will returns to the South to face the cause of his narcissism and incipient madness.

In 1930 Tate and his wife, Caroline Gordon, also an important figure in modern southern literature, moved to a farm near Clarksville, Tennessee. There he worked on a biography of Robert E. Lee, continued publishing poems and essays, and wrote a novel about the antebellum South called *The Fathers*. By the end of the thirties he had worked through some of his most important personal problems, aided by the continuing friendship and inspiration of Ransom and Eliot. He gained much, as he has suggested, by his contact with the southern community, but he was finally too restless and too much an urban man to sink deeply into a single southern community as Faulkner and Eudora Welty did. Welty, Gordon, and Katherine Anne Porter emerged in the thirties as writers who could depict in their fiction the still living southern community. Richard C. Moreland speaks of Welty's "vision of love and community" and of her awareness of "the inevitable isolation and limitation of that vision in its repeatedly losing battle with time."[31] What Tate sought, on the other hand, was to move beyond a kind of literary vision that was caught up in isolation and a battle against time; he sought a revival of values in order to develop a new community with which to replace the old one. Therefore his chief concern in the thirties and later was not a close literary inspection of the southern scene of the sort that Gordon and Welty pursued but, rather, a search for ways of overcoming the dualisms that he thought were destroying the southern community.

The most pressing form of dualism that Tate perceived was that between the individual and society. In the late thirties he wrote one of his best essays on the subject. As his views on narcissism began to crystallize, Tate wrote "Narcissus as Narcissus," an essay about his own poem written in the twenties, "Ode to the Confederate Dead." He states that the poem's subject is solipsism or narcissism or "any other *ism* that denoted the failure of the human personality to function objectively in nature and society." In detailing the problems of what he calls the "locked in ego," Tate in effect says that man must have basic cultural values to help him maintain the unity of his personality. "Without unity," he says, "we get the remarkable self-consciousness of our age." Thus, "man wastes his energy piecemeal over separate functions that ought to come under a unity of being."[32] With this concept of unity of being Tate hoped to elucidate what his poem had already said—that the modern "hollow man" can through contact with art and the past achieve what in "Ode to the Confederate Dead" he calls "knowledge carried to the heart."

For readers of Ransom and Eliot, Tate's thought processes in both the poem and the essay are familiar. Eliot in the twenties spoke of a "dissociation of sensibility" that he first thought could be healed through myth and poetry; later he came to believe that the practice of religious ritual was necessary to realize the underlying unity of personality and society. His thinking in this matter was paralleled by other well-known English figures of the thirties and forties like Arnold Toynbee and C. S. Lewis. Tate followed Eliot's thinking so carefully that by 1950 he became a convert to Catholicism, a branch of Christianity that puts even more emphasis on ritual than does the Anglican Church, which Eliot joined in 1927. Ransom's influence can be seen in the idea that poetry strengthens man by relating him to the concrete world he must live in every day. In another essay, "Literature as Knowledge," Tate writes at length on the Ransom view of poetry as a higher and necessary knowledge, related to what Simpson calls Tate's view of the "grace of the spiritual unity of a traditional community as opposed to the evil of a specialized, mechanized society, with its demand that each individual be at best some fragment of a man."[33] Yet Tate, unlike Ransom, whose ideas about society Tate often drew upon, could not be at ease with traditional southern society as Ransom—and also Tate's wife, Caroline Gordon—saw it in the early twentieth century. He no doubt detected in the views about southern community held by most of the

Agrarians a dualism in which individuals stood either alone or in small groups against a gnostic society.

In his novel *The Fathers,* which represents much of his thinking about traditional community in the decade of the thirties, Tate views the South as a community that was collapsing even before the Civil War. In the character Major Lacy Buchan, a representative of the antebellum gentry, we see the results of a narcissism in which an individual so worships the forms of society that he is consumed by them, losing his individuality. Tate contrasts Buchan with the character of George Posey, who, Young says, is a "romantic hero," one who "destroys the fundamentals of its [traditional society's] civilizing influences and is left naked and alone." Tate himself is both characters, the romantic hero probably becoming dominant in him when he wrote the novel. The point of the novel, Young tells us, is that between the two extremes of Buchan and Posey "is the appropriate place for a vital and healthy society." [34] Tate could never renounce tradition, but he knew that unless, like Posey, one took a dualistic attitude toward an ossified tradition he might lose his individuality. He also knew that this dualism had to be overcome by a new unity—a revival of some principle that would allow tradition to help individuals develop themselves. Like Ransom in 1930 he had reached the conclusion that religion, along with poetry, was necessary for a good society. But in his essay in *I'll Take My Stand* he claimed that the failure of the Old South's religion had spelled its social decline. The problem lay partly, as Tate later saw under Eliot's influence, in a religious dualism like Ransom's that saw God and man as separate. By 1932, even as *I'll Take My Stand* was making its mark, Eliot's influence on Tate was becoming more profound than Ransom's. In the late thirties and forties Tate came to accept Eliot's view that through grace received in religious ritual one could again experience unity.

Before considering the implications of Tate's religious views it is necessary to examine briefly how he arrived at them. Buffington calls attention to a letter Tate at twenty-four wrote to Davidson, in which he describes the literary vocation as a life of adventure because "it is the life of the soul." [35] Early in his career Tate found in Eliot and the French symbolists this same concern for the individual soul in the modern world. The older cultural critics like Arnold tended to forget the agonies that the modern soul had suffered as cultural forms decayed. Tate joined Eliot in suggesting that every person was subject to intense pressures that often split the soul in two. Though he also followed Ransom's lead, in rejecting romantic formlessness and abstract idealism in favor of an eighteenth-century sense of wit and form, Tate remained always something of a southern romantic. Rubin identifies this paradox in Tate's creative life: "My observation is that as an imaginative writer Allen had a gift that was highly and intricately autobiographical. This may seem odd, in that his poetics placed a premium upon achieved anonymity, classical restraint, the primacy of craftsmanship over subject—the antithesis of the romantic subjective artist."[36] Tate, in short, was often a confessional poet, not unlike his friend Conrad Aiken, whose admiration for Tate and his work was always great. Ironically, as Tate's reputation as a poet and critic declined after 1960, the poet who received highest accolades in the sixties was his close follower Robert Lowell, the greatest of modern America's confessional poets and, like Tate, a convert to Catholicism.

The confessional poet Tate meditated upon most deeply was Edgar Allan Poe, a poet who confesses the terrors of his own soul but does so with strict regard for craftsmanship, design, and even a neoclassical sense of order. In Poe, Tate found a sometimes powerful artist suffering from what Tate and other modern critics referred to as the Cartesian split (Eliot's "dissociation of sensibility"), in which mind and emotions often seem to work against each other. He also found in Poe the narcissism that he saw in himself, and he examined in Poe the violence resulting from the narcissist's will to break out of the shell of isolation. Thus Tate went to the heart of the causes of Poe's personality disintegration. In Poe, he says, we see "the intellect moving in isolation from both love and the moral will, whereby it declares itself independent of the human situation in the quest for essential knowledge."[37] In his essay "The Angelic Imagination," Tate describes the process whereby Poe turns himself into God, thus fulfilling the essential quest of the narcissist. In an even more profound essay, "Our Cousin, Mr. Poe," Tate deals with the demonic element in Poe's poetry and acknowledges his own closeness to Poe: "he is so close to me that I am sometimes tempted to enter the mists of pre-American genealogy to find out whether he may not actually be my cousin."[38] It is time, Tate tells us, to believe Poe's statement that from boyhood he had been possessed by a demon that expressed itself in his writings about the kind of vices that we also see in some of Tennessee Williams's works (vampirism, cannibalism, necrophilia), arising from "persons eating one another and calling it spiritual love."[39]

Tate's plunge into the terrors of Poe's soul paralleled his plunge into his own soul. He was, of course, following the lead of the French symbolists from Baudelaire, whose chief mentor was Poe, to Valéry, a poet who often resembles Tate. The French symbolists wrote primarily about isolation and death, but certain modern poets, novelists, and dramatists from this tradition found it possible to push on past visions of death to mythic visions suggesting the possibility of a rebirth of the psyche, visions that Joyce called epiphanies. Yeats, Joyce, Eliot, Aiken, Stevens, Mann, Hesse, Bernanos, Mauriac, Greene, and many others have worked through problems of isolation to bring forth imaginative statements about rebirth and personality development. They have seen the possibility of overcoming the seemingly endless tyranny of time and history by making brief mythic contacts with a supra-sensible reality, as Tate called it. Some writers in the symbolist tradition prostrated themselves in their personal lives before an authoritarian church, but others like Eliot and Tate approached religion from a mythic sense of renewal rather than a blind acceptance of authority.

Renewal for Tate meant, of course, an acceptance of religious ritual. He followed Eliot not only in this respect; by 1950 he had also adopted the view that Dante was Western civilization's greatest poet and that his work deals more deeply than that of any other European poet with humanity's quest for the development of the soul. Tate called the high-water mark of modern poetry Eliot's "Little Gidding," specifically the passage in terza rima that echoes Dante. In his book *The Forlorn Demon*, Tate counters his essay on Poe called "The Angelic Imagination" with one on Dante called "The Symbolic Imagination." He announces that the work of true poetry is "making the supra-sensible visible." For Poe, caught in the Cartesian net, the only supra-sensible visions possible were those of the demonic. Poe thus resembled Nietzsche, who said that if God is dead then man must become God. For Dante, God lives and the "symbolic imagination" does not reject the world of matter to try to find a perfect world of beauty, which must always be lost and followed in turn by a world of demons. The symbolic imagination "does not reject, it includes; it sees not only with but through the natural world, to what may lie beyond it." This way of writing poetry, Tate concludes, never begins at the top but "carries the bottom

along with it, however high it may climb."⁴⁰ Thus in Dante Tate
found the unity which made culture possible and which was
shattered by Cartesianism. He also found a way out of Ransom's
structure-texture dualism in defining the nature of poetry. With
the help of Dante, Tate thus drew close to the Coleridge-Yeats-
Richards tradition of theoretic criticism that sees the art work as an
imaginative unified organism containing mythic and religious
values.

The peak of Tate's philosophical vision in essay form was reached
in his Phi Beta Kappa address at the University of Minnesota in
1952. Its basic ideas are the same as Eliot's; though a lesser poet
than Eliot, Tate is a better essayist—he is more urbane, more lucid
than Eliot. The address, also given in part at an international congress in Paris in 1952 and entitled "The Man of Letters in the Modern World," sums up thoughts about humanity and culture that go
back to the early twenties in Nashville. Tate begins the essay with an
examination of Eliot's statement about the "dissociation of sensibility" (made as early as 1921 in "The Metaphysical Poets"), assert-
ing that the Cartesian way of thinking has split man and culture:
"When René Descartes isolated thought from man's total being he
isolated him from nature, including his own nature; and he divided
man against himself." Moving past Descartes, Tate quotes the father of modern urban poets, Baudelaire, concerning the essence of
culture: "The state is the mere operation of society, but culture is
the way society lives." It is the "medium through which men receive
the one lost truth which must be perpetually recovered, the truth
of what Jacques Maritain calls the 'supra-temporal destiny' of
man."⁴¹ For Tate the role of the man of letters is primarily to accomplish that task set by Mallarmé and restated by Eliot in "Little Gidding": to purify the dialect of the tribe. He defines this purification
as the act of communicating through love: "Communication that is
not also communion is incomplete. We *use* communication; we *participate* in communion." Tate tells us, "the true province of the man
of letters is nothing less (as it is nothing more) than culture itself."⁴²
Tate thus puts literature firmly behind what was for him the great
modern problem, the revival of culture.

Lewis Simpson has said that Tate's 1952 address "may possibly
mark not only the terminal date of the New Criticism but of the
whole movement toward the renewal of the literary order in America." The reason for this, Simpson feels, is that "American society
today does not conceive literacy to be a central need in the mainte-

nance of civilizational order." [43] Although Tate after World War II was intensely concerned with artistic and religious values, he was also very much involved in the development of educational values, especially during the seventeen years he taught at the University of Minnesota. For this reason I cannot agree with Simpson's view of Tate that sees him "dreaming of finding himself somewhere in the twelfth century in a small company of clerks." [44] Tate had a side that was clerkish, but he was primarily a twentieth-century urban man of letters. He was a complex, restless man, and a man of masks; but the facts of his biography show that, like Ransom, he spent most of his mature life as a writer and educator, one involved in a form of "religious humanism," a term that he believed summed up the essential nature of the Vanderbilt Agrarian movement.

For many modern writers religion by 1920 seemed outmoded, but the Agrarians were typically southern in their insistence not on the evangelical values the South has been noted for in this century but rather on the sense of ritual and tradition that was basic to the religious expression of the South in the eighteenth century and earlier. After all, religious humanism was a movement of the Renaissance, and in many ways the early eighteenth century was, as Tate's friend Samuel Holt Monk liked to say, the silver age of the Renaissance. Like Eliot and many of the French symbolists and their followers, the Agrarians felt that romanticism alone could not sustain modern man and that the virtues and views of an earlier, more stable age were necessary to stabilize the life of this century. What they believed the age needed was what they believed the South, more than any other American region, had in some part preserved—hierarchy and community. For them tradition and ritual were inevitably linked to both of these concepts and in some form or other had to be preserved if cultural values were not to become amorphous and meaningless.

The Agrarians, it is now believed by many, failed in their common action against what they thought in 1930 was too exclusive an emphasis in America on the "industrial drive." In 1981 Andrew Lytle confessed to this failure: "Certainly we failed to get the kind of attention necessary to delay or modify the evils of Industrialism." He went on to say that "we did not think of ourselves as prophets" and that "after the stock market crash of 1929 and the Depression, our hopes were raised for a time that we might be listened to." [45]

What Lytle and others have failed to see is that 1929 did mark a new period in all of American life. The Agrarians were not so much prophets as harbingers of this period. In the eighties we now speak of the emergence of a postindustrial age when robotics and computers will eliminate any significant human involvement in the industrial process. Ours is increasingly a service economy, and in both our service industries and our remaining heavy industry we now seek communal work rituals similar to those prevalent in Japan. In the eighties Ransom's belief in necessary "economic forms," by which he meant rituals of work, does not sound so very strange: the old assembly line methods are in many industries giving way to new communal work activities. This contemporary movement to improve work rituals is but one part of the socio-political-economic revolution in America that began with Roosevelt's New Deal and promised a wider inclusion of various groups in the mainstream of American life—southerners, blacks, Hispanics, sharecroppers, to name only a few. Paradoxically, the New Deal liberalism that many Agrarians believed reprehensible began a socioeconomic revolution responsible for instituting changes that saved the nation from some of what the Vanderbilt group called "the evils of industrialism."

We can, as I have suggested, still learn something from the Agrarians about the rituals and forms of work, but their greatest contribution is their exploration of aesthetics and education. The basis for both art and education should be, Ransom believed, certain rites and forms that lift these activities above the random competition of individuals. Thus Young explains Ransom's view of the aesthetic forms: "By extension, too, the social order that cherishes its aesthetic forms as well as its economic forms provides for a fuller life than is otherwise available. But of even greater significance is the fact that a civilization is often protected and perpetuated by its aesthetic rather than by its economic forms."[46] Ransom thus led his followers in the direction of aesthetic revival, which for him was the necessary path toward a larger cultural revival. The wide acceptance of Ransom himself (as well as Warren, Tate, Brooks, and others) in important institutions of higher learning in the North is an indication that the nation's educational establishment was willing to listen to the ideas of the Agrarians. Yet their ideas were never prophecies leading people to a promised land. Rather, the Agrarians from the beginning were stating certain general ideas whose time had come, or was about to come.

As for Nashville, Ransom first found it a New South commercial city. Today it is America's country-music capital. This seems appropriate, because Ransom believed that folk art was necessary for a living culture. Nashville, contrary to expectation, did not in the years after 1930 become known primarily as either a commercial or an industrial center. The city that helped launch Ransom and the Agrarians has at last become the center for a kind of artistic endeavor that is at once both communal and traditional, one that grew from a pattern of aesthetic rituals that Ransom himself could accept.

Finally, what the Agrarians, more than anything else, gave their native region was a belief in its own aesthetic forms. After Mencken's castigation of the modern South with terms like "Bible Belt" and "Sahara of the Bozart," most southerners had come to believe that they had little to contribute to the nation. Deeply embedded in the New South's philosophy as stated by Henry W. Grady and his followers is the belief that the region could only try to imitate northern commercialism and industrialism but that it would otherwise remain separate from the nation, cherishing its old ways. The Agrarians, on the other hand, pointed to the green shoots of southern culture still in the region's soil. The correctness of their view is seen generally in the growth of the arts in the South after 1930 and in the restoration of the region as an integral part of the United States, even to the point where the large majority of southerners could at last accept laws put forward by a southern president, Lyndon Johnson, to end racial segregation.

But the greatest proof that the South could bring forth the fruits of a revived culture that was both southern and American was the appearance of a writer hailed throughout the world as a major figure in Western literature. This was William Faulkner, a religious humanist like the Agrarians but also a liberal humanitarian who actively sought in his life and work to bring about racial harmony in the South. Faulkner was aware of the need for religious and artistic rituals. He was the writer, more than any other, who explained the South to itself and to the rest of the world and who confirmed the belief of the Agrarians that the South still had much to offer the nation.

3

William Faulkner
The Memphis-Oxford Connection

More than any other modern writer William Faulkner fulfilled the Agrarians' demand for a poetic genius who would examine southern culture both historically and in the modern context. Yet to approach Faulkner the way scholars approach the Agrarians, through a study of their concepts and their biographies, provides little understanding of his poetic vision. Faulkner's biographer, Joseph Blotner, has demonstrated that many of the characters and events in the Mississippian's fiction spring directly from life; yet the South that Faulkner created in his novels was dramatically transformed by his complex imagination. Thus it is impossible to put Faulkner's biography alongside his literary works and thereby find clear-cut correspondences. Faulkner at his best was not a confessional writer. Like Ransom, on the surface he was a man bound by tradition, but, unlike Ransom, his literary output was prolific, complex. Unlike the Agrarians, Faulkner never expressed himself in terms of complex ideas. When his major creative period had passed, he often wrote in an abstract style that was embarrassing (see *A Fable*, for example). But at his best, in the great novels and stories of the thirties, he was unmatched by any American writer of the century in imaginative power.

How Faulkner differed from the Agrarians as well as from Wolfe or Aiken can be seen in his portrait of Memphis in the early novel that captured the imaginations of many European intellectuals, *Sanctuary*. In this and other novels Faulkner sees Memphis as part of the American megalopolitan sprawl engulfing traditional southern communities and destroying all memory of ordered moral life. Little matter that the Memphis Faulkner knew as a young man was a New South commercial city similar in many ways to the Nashville that the Agrarians knew. Faulkner's imagination, instead of presenting a commercial river city still redolent of the Old South in some ways, successfully transforms Memphis into a city that is represented by an impotent gangster character named Popeye. This gangster, whose malice, Robert Langbaum says, "stems from the sense of his own nothingness," invades the town of Jefferson (modeled on Faulkner's hometown of Oxford).[1] He also rapes a southern belle, Temple Drake, and then carries her off to a Memphis whorehouse.

Here and elsewhere Faulkner suggests that the megalopolitan spirit is gradually annexing a once provincial world to its own disorderly way of life. The provincial town is no longer a pristine example of agrarian tradition and order; it has already been undermined by the great urban sprawl. For instance, Temple Drake, the belle of Jefferson, finds herself right at home in Miss Reba's whorehouse. Popeye and Temple, different as they are, become united by their emptiness. Their psychic connection is Faulkner's way of suggesting that a deep tie unites the world's exploding megalopolis with the culturally decaying towns that surround the great cities, one of these towns being Faulkner's own Oxford, Mississippi.

When *Sanctuary* appeared in 1931 it shocked a section of the American public, but it (and its author) were eventually lumped with other "shocking" southern novels by writers like Erskine Caldwell. Fashionable New York critics like Clifton Fadiman, for instance, admired Robert Penn Warren's *Night Rider* more than one of the masterpieces of the century, Faulkner's *Absalom, Absalom!* Warren's work contained that "violence and passion," in Fadiman's words, that the reading public of the thirties had learned to expect in new southern authors; also, *Night Rider* was written in a realistic style that was comfortable for most readers and critics. Faulkner was the most brilliantly experimental of all American novelists of the thirties; *Sanctuary* represented his breakthrough to an absurdist, expressionistic style that later became more readily accepted in works such as Ralph Ellison's *Invisible Man*. In the thirties and forties, French and other continental writers, Jean-Paul Sartre among them, saw what Faulkner was attempting and how well he was bringing it off. Primarily as a result of their efforts, Faulkner received the Nobel Prize in 1950, an event that helped a great deal to bring him to the attention of large numbers of readers. All of Faulkner's books were out of print in 1946, but his Nobel Prize fame brought him a large reading public and helped to make him the center of a scholarly industry. Unlike Melville—a novelist with whom he may easily be compared—Faulkner received widespread recognition in his own lifetime. Faulkner's earliest academic critics compared him favorably with Hawthorne and Melville, and he does have their moral imagination; but unlike them he also has a sardonic side and even an uproarious sense of fun, as in a story like "Spotted Horses."

The great city, as shown by Faulkner in *Sanctuary*, is moving toward some ultimate horror; it is doomed to the ugly future that awaits nearly everyone in the twentieth century. *Doom* is one of Faulkner's favorite words, as is *rapacious*. Rapacity, in fact, leads to a biblical kind of destruction in Faulkner's apocalyptic visions. By contrast, in his last novel, *The Reivers*, Faulkner's view of the Memphis of his youth is nostalgic; the city is even shown realistically as a center of southern culture. To understand the varying role of the city in Faulkner's work one must compare the ways cities appear in individual works. In *Sanctuary* he creates a powerful image of megalopolis, but in other books southern cities offer an escape from a dreary countryside. Usually, the city in Faulkner's fiction is a place where old cultural values are dissolving and where the machine process is imitated—literally, in some cases, as with Popeye in *Sanctuary*.

Louis D. Rubin, Jr., has written that the theme that preoccupies Allen Tate in his fiction and poetry "is the erosion of tradition and the accompanying sense of dislocation inherent in modern urban society."[2] The same can be said of Faulkner. The chief problem that Faulkner's fiction deals with, as Robert E. Spiller wrote in the fifties, is "the fury and dismay that result when the biologic life force comes into conflict with mechanism." Spiller adds that this is "the central theme of thoughtful literature from Henry Adams to T. S. Eliot."[3] For the sixties Leo Marx in *The Machine in the Garden* and for the seventies Lewis P. Simpson in *The Dispossessed Garden* examine many aspects of this basic American theme. Yet only to see human communities pitted against machines in Faulkner's work is to miss some of the complexity of the many problems of southern culture that the author confronts.

Sanctuary deals in a searching manner with the theme of man and machine, though *Pylon* is more concerned with this problem than any of Faulkner's other novels. In Faulkner's other important writing of the thirties his great theme is the growing collapse of southern community and culture, due not to the machine but to human rapacity. The source of this rapacity in Faulkner's characters can be found, as I have earlier noted, in what Langbaum tells us is the chief problem dramatized by major modern writers like Yeats, Lawrence, and Faulkner: narcissism and the need to achieve a personal identity. Thomas Daniel Young's *The Past in the Present* (1981) goes beyond Spiller, Marx, and Simpson by revealing the complexity of the decline and death of old southern values caught up in social narcissism and the inevitable attempts to maintain old values. Young, for instance, examines Tate's *The Fathers* and Faulkner's *The Unvanquished*, compares the different views of the two authors about the reasons for southern cultural decline, and points out that both authors seek to show how values may be revived. In *The Unvanquished*, Young writes, Faulkner shows "how through the Civil War the established social order may be destroyed and, at the same time, suggests the means by which some of the values of a traditional society may be perpetuated."[4] Young is correct to point to the views of Tate, Faulkner, and other writers as attesting to the fact that southern cultural values were declining before the Civil War, before machinery was a major factor in the life of the region. However, I suggest that Faulkner also shows that southern society was damaged but not entirely destroyed by the Civil War.

I believe that Faulkner did not see southern culture and social disintegration as primarily a matter of the "bad" city with its machinery versus the "good," that is, traditional, agrarian world. Instead, for him nineteenth-century southern society, both before and after the Civil War, was an urban-rural continuum, an agribusiness complex built primarily on the concepts of community and hierarchy. He began *Sartoris* (1929) by describing his own great-grandfather in the character of Colonel Sartoris, prototype of the nineteenth-century southern hierarch. The old Colonel Falkner was a Confederate soldier, lawyer, politician, builder, entrepreneur, and novelist. He was clearly a man at home in both Memphis and Ripley and in those other Mississippi towns that he hoped to tie together with his own railroad. How different he was from those southern planters whom Eugene Genovese defines as the "pre-capitalist, quasi-aristocratic landowners who had to adjust their economy to a capitalistic world market."[5] Some planters no doubt resembled the Genovese portrait, but most hierarchs of southern society were far more likely to resemble Colonel Falkner—though few had all of his abilities. Tate points out in his essay "The Profession of Letters in the South" that much of typical eighteenth-century life continued into the nineteenth century in the South. The typical eighteenth-century leader in the South was a Renaissance man capable of both urban and rural activities. For this reason more than any other, southern hierarchs like Washington played such a powerful role in the nation's history between 1770 and 1830. With the rise of the "cotton snobs" after 1820 in the southern uplands, a kind of chivalric "aristocracy," influenced by the cult of Victorian medievalism, briefly flourished in that realm called the Cotton Kingdom before the rise of the New South relegated this way of life to history books.

Rubin believes that the old Colonel Falkner inspired his great-grandson to become not just an ordinary writer but a very great writer. Certainly Faulkner was not inspired by his own father, Murry Falkner, and Rubin may be right when he says that "his great-grandson saw himself as giving to his writing the importance and energy William C. Falkner had brought to railroad building, politics, and to his military career."[6] Faulkner had a certain amount of respect for southern hierarchs and the Old Colonel, as he was called, was the chief hierarch of the family. But, as I will suggest, Faulkner's view of all the older hierarchs was highly ambivalent because he was aware of their narcissism and the rapacity that grew out of their need to establish powerful images of themselves. Faulkner was far more complex than any of his forebears, and this complexity can be seen in his early attraction to the world of modern literature and philosophy. He also reached out to the city, bypassing higher education with only a quarter's work at the University of Mississippi. Fittingly, New Orleans was the city in which he chose to pursue his literary fortune. This city, more than any other, was the chief cultural pipeline before the Civil War for the Mississippi uplands where Faulkner lived. After the war Memphis eclipsed New Orleans as a cultural center for northern Mississippi, but both cities were important culturally for the state. In the words of David Cohen, which Faulkner paraphrased in a *Holiday* article, the state of Mississippi begins in the lobby of the Peabody Hotel in Memphis and ends in the Gulf of Mexico. New Orleans was always important to Faulkner; but because he returned to Oxford to live out the rest of his life, Memphis was the single most important city in his life and work.

In New Orleans Faulkner wrote newspaper articles and met Sherwood Anderson, who helped him publish his first novel, *Soldier's Pay* (1926). In 1927 he published a novel about New Orleans called *Mosquitoes*, which satirizes a gathering of effete sophisticates in a manner that has little in common with the brooding, tragic Faulkner of the later novels. But two aspects of *Mosquitoes* did foreshadow the major Faulkner works: the direct influence of Joyce, also evident in *The Sound and the Fury* two years later, and a concern for ritual. A character in *Mosquitoes* speaks of people who "destroy life by making it a ritual" and contrasts them with others who "put life into ritual by making conventions a living part of life."[7] Faulkner's interest in ritual is essential to an understanding of his mythic approach to life. Massive Faulkner scholarship since 1960 has demonstrated how deeply Faulkner had delved into Joyce, Frazer, and Bergson. Thomas L. McHaney, for instance, has shown in detail how Faulkner made extensive use of basic concepts concerning myth first developed by Frazer in *The Golden Bough*, the work that deeply influenced Eliot in the composition of *The Waste Land*. Faulkner's Oxford friend and literary mentor, Phil Stone, introduced him to Joyce's *Ulysses* early on, and studies of at least one of his masterpieces, *The Sound and the Fury*, show the strong influence of Joyce in matters of technique and style. Yet Faulkner probably learned most about the mythical method from the novels of Joseph Conrad and Thomas Mann. He regularly reread Conrad's *Nostromo* and *Lord Jim* and Mann's *Buddenbrooks*. Mann's work spoke to Faulkner of a dying society, whereas in Conrad he found possibilities of heroism on the frontiers of civilization. These were the themes that Faulkner pondered most when he took Sherwood Anderson's advice to write about the world he knew best, the upland South that he had left when he went to New Orleans to seek in the city, as modern writers have so often done, a more sophisticated way of life than he had known in the provinces.

When Faulkner finally found a fictional style and a subject matter that suited him in the writing of his third novel, *Sartoris* (1929), he had anchored himself emotionally in the upland South. In writing about this region, he went beyond what any American writer has accomplished, defining an entire culture within the context of the past, the present, and even the future. Unlike many southern writers—Caldwell, for instance—Faulkner did not simply select one small area and write about it. Instead his Jefferson (Oxford, Mississippi) and his Yoknapatawpha County (Lafayette County) are seen as part of a much larger area, as a rural-urban continuum that included Memphis and sometimes New Orleans. He saw with a clarity few novelists have ever had that past, present, and future all impinge on one another. Thus his well-known statement that the past is not dead, it is not even past, is rightly quoted as evidence of Faulkner's insight into a southern culture that, more than any other in America, had centered its thinking on the past. At his best, Faulkner sees his community of southern gentry as one of three; no other novelist has ever delved as deeply into the three great southern communities—the gentry, blacks, and yeomanry—and into the interactions of these peoples. Faulkner spent hours silently listening to the conversations of the people around him, and some of his dialogue is itself a great gift to anyone seeking to understand the day-to-day life of the early twentieth-century South.

Faulkner's profound, instinctive understanding of the upland South is based in large part on years of study in residence, but he was not completely anchored in the South. A restlessness and a need for money drove him both north and west. He always loved to walk down Park Avenue in New York, and even though he generally hated Hollywood, where he was often forced to go to make money as a scriptwriter, he could make himself comfortable with friends and other writers there. Thus it is possible to see Faulkner the man (as well as the writer) at ease with a cosmopolitan way of life. One writer on the life and work of Faulkner, David Minter, tells us that "for years Faulkner had regarded himself as a person who had chosen art over the provincial values and prejudices that were a part of his heritage." He goes on to speak of Faulkner's "exploring the social implications of that self-conception," having pointed out that Faulkner in the fifties "directly confronted an issue that was more and more to occupy him: racism, he said, was the world's greatest problem, tolerance its only hope."[8]

Faulkner did have a liberal side, but his best creative efforts must not be confused with his liberalism. When he states liberal opinions in his work he is a spokesman for ideas he himself sometimes has trouble clarifying. Floyd Watkins in *The Flesh and the Word: Eliot, Hemingway, Faulkner* has analyzed in detail Faulkner's artistic failures when opinion and abstract idea take over in his fiction. Faulkner himself often but not always held to liberal ideas; however, his best writing only occasionally deals with these particular values. As

I will later suggest, it is possible, as in the case of Thomas Wolfe, to write powerful novels on the subject of the writer's search to develop himself as an artist and even on the discovery of a national revival based in part on liberal concepts. But, though Faulkner admired Wolfe's novels, he did not very much resemble the North Carolinian. Wolfe was a confessional fictionist par excellence, while Faulkner was Joyce's "objective" novelist, existing like Joyce behind his work rather than confessing his soul in the work.

Though Faulkner was urbane, his heart was always in the provinces. He was, like Ransom the poet, at his best struggling with the failings and the values of the South, which his psyche could never really leave no matter how often he traversed other regions. The great difference between Faulkner and the Agrarians is that he was never an essayist—they are often at their best as essayists—and he had a poetic power unequaled by any of them. Faulkner had at first hoped to write successful verse, but his poems are at best minor. Although he sometimes thought of himself as a failed poet, his best novels are filled with the spirit of poetry. More than any other modern American novelists, Faulkner and Hemingway were read for the poetic power of their prose as well as for their profound analyses of individual psyches. Because of his literary virtues of clarity, conciseness, and elegance Hemingway received widespread recognition much earlier than Faulkner did. The very complexity and variety of Faulkner's various styles misled or discouraged many of his early readers. But by the time he received the Nobel Prize, his poetic powers were being appreciated by increasing numbers of Americans. Careful readers were discovering that Faulkner, far more than the Agrarians or anyone else, had explained certain intricacies of southern culture that had never before been dealt with in any works of art. Though he often wrote in the absurdist style typical of much of *Sanctuary,* he could also write more realistically, clearly revealing the complexities of the various communities that made up the southern culture he knew. Thus, though he resembled the Agrarians in many ways, he went far beyond them in the breadth of his view and the depth of his imagination. And he could accept at deeper levels than any of the Agrarians the decline of the South's culture.

For Faulkner the chief cause of cultural decline was the failure of those hierarchs often loosely called "aristocrats." In his depiction of these leaders Faulkner identifies such internal forces as pride, lust, and anger; for, as Minter puts it, "the forces that threatened or at least troubled Faulkner were internal and psychological as well as external and social."⁹ Faulkner's attitude toward the handful of men who led the South before and after the Civil War is always ambivalent, and this ambivalence adds depth to his portrayal of them. For instance, the stories about his great-grandfather, told and retold within the family, were myths and legends to Faulkner and often were treated as such in his fiction. Yet Faulkner was also deeply aware of the failures of leaders like the Old Colonel, who successfully led his regiment at the Battle of Manassas but who was voted out of his command by his troops because of personal failings. As Minter writes, "All of the Falkners thought themselves aristocrats; they could be stiff, proud, overbearing. But they were not snobs, and they enjoyed much casual intercourse with every segment of Mississippi society."¹⁰ The Old Colonel was an "aristocrat" in both the American and the upland southern sense. He had risen from obscurity, had acquired money, power, and estates, and had commanded men. His life illustrates fully the concept of the southern urban-rural continuum; he was, unlike some of the lesser gentry, as much at home in the Peabody Hotel in Memphis as he was on the courthouse square of his small hometown. But Faulkner's story of the Old Colonel and his family, extending from a time shortly before the Civil War to the 1920s, could not be presented as heroic legend, even though the author had heard it told as such. Instead, because he was so acutely aware of the failure of southern cultural values and because his family and others like it were so much a part of that failure, Faulkner could only present the fictionalized version of his family's life as a tragedy, not an unmitigated tragedy but a tragedy nevertheless.

In his four greatest novels—*The Sound and the Fury* (1929), *As I Lay Dying* (1930), *Light in August* (1932), and *Absalom, Absalom!* (1936)—Faulkner exposed the psychological roots of the southern hierarchy's failure in the period between 1865 and 1930. Two types of hierarchs emerged and held power in this period. One is represented in Faulkner's fiction by the Compson family, which wraps itself in a narcissistic dream of earlier glory associated with the Old South. Thomas Sutpen represents the other type—those who seek a sense of identity by forcing themselves to the top of the hierarchy and, in their efforts to maintain the grand style, tend to crush others below them in the social scale. The Sartoris family, modeled on the Falkners, stands somewhere in between, having characteristics of both groups. The dreams of glory of these aristocrats bring on their decline, and the way is thus opened for the rise of yeoman families like the Snopeses, prototypes of southern "rednecks" who seek to supplant the old hierarchy by acquiring land, money, and power. At the core of his drama of the fall of the old families and the rise of new people from the lower levels, Faulkner shows the failure of love, a failure that tears apart families and social groups. This failure is also related to an obsession with race and sex that drives apart the black and white communities as well as men and women. No southern writer explores the agony of southern decay as deeply as Faulkner, and yet for all his probing of psychological and social ills, no novelist of the region so convincingly portrays the possibility of the revival of values.

Like the Agrarians, Faulkner believed in values associated with ritual and religion. His approach to religion is examined by Cleanth Brooks in *The Hidden God* (1963). William Bedford Clark suggests that Brooks sees a "close analogy between the search for self-knowledge . . . and the Christian quest for redemption."[11] He describes Faulkner's work as influenced by both Ransom and Eliot—essentially Christian, though not specifically orthodox. Certain characters in Faulkner search for ways to develop their souls—to develop an inner belief—as well as ways to give life to outdated rituals and codes. These characters become capable of self-knowledge. Those who cling instead to their narcissistic dreams as well as to their ideals and images of the past and future lose the very identity they seek. Brooks, like Eliot, emphasizes the importance of both ritual and dogma for a meaningful life. Faulkner does the same, but he also expresses a basic idea in Tate's philosphy: through grace the individual can share a communion with others.

In his first great novel, *The Sound and the Fury*, Faulkner clearly demonstrates in certain characters the possibility of encountering what Mircea Eliade calls the element of the sacred in religious ritual. For Eliade this encounter with the sacred is the basis of the mythic experience; it is what makes possible a giving up of outdated values in order to achieve new, creative life in the present. The chief character in the book who encounters the sacred—or grace, an older name for this religious quality—is Dilsey Gibson, a black woman whose portait in the book is based on a Falkner family servant, Caroline Barr. Dilsey's encounter with the sacred enables her and other members of her family to live with love and dignity, with what Faulkner calls the "old virtues," although they are caught up in the madness of the Compson family and the racial persecution of Mississippi. In his description of Dilsey and her family and friends in the Compson Appendix sometimes published at the beginning of the book, Faulkner simply says, "They endured." In the context of the book Faulkner shows a group of blacks whose spiritual leader is Dilsey, not just holding on in stoic endurance but going on with their lives while the white aristocrats who employ them are dying psychically and literally before their eyes. Thus in the Compsons and others like them Faulkner depicts the disintegration of the cultural values of the gentry, living side by side with their servants, who manage to survive and, on a religious level, even flourish. Dilsey herself proclaims the end of the old order and her religious life becomes a symbol of renewal.

The section of *The Sound and the Fury* titled "April 18, 1928" epitomizes the Faulknerian vision of the life, death, and rebirth of the South. To introduce this vision the author first shows the pain and the pettiness of Dilsey's community of black servants. They are neither idealized nor stripped of their dignity. They suffer from persecution, but they are not primarily working the land, nor are they part of the neoslavery of certain twentieth-century plantations. The black urban-rural continuum is always evident. Frony, for instance, is presented in the Appendix as one "who married a pullman porter and went to St. Louis to live and later moved back to Memphis to make a home for her mother since Dilsey refused to go further than that."[12] The black community in Faulkner's fiction is depicted in its relationship to family and church, and the hierarchy of the black community includes women like Dilsey among its leaders.

Dilsey's leadership is based chiefly on her spiritual and moral strength. Though she has her faults, she constantly shows, by the way she lives her life, that a loving community is possible—even while her white employers, who claim leadership, are in effect betraying this possibility. When Frony says that she wishes Dilsey would not keep bringing the retarded Compson son, Benjy, to church, Dilsey gives an answer based on her belief in the unity of all human beings: "Tell um de good Lawd dont keer whether he smart er not. Dont nobody but white trash keer dat." Yet she also suffers from a feeling of inner pain, and she goes hopefully to church one day when the service is to be led by a preacher from St. Louis, who it is said "will give her de comfort en de unburdenin."[13] This man, the Reverent Shegog, is no ordinary preacher, but a shaman who promises a vision of "the power and the glory." He invites all to a mystical participation in a shamanic ritual in which those who give themselves to the experience encounter the same vision as the preacher.

After the service all are amazed by the shaman's visionary act, but the effect of mystical participation is strongest on Dilsey. She walks away from the church, head held high, weeping. She tells Frony, "I've seed de first en de last," and then, "I seed de beginnin, en now I sees de endin."[14] She has achieved that momentary glimpse of unity, the connection between end and beginning that is in all creative acts and in the life of her own culture: its pristine power as well as its tragic downfall. Dilsey thus affirms what Eliade calls the mythic continuum of life, death, and rebirth. She has experienced the life and death of one phase of southern culture, and through her ritualistic experience she deepens her own inner life, from which springs her strong moral sense. Thus strengthened, she can return to the painful task of taking care of the disintegrating Compson family.

The primary juxtaposition of *The Sound and the Fury* is that of Dilsey and her family on one side and the Compsons on the other. Her opposite, Mrs. Compson, also has "religion," but it is a religion of words that has little real effect on her character or her emotions. In fact, for Mrs. Compson words and concepts block the natural flow of human emotion and insight and erect barriers between people. As Panthea R. Broughton says of the best of the Compsons: "Quentin cannot move with any current. He would prefer to find shelter in a few rigid and clean concepts."[15] Quentin, who lives chiefly in a narcissistic world that he creates from the history of the Compson family, acts out his death wish, which springs from the pain of his isolation and guilt. He is a tragic figure in that he has the ability to love as well as a searching mind, but he cannot break out of his narcissistic shell. The one person he loves, his sister Caddy, he loves for "some concept of Compson honor."[16] Like many southerners, Quentin went north—to Harvard and Boston—to find himself, but he never learned how to extricate himself from his family.

In his earliest and most brilliant works Faulkner portrays the southern gentry of the upland South as a community caught up in guilt and rage, burdened by their worship of past exploits and lost ideals. In his obsession with the past Quentin represents his community. Cleanth Brooks rightly says that this obsession "is in fact a repudiation of the future. It amounts to the sense of having no future." [17] Dilsey on the other hand, through participation in religious ritual, can hold both past and future before her eyes, seeing alpha and omega as essentially one. Her vision of an underlying metaphysical unity enables her to love others and gives her an inner sense of the triumph of life over death. Quentin, haunted by a doomed past and sensing a doomed future, can only sink into death, never having really known his inner self. He is a victim of Cartesian duality—that is, concepts of honor and family are separate from the emotions of love and hate struggling within him. Tate in his Phi Beta Kappa address quotes Auden's line "We must love one another or die" and states that "man loves his neighbor, as well as the man he has never seen, only through the love of God." [18] Quentin must die at last because he loses his ability to love; he becomes entangled in dead concepts and empty images of a glorified past. This fate is inevitable for Quentin, but not for Faulkner, who would always "decline to accept the end of man" as he put it in his Nobel Prize speech. His best novels and stories from 1929 on would be partly a search for the connecting unity that frees man from Cartesian dualism and makes possible human freedom and love.

The very next year, 1930, brought another major work, *As I Lay Dying.* In it Faulkner turned away from white aristocrats, who through narcissism were leading their communities to cultural death, and away from their black attendants, who with the help of ritual carried on the leftover life of southern culture. Instead he took up the story of the yeoman community of the South, not in the expressionistic manner of Caldwell or O'Connor but in a sympathetic manner based on his own careful observance of their communal way of life. Many Faulkner critics do not regard the Bundrens as being members of the yeomanry, but clearly they are because, though poor, they own land and have a sense of belonging to a community of their own. They are not part of that dispossessed group of southerners consisting mainly of sharecroppers and "poor white trash" who possess little sense of belonging to a community. It was as if, after creating Mrs. Compson, a white southern woman who exemplified the death process of the South, Faulkner had to draw the portrait of another white woman, Addie Bundren, who, though dying, was still seeking self-knowledge. Addie does not think of herself as poor or rich or of any particular class. She reveals the vein of iron that is also in some of Ellen Glasgow's characters, the kind of women who were once the central figures of much of southern life. Addie's tragedy is that she is dying in loneliness, watching her family disintegrate. Her Protestantism has failed to give a ritualistic significance to her life. Of Addie's tragedy Minter writes: "Like the society of which it is a part, the family restricts yet no longer sustains its members. The problem lies at the center: possessing no principle of order and no capacity for love, the parents fail to spread order and love around them." [19]

The failure of Addie's marriage and her family life can in part be attributed to the hypocrisy of her husband, Anse, and that of the Reverend Whitfield and her friend Cora. As she is dying she refuses to hide behind words and concepts as these three do, but searches her own soul for the meaning of her pain and the pain of her family. This inner searching, carried on through much of her life, gives her a dignity the other three lack. In her, Faulkner has shown one aspect of the Protestant South. The collapse of Protestantism as an effective mythic force has much to do with the community's failures, Faulkner seems to be saying. In the Reverend Whitfield, Faulkner presents a character who, like Mrs. Compson, knows all the right words about religion but has none of the inner grace necessary for meaningful religious experience.

We see in *As I Lay Dying* that the inevitable tendency of humans, when deprived of ritual and symbolism, is to make rituals of their own. In her classroom, Addie as teacher conducts a sadomasochistic rite of whipping her students and effects a kind of perverse relationship with her students that parallels the racist fanaticism of the larger community. Deprived of meaningful ritual in her life, Addie tries to create rituals that will bind her in an emotional relationship with her students, but the result is an increase in alienation. The same kind of pain and alienation is revealed in *Light in August* in the relationship between white racists and their black victims.

Individual attempts in *As I Lay Dying* to create rituals do not always result in pain and alienation. Addie's children, for instance, invent rituals that serve, at least briefly, to relate them creatively to nature and to other people. In his pioneer study of the Christian symbolism in *As I Lay Dying*, Hyatt Howe Waggoner points to the sacramental use of nature by Addie's children, who, deprived of religious ritual, seek symbol and ritual wherever they can find it. The greatest symbol of the book is the fish, which, in its bleeding, is symbolic of both the suffering of Addie and the love of Christ. Vardaman, for instance, cries out: "'Where is ma, Darl?' I said. 'You never got her. You knew she is a fish but you let her get away.'" [20]

Addie becomes the Christ-fish, momentarily held and then lost but still offering herself to the suffering community of her family. Some of the most powerful scenes in the novel are those portraying the brief insights of Addie's children into their own need for symbols and rites that will renew the dying family and community relationships all around them. Even as Faulkner shows the dying community of white small farmers, he also records the dignity and emotional warmth of at least some of its members.

The greatness of *The Sound and the Fury* and *As I Lay Dying* consists partly of Faulkner's unearthing of the folk communities of blacks and yeomanry, especially the hill people, in Mississippi. Studying Faulkner in relationship to these two communities of the South, the way Constance Rourke studies the painter Charles Sheeler in connection with the Shaker community, one finds an amazing richness of detail. Though he was a member of the gentry, Faulkner spent many hours in Oxford listening to poor farmers talk, and he studied carefully the inner workings of the black community and its religious ritual. Unlike any other southern author, he made a deep commitment to understanding both the black and the yeoman communities. In *Light in August,* one of his greatest works, he presents a member of the gentry, the Reverend Gail Hightower, who reaches out to individuals of these other two communities and thereby suggests the possibility of communal relations based not on hatred and distrust but on concern and mutual respect.

The central figure of *Light in August* is Hightower, not the mulatto Joe Christmas, as some have thought. Faulkner seems to have begun the novel with Joe Christmas as the symbolic center, but the symbol got away from him and developed a life of its own. Thus the story of a man caught between blacks and whites—searching for his identity and forced to wander aimlessly until at last he is lynched by a town mad with racial violence—becomes for Faulkner not the central event of the novel but rather the tragic background against which a mythic comedy is played out. The central event of the novel is based on Hightower's searching for the meaning of his life and finding it in his relationship with a member of the southern yeomanry, Byron Bunch. Bunch, like Addie Bundren, represents the struggle for dignity of the small southern farmers and tradespeople who formed the backbone of the southern yeomanry. Byron is a rustic knight who finds his lovely lady in Lena Grove, who is engaged in a search for the man who made her pregnant. Gail

Hightower becomes Byron's priest and even helps in the birthing of Lena's baby. This part of the novel, against the background of racial fury and the lynching of Joe Christmas, is essentially comic. In fact, the story of Hightower and Bunch is comic in the Chaucerian sense, implying the hope of renewed life for the shattered old southern community. The story also contains the serious matter of the mythic death and rebirth of Gail Hightower through his participation in the birth of Lena's baby.

In achieving his own renewal by reaching out to those he had once stood apart from, Gail Hightower discovers the meaning of religious values that help to liberate him from his guilt and narcissism. Robert Jacobs describes the meaning of the delivery of Lena's child for Hightower: "Having performed an act of human responsibility, having breached the wall of his own person, Hightower manages a kind of redemption." Jacobs goes on to suggest that Hightower, like Quentin Compson, had been narcissistically caught up in the past: "He had bought and paid for his dream of the past, that past that became his person. In his final recognition, however, he became aware of his solipsism, of how he had sacrificed his wife to live in a dream world."[21] Unlike other Faulkner characters who seek to escape their past through violence, Hightower creatively chooses to admit his flaws and walk out to meet and relate with others. He prepares for his redemption with a long period of introspection. In examining his soul, he sees how he has been a failure as a minister and as a husband. Admitting his errors, Hightower relearns the ritual of private prayer. He sees that his earlier failure was a result of his flight from life: "He believed with a calm joy that if ever there was shelter, it would be the Church."[22] In seeking to withdraw into a kind of religious sanctuary, he had become "the instrument of her [his wife's] despair and death."[23] His flight from life had been a flight from encountering evil, and had led to his joining the "professionals" who control the church and "who have removed the bells from its steeples." He sees that religion in a time of social decay can become "sky-pointed not with ecstasy or passion but in adjuration, threat, and doom."[24] According to Jacobs, Faulkner views the failure of Protestantism as a consequence of its inability to allow individuals, through penance, to be freed from their guilt.

The Protestant tyranny that Hightower confronts everywhere always speaks threateningly of doom and never offers the possibility of forgiveness, or release from the past, or the continuing rebirth of the soul. The greatest racial bigots in Faulkner's novels speak with complete assurance that God is directing them as instruments of destruction against all who disagree with them. Their dualistic minds see only those who are for or against them. They have not searched their souls for sin; therefore they project their own destructiveness onto others, particularly blacks, whom they view as repositories of everything negative in their community. Percy Grimm is the sum of these characters; it is he who leads the lynching party that castrates Joe Christmas and it is he who shoots Christmas. Grimm is Faulkner's symbol of a dying culture and the failure of all communal values.

In *Absalom, Absalom!* Faulkner presents an even greater symbol of communal destructiveness in the person of Thomas Sutpen. *Absalom, Absalom!* is Faulkner's ultimate statement about the rage and power of a man obsessed by certain images in his search for identity. It also contains an apocalyptic statement of rebirth: out of the destructiveness of an obsessed individual will ultimately come, Faulkner tells us, new life and new forms of culture. As an instrument of the destruction of southern culture, Thomas Sutpen is caught from childhood in the grip of a dualistic vision. As a poor boy in Virginia early in the nineteenth century he comes to the front door of a great white mansion, symbolic of southern aristocracy, and is told by a black servant to go to the back door. From then on he believes that rich is good and poor is bad, that white money means the good life and that black or white poverty means subservience; he develops a view of life that sets black against white and wealth against poverty. He can never escape this dualism and builds his life upon it. Like Scarlett O'Hara after the Civil War, he realizes that to possess the symbol of wealth and power—that is, the great white house on a large estate—which he needs to believe in his self-created identity, he must go where the money is. He becomes involved in the web of agribusiness, which carries him to the West Indies and thus to the commercial web that links four continents—the two Americas, Africa, and Europe. But for all his monetary success, he cannot realize his dream of power until he has erected the great mansion in Mississippi.

When the mansion and the estate are ready, one more thing is needed: a dynasty. But, despite the fact that he has both white and black children, he cannot bring to life a family tradition. His own racism infects all his family relationships and leads ultimately to the collapse of the dynasty he seeks to create. Sutpen's evil springs from his willful desire to possess people and land; but Faulkner also shows the pitifulness of Sutpen's inner life, how he is possessed by the image of the great mansion. As Shakespeare shows the damnation of Macbeth, Faulkner shows the psychic destruction of Sutpen: "That this Faustus, this demon, this Beelzebub fled hiding from some monetary flashy glare of his Creditor's outraged face exasperated beyond all endurance, hiding, scuttling into respectability like a jackal into a rockpile." [25]

By the time Sutpen erects the mansion, Faulkner has made it clear that he is the instrument of a diabolical force. For a long time Faulkner reread Conrad's *Lord Jim* once a year, and there he found a strong sense of what Conrad called the "dark power." Faulkner uses his psychic sense of other worlds intruding upon the flesh-and-blood world to describe the sudden appearance of this rootless man, devoid of culture, who builds a mansion and a dynasty: "this Faustus who appeared suddenly one Sunday with two pistols and twenty subsidiary demons and skulldugged a hundred miles of land out a poor ignorant Indian and built the biggest house on it you ever saw." [26]

On the rock of miscegenation Sutpen's ship founders. His empire collapses mainly because of his failure to provide for his black offspring, as well as his abhorrence of any ritual liaison between black and white. But out of the fires of lust and greed—as well as the literal fire, set by his own black child in 1910, that destroys the mansion—springs the hope of a new life to be carried on by descendants of the family. The prophecy of new life is fittingly supplied by Quentin Compson's roommate at Harvard, Shreve McCannon. After the entire story of the Sutpens has been told to him, Shreve says of Jim Bond, the last black descendant, who disappears from the estate in 1910: "I think that in time the Jim Bonds are going to conquer the western hemisphere. Of course it won't quite be in our time and of course as they spread toward the poles they will bleach out again like rabbits and the birds do, so they won't show up so sharp against the snow. But it will still be Jim Bond, and so in a few thousand years, I who regard you will also have sprung from the loins of African kings." [27]

The final statement of the novel is Quentin's; he replies to Shreve's question of "Why do you hate the South?" by repeating "I don't hate it" over and over as he tries to repress his own bitterness at having become hopelessly involved in the downfall of the southern ruling class. [28] Quentin represses the hate he feels because of his suffering at the hands of his family who, like Sutpen, live only for the sake of using people and things to satisfy their desires. In the telling of his intolerable tale he begins to realize that only those who are capable of lasting human relationships can bring forth new life, that he and his sister and those who followed Sutpen's way are too broken by dualism and despair to flourish and to replenish the land. Thus Quentin affirms that only through reviving family and communal relationships can the culture of the South be revived. What Faulkner reveals in *Absalom, Absalom!* is how Quentin becomes possessed by a narcissistic fixation on the past, making it impossible for him to ever free himself from hopeless images and ideals.

William Faulkner himself doubtless had many of Quentin's characteristics. Rubin writes: "If we equate Quentin's general background and station with that of young William Faulkner, we realize, from reading Blotner's biography and from the evidence of the novels themselves, what the young William Faulkner had that Quentin Compson lacked—the Sutpen-like dream of greatness, which for him took the form of vocation, the desire to be an author, and the imagination and self-knowledge that could make that dream a reality." [29] I have earlier suggested that Faulkner went to cities like New Orleans, New York, and Los Angeles in order to develop and practice his vocation as a writer as well as to develop an urbane side of himself that manifested itself early in his life. Unlike Quentin—or Thomas Wolfe—Faulkner never tried to find himself at a place like Harvard. He did, however, serve a kind of educational apprenticeship to his friend and mentor Phil Stone; in addition, Faulkner's later visits and addresses at educational institutions were an important aspect of his declining years. With all this in mind, I would still say that the chief way in which Faulkner moved beyond an inherited narcissism similar to Quentin's was in his continuing search for self-knowledge within the Oxford-Memphis cultural continuum. Applying Brooks's theory that the quest for self-knowledge in Faulkner and other southern writers like him is tied up with the religious quest, one can see that Faulkner related his observations about the rituals and moral actions of people in his own community to his inner development. In his fiction, individuals who have developed some degree of inner life based on self-knowledge have a depth of character others lack. Jacobs says that Addie Bundren's life "was an attempt to break through the walls of her solitude and find some meaning." [30] Addie never finds the meaning she seeks because she is separated from meaningful cultural institutions, but her search nevertheless gives her a kind of nobility. Faulkner himself, both personally and in his novels, found a kind of self-knowledge that led him to accept communal responsibility—and to move beyond solitude and isolation to meaningful relations with others. In studying the Falkner family servant Caroline Barr, the model for Dilsey, he found an example of one who continually reached out to others. For Faulkner the hope for revival of the shattered southern community he saw everywhere around him lay in the actions of people like Caroline Barr.

There are more characters like Dilsey in Faulkner's fiction than one might imagine. Not only are there blacks and poor whites but there are also representatives of the gentry who seek self-knowledge and true communication with others. Caught up in a sense of fatality, or "doom," two of the old families of Yoknapatawpha, the Sartorises and the Compsons, collapse; but members of a third "great" family, the McCaslins, "possessed a capacity for penance almost as great as their pride."[31] McCaslin repudiates not only the pride that isolates members of the gentry from other groups but also the destruction of nature by people who have rejected the cultural values inherent in their community. These people, McCaslin sees, are destroying not only the community but the very biosphere. In the story "Delta Autumn" McCaslin at last sees clearly the connection between the destruction of nature and the obsession with power and pleasure that draws men once tied to the land to cities like Memphis and Chicago: "*This land which man has deswamped and denuded and deriuered in two generations so that white men can own plantations and commute every night to Memphis and black men own plantations and ride in jim crow cars to Chicago to live in millionaires mansions on Lakeshore Drive.*"[32] The Memphis-Oxford connection had once been a union of urban civilizing influences stretching into the villages and the countryside, but in modern times, Faulkner is saying, the connection has become a matter of individuals from the country seeking the wealth of cities. The obsession with wealth and power is based on the need for identity that is missing from lives in which no search for personal development or self-knowledge has been undertaken through education, religion, or even within the lonely isolation of the individual ego. Those who seek their identity in a past of supposed family glory (or shame), like Quentin or Horace Benbow, can only look on impotently while families like the Snopeses discard all values in a mad rush to get enough money and power to take over the towns and then move on to the cities in search of even more money and power. Finally, in narcissists like *Sanctuary's* Temple Drake, a belle whose identity resides in the greatness of her family, we see the lure of the megalopolitan aspects of Memphis. Her acceptance of Popeye and Miss Reba's whorehouse is based on a belief that the megalopolis offers ultimate pleasures.

By 1940, when Faulkner published *The Hamlet,* his first book devoted to the career of the Snopes family, the author's creative powers were beginning to wane. *The Hamlet,* nevertheless, is a comic triumph; it represents, in one sense, Faulkner's acceptance of the rapacity of those southerners who were driven, like Sutpen, to find their identity in money, prestige, and power. Unlike Sutpen, however, the Snopeses are incapable of real tragedy. Lacking Sutpen's complex personality, they are presented as human termites, who in time become symbolic of the ravenous lower orders who will do anything to get money and power. Like Sutpen their eye is always on the white mansion and all it stands for; thus Faulkner fittingly entitled his last novel about the Snopes clan *The Mansion.*

Faulkner's final fictional statement in his declining creative years during and after World War II deals not so much with destruction and rapacity as with the possibility still latent in southern culture for the revival of both communal and hierarchal values. Out of his strongest creative period had come figures like Reverend Hightower, Byron Bunch, and Dilsey Gibson, who seek ways of restoring the values of religion and family in their lives. In later characters like Sam Fathers and Boon Hogganbeck in *Go Down, Moses* (1942) he presents individuals who still live by the rituals of the forest and the hunt. In the character of Isaac McCaslin he suggests the possibility of modern individuals returning to rituals that will allow human beings to interact creatively with nature. As he grew older Faulkner became increasingly aware that ritual undertaken with faith and concern for human development was necessary for sustaining culture. *The Reivers,* published shortly before the author's death in 1962, looks back to a more tranquil period of history when ritual and belief actually sustained connections between Memphis and the surrounding town and countryside and, to an extent at least, served to hold in check the destructive impulses of humanity. Even in *A Requiem for a Nun* (1951), a continuation of the story of Temple Drake and her destructive ways, Faulkner describes the development of political rituals that sum up the life of the community. The second section of the book, "The Golden Dome," is about the state capitol, which symbolizes the political aspect of that culture which molded pioneers into living members of a law-abiding community. In *A Fable* (1954) Faulkner writes allegorically about the death and passion of Christ, thus invoking that essential action of death and rebirth which ritual encompasses. *A Fable* records Faulkner's mature judgment that humanity, despite its mistakes, will at last prevail. Faulkner had hoped it would be his "great book," but critics agree that it does not represent the author at his best; nevertheless it does reveal Faulkner's continuing meditation on the revival of religious and humanitarian values.

It is Lucas Beauchamp, a black man who appears in several works, who summarizes the virtues Faulkner enumerated in his Nobel Prize acceptance speech: "courage and honor and hope and pride and compassion and pity and sacrifice." Beauchamp is a natural aristocrat in the Jeffersonian sense, a man who represents the triumph of human dignity over racial prejudice. He last appears in the novel *Intruder in the Dust* (1948), a minor masterpiece about heroism; from this came the only good motion picture ever made of Faulkner's works, mainly because the author himself insisted on having a hand in the picture's production. Ralph Ellison wrote that blacks could identify with this motion picture: "the factors that make this identification possible lie in its depiction not of racial but of human qualities." [33] In Beauchamp, Faulkner created a character who represented much of his best thinking about ritual and about the humanitarian tradition to which he belonged.

The Agrarians believed that through a reestablishment of myth and traditional rituals, human dignity could be preserved. Yet the Agrarians never viewed the problem of racism as an aspect of the decline of southern culture. Faulkner, on the other hand, brings to his fiction a powerful critique of the old southern biracial society and thus firmly establishes himself as a writer of the restored South. His books and pronouncements on the South, though often eccentric, point to the region's return to the national mainstream, particularly on matters of race. Faulkner's attitudes toward race were by and large ignored, at least until the early eighties, when Eric J. Sundquist's *Faulkner: A House Divided* examined in detail his vision of racial agony in the South and its relationship to the collapse of old communal values.

In summing up Faulkner's accomplishments, I believe it is necessary to maintain a balance between his imaginative grasp of the revival of cultural values and his dark, apocalyptic vision of cultural decline. Faulkner was aware of an element of chaos in his own society even as he was aware of its healing powers. Blotner, Minter, and others who have written about his life have told us about the personal chaos of his family life and his struggles with alcoholism. Yet we are also aware of his continuing ability to act creatively. The life and work of William Faulkner demonstrate that southerners can face racism and moral decay and emerge with a vision of hope and renewal. Thomas L. McHaney reminds us that "the suicide Quentin Compson was reincarnated happily as Lucius Priest, whose life-restoring adventure also begins with the death of a grandparent."[34] Not least among the reasons for hope Faulkner has given us is that he was able to fulfill the prophecy of Ransom and others that the South as a culture could continue to nurture artists. Faulkner's presence in the South as a major international author helped to strengthen the belief of other southern writers that they did not have to turn to other cultures for their art. He has inspired writers like Robert Penn Warren, Flannery O'Connor, Walker Percy, Tennessee Williams, and Ralph Ellison. None of these writers rose to Faulkner's heights, but they were all strengthened by him and they have achieved international recognition.

To have achieved even a measure of harmony and creativity amid personal disorder is a triumph for any artist. Faulkner's books moved Malcolm Cowley to write to him: "your Mississippi work hangs together beautifully as a whole—as an entire creation there is nothing like it in American literature."[35] Faulkner by no means solved all of the artistic problems facing modern American writers. He began as a verse writer under the influence of Conrad Aiken, whose "minor music" had early moved him, and he always honored this poet, even as Aiken in his criticism honored Faulkner's work. Yet Faulkner's creative task was not like Aiken's, which was to sing about his native city of Savannah and search for a kind of self-knowledge that Faulkner never achieved. Faulkner later held up Thomas Wolfe as a great American novelist who had worked to get all of America into his writing, revealing those connections between northern and southern culture that hold the nation together, connections for which Faulkner in his concentration on the South had little time. Nor was his task the same as that of the Agrarians, though he held views similar to theirs concerning nature, myth, tradition, and ritual. Faulkner's great artistic task was to dramatize poetically the depths of cultural decay and the heights of virtue achieved by some individuals amidst this decay and, in presenting a panorama of southern history, to reveal a hope of both southern and American renewal. It was a large task and he performed it well.

4

Conrad Aiken
Culture and Violence in Savannah

In his study of the relationship of geography to literature, *Three Modes of Southern Fiction*, C. Hugh Holman asserts that there are three Souths: the Tidewater, the Piedmont and Appalachia, and the Deep South.[1] Holman makes his case well, but he does not suggest the complexity of the different types of urban settings that have contributed to the formation of his three southern regions, and he does not take into account southern culture as a whole.

Holman selects Ellen Glasgow as representative of the Tidewater South. But her city, Richmond, is only one of several cities on or near the southern coastline that have made significant contributions to the development of southern culture; and, because it came into its own only in the early nineteenth century, Richmond is one of the least important of the major centers of southern culture. Southern culture was first developed on the coast and later carried into the uplands—Baltimore, Williamsburg, Charleston, Savannah, St. Augustine, Mobile, and New Orleans all played earlier and more significant roles than Richmond. The last three with their Spanish and French origins have been largely ignored because of a southern bias against the Latin element in American cultural life. In three of the cities—Charleston, Savannah, and New Orleans—Latin culture and British culture mingled to produce a way of life that decided the destiny of the largest part of the South, extending from South

85

Carolina to Texas. Savannah, the birthplace of Conrad Aiken and
Flannery O'Connor, has since World War II aroused increasing interest. Unlike New Orleans and Charleston, it has not turned its
inner city into a museum for the tourist trade. Since 1960 it has
undergone an inner-city transformation that has become a model
for the renewal of other early centers of American culture.

Savannah in the 1980s still contains many reminders of its
eighteenth-century Tidewater culture, yet it is also a medium-sized
modern American city with all of the accompanying urban tensions. When Conrad Aiken was born there in 1889, those tensions
were hidden but growing in intensity. Savannah at the end of the
nineteenth century, though still dreaming of its antebellum brilliance, was becoming a new city in a republic soon to be a world
power. In his brilliant short story "Silent Snow, Secret Snow," in the
metaphysical poems known as the *Preludes,* and in his masterful autobiography *Ushant,* Aiken evokes the Savannah he knew as a child,
a city looking backward at its dying past and at the same time forward to a commercial-industrial future. For all his memories of its
beauties, based as they were on both a cultivation of nature and the
careful preservation of the buildings of the old inner city, Aiken
saw Savannah primarily as the place where an act of violence
robbed him of both mother and father at age eleven. His father
murdered his mother and then committed suicide, and Aiken was
plunged into a profound psychic trauma that became the central
influence on his personal and literary life. All serious critics of
Aiken have viewed this murder-suicide as the major event in the
writer's life and work, but none has taken into full account the author's depiction of the web of culture and violence in the modern
city of Savannah that provided the context for the death of his
parents.

Aiken, his two younger brothers, and one sister were taken north
to live with relatives after the tragedy; Conrad eventually attended
high school in Cambridge, Massachusetts. By the time he was a student at Harvard, working with T. S. Eliot on Harvard's literary
magazine, the *Advocate,* Aiken was already immersed in the modern literary movement that was seeking to renovate the cultural values of the nation. Like so many other writers trying to escape from
a constricting puritanism, Aiken turned to cities, first New York
and then London; but in his best writing—his stories, poems, and
the experimental novel *Blue Voyage,* published in 1927 and written
under James Joyce's influence—Aiken was continually returning to

the decaying culture and violence of his childhood Savannah. Finally, in the thirties, he came to grips with Savannah both in the *Preludes* and in his first visit to the city since he had left it as a child. The painful rediscovery of the city in the *Preludes* was paralleled by Aiken's personal rediscovery of Savannah. The literary struggles that produced the *Preludes* led to the spiritual revolution described in *Ushant*, generally acknowledged as one of the greatest American autobiographies.

Aiken's personal confrontation with Savannah also led him to settle there in the early sixties. Until his death in 1973, when he was buried beside his parents in Savannah's Bonaventure Cemetery, Aiken spent the cold months of the year in Savannah and the warm months in Brewster, Massachusetts (also maintaining a small apartment in New York, a city for which he always had a strong attachment). Savannah remained the city most important to his soul. As Aiken's biographer, Joseph Killorin, says, "All his life Savannah and the house where he grew up were like a lodestone drawing him back." [2] Killorin claims that Aiken "said everything he did in his life was an attempt to get back to his house where he had read and written his first poems." [3] In doing so he became, like Ellen Glasgow, an interpreter of a southern Tidewater city.

Hugh Holman rightly sees Ellen Glasgow as the southern writer most dedicated to explaining the culture of the Tidewater South. In her Queenborough novels she dissects the social life of Richmond, and in possibly her best novel, *The Sheltered Life*, she shows in detail how violence can break through the polished surfaces of a dying culture. Glasgow is credited by many with founding modern southern letters by recognizing that what the new literature of the South needed was, in her own words, "blood and irony." In *A Certain Measure*, the book she wrote about her novels, Glasgow tells her readers that she put into General Archibald in *The Sheltered Life* much of her own "ultimate feeling about life. . . . He represents the tragedy, wherever it appears, of the civilized man in a world that is not civilized." [4]

Like Glasgow, Aiken saw himself and a few others as representative of civilized values. He remembered his father and mother as two of the most cultivated people he had ever known, whose rich heritage had not saved them from tragedy. Unlike Glasgow, Aiken could never be satisfied merely to record the triumph of violence over dying values. Glasgow in her most brilliant novels depicts the few people who maintain their cultural values amid the subtle underground violence of Richmond society. Aiken, on the other hand, writes in most of his best work about a quester—himself, in effect—who ventures into realms other than his own in order to find new life. But as Aiken began to discover that new life, he found it necessary to return to Savannah to complete his quest.

In one sense Aiken's personal quest began with the first poems he wrote as a boy in Savannah. In another it began with his work at Harvard on the *Advocate* and with his continuing association with T. S. Eliot, as well as his encounter in the classroom with George Santayana, a philosopher who influenced him a great deal. In the deepest sense it began with an early poem that is probably his most anthologized work, "Tetélestai," a poem in which he reenacts his father's suicide; and it continued with the story "Silent Snow, Secret Snow" in which he deals with his own childhood terrors and his schizophrenic retreat from the violence that was a consequence of his father's growing insanity. He continued the pilgrimage with poems of the twenties, the *Symphonies,* and with his first two novels, *Blue Voyage* and *Great Circle.* Unlike most American authors, whose creative lives have only one or at best two acts, Aiken entered a major literary phase in middle age when he wrote the *Preludes,* a phase that continued into old age with the publication of his autobiography. All his life Aiken was a pilgrim, a quester, a voyager—he continually uses these and similar terms when he refers to his spiritual journey—but by the time he wrote the *Preludes* in the thirties he had begun to find solutions to the problems of violence and cultural decay that had destroyed his family and had nearly cost him his own sanity. The problems, he saw, lay within the bounds of the beautiful city of Savannah, which contained a canker that was destroying the very values on which the cultural centers of the Tidewater were erected. If he could explore his early life in Savannah and the lives of his parents, he reasoned, perhaps he could find where southern and even American culture had gone wrong and how matters could be set right.

Aiken's awareness of the importance of Savannah in his life dawned more clearly than ever upon him after his painful reenactment of his father's violence in the writing of "Tetélestai" in 1917. A sense of his father's growing mental collapse and of the rich natural surroundings of the city pervades the poem. By the time it was published Aiken was deeply engaged in the new movement of modern letters. After leaving Harvard he went to Boston and New York, working with poets as diverse as Ezra Pound, John Gould

Fletcher, and William Carlos Williams to explore the meaning of the new American style in poetry. At the same time he began to study Freud and other depth psychologists such as Jung and Adler. He moved on to London, where his friend Eliot was beginning to establish himself as literary dictator, and became in the early twenties a part of the rich literary life there. He withdrew in the late twenties to Rye, a small town on the southern coast of England where Henry James had once lived. After World War II Aiken returned to America and divided his time first between New York and Brewster; later between Brewster and Savannah. He taught for one year at Harvard and another at Florida Southern College. Like his friend Allen Tate, Aiken often felt the need to visit cosmopolitan centers of the world while at the same time seeking retreats in the country, small towns, or universities. Both sought solitude to continue their long careers of free-lance writing, but both also sought cosmopolitan experiences. Aiken and Tate always felt an affinity for Poe, the first truly international American writer, and like him they wandered for years through several cities of the world. But unlike Poe they defused the violence within themselves and lived creative lives into old age.

In his poem "Ode to the Confederate Dead," and in the essay he based on the composition of this poem, "Narcissus as Narcissus," Tate put his finger on the problem central to the destructive element within himself and southern society. It is summed up in the word *narcissism*. In "Tetélestai," a poem he never commented on, Aiken dealt with the same problem, seeing his father's egocentricity as the malign element that drove him to murder and suicide. Unlike Tate and Eliot—both of whom steered clear of depth psychology—Aiken turned to Freud, who became one of his chief mentors, to discover the meaning of narcissism and of what Freudians then considered a related psychic disorder, the Oedipus complex. Seldom has a modern writer applied modern psychology to his own problems so effectively in the act of literary creation. As Aiken has often suggested, his chief literary mode is personal confession, and that confession is often based on his knowledge of depth psychology. Aiken did not stop with Freud; he went on to Rank, Ferenczi, Adler, and Jung and then back to the Unitarian beliefs of his grandfather William James Potter in order to create for himself a philosophy with which to combat his narcissism. Tate, on the other hand, followed Eliot, studying Dante and embracing ritualistic Christianity.

Aiken's studies of Freud gave him an understanding of narcissism that neither Tate nor Eliot had. He learned that narcissism, the individual's worship of his own image, was also a cultural phenomenon and should be treated as such. For this reason, places—Savannah, Boston, New York, London—are always involved in Aiken's depiction of his own and others' narcissism. In the late seventies Christopher Lasch wrote in *The Culture of Narcissism* that "recent critics of narcissism" by "ignoring the psychological dimension" also "miss the social" implications.[5] Psychologists have studied the many clinical aspects of narcissism, but commentators, Lasch tells us, have failed to link its symptoms, such as "a sense of inner emptiness, boundless repressed rage, and unsatisfied oral cravings," to the decline of civilized values in a culture.[6] Aiken did explore the connections between the narcissistic personality and the culture from which he sprang. His third novel, *King Coffin*, which shows the growing rage of a narcissistic protagonist, was in the thirties used as a psychology textbook at Harvard. Pioneering psychiatrists like Henry A. Murray, who became a good friend of Aiken's, used his literary work in conjunction with their own psychological studies. Freud himself placed Aiken's work *Great Circle* on a waiting room table for his patients to read.

Like Tate, Aiken saw early in his literary career the connection between narcissism and the always latent, sometimes erupting violence of the South. The South had suffered a painful blow to its pride in the Civil War, and from 1865 onward, particularly in the Tidewater areas from which southern culture had first been diffused, diligent attempts were made to arrest the development of the region's culture. Glasgow in *The Romantic Comedians* describes Richmond society as having "never outgrown an early stage of arrested development."[7] This atmosphere caused many creative people to feel that they were caught in a kind of web, the image Thomas Wolfe used to describe the constricting southern society he knew in Asheville. Many escaped from this web by flight to the great city. Others were imprisoned by violence that stemmed from repressed anger, as was true of Wolfe and Aiken's father. This sense of a constricting community, however, was not limited to the South; Eliot's poem "The Love Song of J. Alfred Prufrock" is based on his evocation of Boston society early in this century. James Joyce's *Portrait of the Artist as a Young Man* explores what Joyce called the modern "paralysis." For Joyce, as for so many younger writers in modern literature, the only escape from such paralysis was life in one of the new megalopolises. Aiken and Tate both joined the trek to the great cities, but they found it necessary to return to the South, both mentally and physically. Aiken did not return physically until many years after his departure, as he was beginning to discover the answers to problems springing from his own psychological frustrations.

Aiken's fiction is important in understanding many aspects of his psychological development, but it is in his poetry that we can best trace his quest for answers to his personal problems. His poems from the twenties, *Symphonies,* are collected under the title of *The Divine Pilgrim.* In long poems like *The Charnel Rose* and *The Jig of Forslin* he records the adventures of the fragmented ego's encounters with woman as both goddess and temptress. The witch-temptress in Aiken's work is a Freudian symbol of the Oedipal attachment to the mother. This attachment is also explored in *Great Circle,* the novel that delighted Freud as an example of what the literary artist could do with Freudian psychological concepts. In *The Jig of Forslin* Aiken shows an ego bewitched by the temptress, withdrawing into fantasies of sexual pleasure that in turn lead to dreams of lust and horror, manias and vampire images. Bewitchment by images that initially bring pleasure, then a sense of being possessed, and finally rage are common in the poet's early work. The early poems show that psychic bewitchment can be traced back to two sources: bewitchment by one's own self-image, called narcissism by Freud, and bewitchment by the image of the parent of the opposite sex, which Freud termed the Oedipus complex. This bewitchment, Aiken shows, frustrates psychic growth and stops the pilgrim's journey in his early poems. Yet the pilgrim in Aiken's work is awakened and rescued from lust and horror by images of a goddess who has restorative powers. Like Freud, Aiken shows us that the human psyche contains images of the positive, life-giving aspects of its parents as well as their castrating, destructive side.

In one of his best earlier works, *Priapus and the Pool,* Aiken reveals the connection between devouring, destructive lust and the narcissistic lover who has fallen in love with his own image. The destructive woman appears as Medusa; she is contrasted with lovers who have the power to lead the pilgrim to a higher life. These lovers, coming from a paradise called Atlantis, symbolize what Aiken calls divine powers. His pilgrim, as the title of the collection, *The Divine Pilgrim,* suggests, moves toward achieving the power of divinity and is aided by energies within the soul that whisper secret words: "they have heard / Out of the infinite of the soul / An incommunicable word." [8] The word is *love* and it is at once the guide and goal of the divine pilgrim. For Aiken love is the central concept necessary for the development of the individual psyche as well as for the revival of values needed to restore a true communal spirit.

In most of the poems of *The Divine Pilgrim* the author describes his retreat into narcissism. For the narcissist, the possibility of retreating into insanity or death hovers constantly; this retreat produces feelings of rage and isolation. Along with this rage come visions caused by the destructive energies that spring from an unresolved Oedipus complex. Aiken's work and life record the pilgrim's movement toward what Freud called the reality principle, that is, a full acceptance of one's own and others' lives and the interrelationships that are necessary for fruitful human interchange, first in the sexual and then in other creative areas of life. In his search for fulfillment Aiken remembered the love he knew within his family and city. Because he accepted and forgave the problems they caused him, his psyche was gradually released from their obsessive hold; thus narcissism and the Oedipus complex gradually lost their power over the pilgrim.

At the end of *The Divine Pilgrim* there is a long poem called *Changing Mind* that records the actual process of pilgrimage leading beyond narcissism to an acceptance of the reality principle. Aiken once told me that the poem, based on a dream, records the pilgrim's descent into his own soul, where he encounters the creative powers that enable him to overcome Narcissus, whose power bewitches the consciousness and seeks to arrest its growth. It is necessary to face Narcissus in order to begin the symbolic journey that leads to a release of psychic energies. Delving into his soul, the pilgrim encounters Mephistopheles, symbol of the destructive power within everyone, which Jung called the shadow. Every day, the poet tells us, the pilgrim fights a giant and is defeated—but each crucifixion by the giant means another victory over narcissism, and with each victory the creative powers within the pilgrim's soul cry out: "Alas, Narcissus dead, / Narcissus daily dead, that we may live!" [9] Christ and Socrates also dwell within the poet, and they journey with the other figures to the symbolic Golgotha, which is the scene of the daily crucifixion. The poet himself cries out: "Daily I fight here, / Daily I die for the world's delight / By the giant blow on my visible heart!" [10] Thus through acceptance of traumas within his own unconscious mind, the individual's creative power can grow; with the release of these powers, cultural values are revived.

With his first group of *Preludes,* called *Preludes for Memnon,* Aiken directly attacks the problem of individuals and societies that are held in the grip of narcissism and the obsessive images that accompany this condition. In *Preludes for Memnon,* the individual psyche and its problems are always most prominent. Aiken during the thirties was still working through the psychic problems that had bedeviled him since childhood. These problems were exacerbated by his painful divorce from his first wife and a second unsuccessful marriage in 1930, to Clarissa Lorenz. By 1932 his personal problems seemed so great that he attempted suicide. The next year he published what many consider his best novel, *Great Circle,* in which, among other things, he faced the problem of his unresolved Oedipus complex. In 1935 he published the novel *King Coffin,* a mediocre work valuable chiefly for its analysis of the destructive emotions that grow out of the narcissist's inevitable alienation. By the mid-thirties Aiken's fiction was not nearly as important as his poetry in recording his development; yet both the fiction and the poetry revealed the truth of a remark he once made about all of his work: "Freud was in everything I did from 1912 on."[11] Freud—but also Jung, Rank, Ferenczi, and Adler—provided the conceptual framework for the work of Aiken's greatest creative period, the thirties; but his own experience was the foundation of this work.

Aiken begins to consider communal values in the second set of *Preludes,* called *Time in the Rock* and published in 1936. In these poems he shows how positive values like knowledge and love can emerge after repeated encounters with psychic traumas. Armed with these values, he was able to face his own inner corruption and that of others. As mythic quester moving into the depths of suffering that springs from inner decay, the poet in *Time in the Rock* at last glimpses his real destination: "And it is you: toward the light you move / as silently, as gravely, as a ship / counters the evening tide."[12] The quester moves past chaos and pain, past the wreckage of dissolving civilizations, encountering along the way glimpses of visionary light that lead to creativity. Chaos, symbolized by a maelstrom that threatens the pilgrim's destruction, is in fact necessary for the refinement of his heart. This refinement through pain makes possible the poet's deepening awareness of an underlying unity between the blood and the rock, the individual and the Self, that is the spark of God within the soul:

Yes, and you have noted
how then the chemistry of the soul at midnight

secretes peculiar virtue from such poisons:
you have been pleased: rubbed metaphoric hands:
saying to yourself that the suffering, the shame,
the pity, and the self-pity, and the horror,
that all these things refine love's angel,
filth in flame made perfect.[13]

Aiken ends *Time in the Rock* with an admonition to himself:

Simple one, simpleton,
when will you learn the flower's simplicity—
open to all comers, permit yourself
to be rifled—fruitfully too—by other selves?
Self, and other self—permit them, permit them—[14]

The *Preludes* are firmly based on a full acceptance of human
narcissism and Oedipal connections present in every unconscious
mind; Aiken believed, as Freud taught him, that through self-
knowledge one could overcome most of the ill effects of these inevitable psychological flaws. The *Preludes* also contain the kind of
modern nay-saying Aiken learned from Herman Melville, a questioning of the extravagant, overly optimistic claims of an earlier
transcendental idealism, a modified form of which Aiken accepted
because of his continuing adherence to his grandfather Potter's
views. As Frederick J. Hoffman has pointed out, "an idealism that
does not face the continuing facts of human pain and death can
become not only meaningless but also dangerous."[15] Aiken's father
and mother had been heirs to the American transcendental tradition and had ultimately failed to benefit from it. Was it not true,
Aiken was forced to ask himself, that they and others whose cultural values had been declining throughout the late nineteenth
century had not fully faced their own inner suffering? And had not
his parents too readily accepted certain false values based on the
prevailing social narcissism that they found in Savannah? Aiken
continued to ask himself these questions because he knew that writing the *Preludes*, his greatest poetic accomplishment, did not mean
his pilgrimage was finished—that indeed, it had to be continued at
an even deeper level—so in 1936, the year of the publication of
Time in the Rock, he visited Savannah for the first time since leaving
in 1901. This journey to the city of his birth and early sorrow was a
necessary step leading to what many believe is his greatest work, his

autobiography *Ushant,* which Malcolm Cowley called one of the greatest American autobiographies.

In the period between *Time in the Rock* and *Ushant* Aiken published an important volume entitled *Brownstone Eclogues and Other Poems,* in which he depicts modern humanity as bound up in an urban environment, yet still seeking a paradise beyond the city. By 1942, when the volume was published, Aiken's religious vision had deepened, allowing him to use the modern urban setting in his work and at the same time offer the hope that new cities would reflect the transcendental vision of Emerson and Whitman and of others like his grandfather. For Aiken this meant a national vision of the regeneration of both the individual and his urban and natural environments:

> Lord, Lord—all voices say, and all together,
> stone, steel, and waking man, and waking weather—
> give us thy day, once more we may be
> the endless miracle that embodies thee.[16]

In *Brownstone Eclogues and Other Poems* Aiken was preparing himself for the full acceptance of modern urban existence and the affirmation of transcendental insights that he would reveal in *Ushant.*

When *Ushant* finally appeared in 1952 Aiken was able to take into account the chaotic nature of modern urban expansion as manifested not only in great cities like New York and Boston but also in his own Savannah. The chaos that had broken through the surface of Aiken's family life in 1901, recalled in vivid detail in *Ushant,* seemed prophetic of a larger social disorder of the new century. By accepting the tragic events in his life and the lives of others (becoming in the process what Henry A. Murray would call a poet of "creative dissolution") Aiken gradually found the three values he prized most highly: knowledge, vision, and love. He was able to discover these values even while confronting calamities that included shattered marriages and lost friendships (the painful deaths of John Gould Fletcher and Malcolm Lowry among them), depression that led to attempted suicide, and a sense of literary failure despite a Pulitzer Prize, a Bollingen Prize, a National Book Award, and the National Medal for Literature. The most important fact Aiken reveals in his autobiography is that despite the many chaotic events in his life, and even because of them, he emerged a stronger person as he entered a renewed period of creativity after 1945. Reuel Denney writes that despite Aiken's "reputation as a poet of chaos his work embodies a total, consistent, and normative view of man." [17] To be more precise, a consistent and normative personality begins to show in the *Preludes* and other important writings after 1930, emerging triumphant in *Ushant*. Aiken's lifelong quest is thus a journey toward a full development of his inner humanity. Actually, this development occurred as Aiken entered his sixties.

Ushant sums up the discovery, after a long search, of a stable set of values that support family and communal life. Aiken in *Ushant* speaks of himself in the third person as William Demarest, protagonist of his first novel, *Blue Voyage* (all of Aiken's fictional protagonists are really himself). As Mary Rountree has written, *Ushant* describes a perilous journey around the "shoals of experience." Aiken "must mark out 'the course of life' . . . around the tragedy of his childhood in order to forgive and finally to love the father and mother responsible for that tragedy." [18] Rountree observes that the most moving part of the autobiography is the depiction of "Aiken's search for a home, for a sense of family and personal identity." [19] Aiken found happiness in his third marriage, to painter Mary Hoover, and in his deepening relationships with his three children by his first wife. His return to America in 1939 to live in Massachusetts and later Savannah marked his emergence as a major man of letters who had undergone personal and family struggles and survived.

Ushant is defined by Aiken as his continuing quest for the self-knowledge with which to overcome inevitable attachments to the self-image (narcissism) and to the images of father and mother (Oedipus complex and mother-father fixation). The word *Ushant* is literally a telescoped version of "you shan't" and was inspired by a dream that Aiken had in which he was a passenger in a ship that nearly went aground on dangerous rocks. The term refers both to the castrating voice of the repressing father, so well described in the story "Silent Snow, Secret Snow," and to the threatening voice of his childhood Savannah. The voice says, in essence, that no one should even attempt the journey of self-discovery. In Aiken's dream the ship nearly crashed on the rocks but somehow got by them. Thus Aiken came to believe, after meditating on the dream, that his psychic journey had led him, in the middle of his life, past the powers of repression and puritanism that he had found not only in childhood but also in the critical forces arrayed against modern writers like himself and his friends Pound, Fletcher, Lowry, and

Eliot. These writers early in the century challenged a narcissistic, dying tradition of romanticism and went beyond it to find first self-knowledge, then an imaginative vision, and finally love. As Freud had promised, love in all its forms, sexual and filial, was indeed often repressed but could, through the efforts of self-examination, be rediscovered. In *Ushant*, moments of exquisite poetic vision are given to the one who breaks the bonds of the narcissistic past. One of Aiken's greatest visions is that of love as a banquet: "How often had the shadow of Eros passed by unrecognized, unhonored, the ethereal wing-beat unheard, or, if heard, mistaken for something else! Once—the poet—Rimbaud?—had said—'If I remember rightly, my life was a feast where all the hearts opened, and joy flowed like wine. How was it all lost, and where find again the little key to that divine banquet?' The key was charity: *caritas*, the love of loves!"[20]

Aiken's answer in *Ushant* to Rimbaud's question of how to find the key to love's banquet is that one must continue the search for self-knowledge, always risking disaster through continual encounters with violence. For instance, the literary scene of London in the twenties is described "as a jungle scene, simply this literary forest," in which Aiken witnessed the hatred and envy between Virginia Woolf and Katherine Mansfield, among many others: "Envy and hatred, alas, yes; one might as well admit it. The rivalries become too intense, and inevitably . . . occasions arose when there must be a fight to the finish."[21] Violence of all types is never far from Aiken's thoughts in *Ushant*, yet the book depicts a quest that is a continual encounter with both the pain of violence and the healing power of a briefly glimpsed harmony. As a child he had known such moments of harmonious joy and love and believed he could find them again. Therefore in *Ushant* we find the pervading symbols of water and death intertwined with dreams and glimpses of divine harmony. Finally, as the book concludes, Aiken tells us that the word *Ushant* also means "journey's end," which for the quester means receiving the vision of complete harmony. He quotes the poem "Juhoohooa" by his five-year-old daughter and then comments: "World's end—for wasn't Juhoohooa another Ushant?"[22] *Ushant*, which at first means a force threatening the pilgrim, comes to mean the ultimate perfection that man longs for, the paradise in the soul continually lost and refound. Children, Freud tells us, apprehend early the possibilities of psychic development, of full sexuality, but the threatening, castrating side of their parents orders them to live by "thou shalts" and "thou shalt nots" instead of by an affirmation of Eros. Narcissistic societies threaten the quester with puritanical injunctions long after he has grown up, but if the quester continues his pilgrimage he bypasses these forces to discover visions of harmony and love. Thus in *Ushant* Aiken initially takes his philosophy from Freud, but then he traces its essential ideas back through his grandfather's transcendentalism to Socrates' vision of man's possibilities: "Freud had merely picked up the magic words where Socrates, the prototype of the highest man, had let them fall, and now at last the road was opened for the only religion that was any longer tenable or viable, a poetic comprehension of man's position in the universe, and of his potentialities as a poetic shaper of his own destiny, through self-knowledge and love. The final phase of evolution of man's mind itself to ever more inclusive consciousness: in that, and that alone, would he find the solvent of all things."[23]

The above passage is possibly Aiken's best definition of the fruit of self-knowledge, but he does not choose to end *Ushant* with a philosophical statement. Instead, the final vision in the autobiography is of a sheet of illuminated music: "—Yes, now we are drowning— and all of us are drowning; but as we drown, we seem somehow to be floating upward, we are all floating upward and singing. Floating upward to that vast, that outspread sheet of illuminated music, which is the world; and above which, as we now dimly make out, is—what exactly: the fact of the Teacher of the West."[24] Thus Aiken ends *Ushant* with the symbol of music just as Eliot uses both music and the dance as key images in the *Quartets*. For both poets, music and dance symbolize a divine harmony that undergirds the universe and that man seeks in his quest for knowledge, vision, and love. Aiken's "Teacher of the West" is an image in one of his dreams that seemed to guide the direction of his quest. Fittingly, the image of the teacher stands as a central symbol of the book—fitting because Aiken sees himself as both a mythic quester and a humanist teacher who has through suffering and perseverance at last earned the right to make philosophical and poetic statements about human values.

Only once more in his life would Aiken rise to the level of *Ushant*—in his poem "A Letter from Li Po," from the volume *A Letter from Li Po and Other Poems*, published in 1955. This poem, as E. P. Bollier says, "not only recapitulates the earlier themes and attitudes, but transforming them, goes beyond them—goes beyond even *Ushant* perhaps. . . . [The poem's] initial theme is change, and the one constant within all change, the heart's tears for lost children, lost lovers, lost friends."[25] In the poem there are also themes of the pride and loneliness of the self and, finally, Li Po's ultimate wisdom: that the poet writes of the world he views and, through his vision, creates his own life by rising to higher levels of consciousness.

Li Po, a philosophical poet of ancient China, represents Aiken in his old age when he had become one of America's authentic men of letters. He had begun writing verses as a child in Savannah, and his young life had been shattered by violence. Later he saw that the culture his life had been based on was paralyzed by a collective narcissism. As he rediscovered Savannah, both in person and in his writings, he saw that time shatters all attempts to arrest cultural development. In his last two great works, *Ushant* and "A Letter to Li Po," he summed up his acceptance of change and pointed at the same time to the one constant beneath all change, love. The love of his family had been shattered, but love could be renewed and could sustain new families, revive communities, and allow old wrongs to be forgiven. These were Aiken's views as a humanistic teacher and writer, as summarized in a series of interviews during the sixties;[26] Alexander A. Alexander has also written at length of Aiken's perspective as an old man on his early days in Savannah.[27] The core of Aiken's life and work was the renewal of values connected with the family and the larger community.

Love, for Aiken, particularly in the family and community, was the most basic human value, the only one that could overcome the decay of time and the one absolutely necessary for reviving other cultural values. A sense of love and true community is basic to one of the most important of Aiken's literary endeavors—his criticism. As early as 1919 he had established himself as a critic who was important to that small group of people who were launching the modernist movement in England and America. He was one of the first Americans to understand the importance of I. A. Richards's *Principles*. Stanley Edgar Hyman points out that Aiken "had made the same basic revolutionary statement *Principles* made in his own *Scepticisms* five years before, in 1919; and . . . with a comparable audience, influence, and documentation, would undoubtedly himself have begun the modern critical movement."[28] In fact, Aiken was the only American critic Richards took notice of in his writing, possibly because he realized that Aiken's theoretical criticism pointed toward the possibility of breaking down the old dualism of science and poetry created in English literature by Arnold and other Victorians but implicit earlier in the Cartesian viewpoint. Richards is more subtle than Aiken in his theoretical analysis concerning the unified vision of literature, but Aiken is far ahead of him in practical criticism. Aiken, in noting the sheer poetic power of Melville, Dickinson, Pound, Eliot, Fletcher, Lorca, Faulkner, Schwartz, and Lowry, maintains what Arthur E. Waterman calls the "consistent" view in his evaluation of essential figures of modern literature; consistent, that is, because Aiken had a way of being right about those and others long before they were all recognized as authentic literary geniuses.[29] His approach to criticism was at its best in his recognition of the community in which the modern writer exists, and in Joseph Killorin's *Selected Letters of Conrad Aiken* we see the richness of Aiken's own participation in the Anglo-American community of letters in the twentieth century.

The concept of literary community as well as the philosophical problem of Cartesian dualism drew Aiken to Allen Tate. Of this friendship Reuel Denney has written that the "mutual regard of Allen Tate and Conrad Aiken . . . is some sort of monument to the transcendence by affection of deep differences in temperament and virtually diametrical perceptions of art and politics."[30] Tate was always a political conservative, and Aiken's political liberalism remained that of his chief philosophical master, his grandfather William Potter. Tate's concept of a unity that underlay the Cartesian dualistic vision grew out of his Catholicism and his study of Dante, whereas Aiken's concept of underlying harmony was based on the transcendental vision of Potter and on his personal discovery of the flow of love that unites not only one individual to another but the individual to his natural surroundings. Aiken far better than Tate understood the underlying connections between the arts and the sciences, and in this he often resembles Walker Percy, another friend of Tate's and the subject of a later chapter. Finally, where Tate and Aiken most resemble each other is in their essential urbanity and in their principles of literary criticism. What Aiken sought for American criticism is best summed up by Douglas Robillard, who notes that he set "high standards, based entirely upon the quality of the poetry and not upon its historical or cultural interest"[31] (although both Tate and Aiken believed that poetry and other arts could play an important role in shaping history and culture).

Aiken and Tate refused to settle for easy solutions to problems. They went beyond romanticism to accept modern narcissism as a problem that had to be overcome. Both survived and transcended their own narcissism, as shown in their later work, which often bears the mark of Eliot, their teacher. Both knew—and this knowlege drew them together—that they would not be very famous during their lifetimes, though they would never lack the respect of their peers. What most readers of serious literature after 1920 seemed to want was the poetry of tragic narcissism—of tortured personalities like F. Scott Fitzgerald, Hart Crane, or Thomas Wolfe—or else they wanted the writing of tough, death-haunted figures like Ernest Hemingway or William Faulkner. Aiken believed that his time would come, that America would discover modern transcendentalists like himself when it was ready for them. He knew that writers who put violence at the center of their work would be popular momentarily, but he believed that the restoration of culture would eventually become the major concern of humankind. Aiken had himself used the various literary styles—symbolism, psychological realism, neo-romanticism, stream-of-consciousness techniques, even a lyrical style in "The Kid"—but style was not central to his work. His indebtedness to the past, which he freely acknowledged, was always important to him; but central to his work, as Joseph Killorin has pointed out, was his effort to write about what was deepest in himself, his "struggles 'on his own' toward his own attitudes and definitions."[32] The struggle is central and his various styles secondary. In a *Life* magazine interview Aiken said that ours would be called the Age of Eliot.[33] He said this because one of the chief concerns of modernism is style; Eliot and Hemingway are the great modern stylists in English and thus receive great attention. But the vision won through personal quest would also have its day, Aiken believed, and the poets who told of their own hard-won victories over themselves to find self-knowledge and love would have their day.

Douglas Robillard has suggested that we should view Conrad Aiken as a man of letters in the mold of that great confessional writer of romanticism, Goethe. I would add that Aiken, like Goethe, believed that life should be an apprenticeship in order to acquire knowledge and imaginative vision to pass on to the young and to evolve into the role of supreme teacher. Fittingly, Aiken at the end of his life created for his tombstone in Savannah's Bonaventure Cemetery a stone bench where visitors could come and have a drink and picnic even as he had once picnicked at the graves of his parents. On the bench are two epitaphs that are at once a confession and a statement of hard-found wisdom. One is "Give my love to the world" and the other is "Cosmos Mariner / Destination Unknown." Even in death Aiken continues to proclaim what he said in *Thee,* his last long poem: the pilgrimage does not end with death because at "no compass-point / is final rest." [34]

5

Thomas Wolfe

The Web and the Rock in Asheville and New York

Perhaps more than any other southern writer Wolfe devoted himself to the search for cultural values in the modern city. The great cities of America and Europe fascinated him; they were places, he thought, that might aid him in his attempt to become a significant literary artist and to escape the provincial culture of Asheville, his hometown, itself on the way to becoming a modern commercial city early in the century. From his encounter with Boston and New York, Wolfe brought forth literary insights into modern urban culture as well as visions in his later work of the possibility of cultural revival in America itself.

The importance of Wolfe's encounter with the modern city has never been very well understood because critics have found the North Carolina author hard to classify. Since Wolfe's day, criticism has largely been formalist in nature, and form was the aspect of literature with which Wolfe had the most trouble. His published writing is also uneven and sometimes immature. The purely autobiographical nature of his fiction has also dismayed certain critics. He reminds us of Whitman's saying that when one touched his work one touched a man. Of Wolfe's two protagonists in his four chief works (Eugene Gant in *Look Homeward, Angel* [1929] and *Of Time and the River* [1935] and George Webber in *The Web and the Rock* [1939] and *You Can't Go Home Again* [1940]), Richard Chase has rightly said, "Yet as everyone must see, Webber is still fundamentally Gant, and both are Wolfe."[1] The four novels are one great confession of Wolfe's struggle to be an artist, and serious modern American critics have generally turned away from autobiography presented as fiction. Probably for that reason, the first modern critic to take Wolfe seriously and to examine his work in detail with the intellectual insight that it demands was English: Pamela Hansford Johnson wrote *The Art of Thomas Wolfe* (1943), which deals with Wolfe as an artist of international significance. Johnson, who also discovered Dylan Thomas, confirmed Wolfe's reputation in Europe, where it has always been greater than most Americans have realized. Furthermore, she appreciated him as an old-fashioned romantic searching the modern world for a culture that would accept him.

Johnson believed that Wolfe's search for artistic self-expression is the basic theme of his work. It is also the basic theme of similar writers in other American regions whose books often begin in a provincial hometown and end in a great city. These writers question the values of both hometown and city; but Wolfe moves beyond questioning to an affirmation and, indeed, a celebration of his own life's quest and that of certain friends he meets along the way. Wolfe sometimes resembles Whitman but, unlike Whitman, he was a satirist, and through his satire he questioned some of the values of hometowns and cities. His questioning of cultural values relating to the family, the male-female relationship, and, later, politics is a statement about his attitude toward American culture. Certainly Sinclair Lewis, once thought to be America's greatest modern satirist, early recognized Wolfe's ability as a writer who probed America's failings, particularly its urban failings. But Wolfe, unlike Lewis, had a deeply romantic side, which Johnson makes much of in her book; by developing the romantic side of his art Wolfe was able to affirm life while at the same time criticizing and satirizing both town and city.

Like Faulkner, Wolfe discovered early the work of James Joyce, which taught him that it was possible to show the shabby side of a city without rejecting the life within the city. Joyce is a mythic writer, as T. S. Eliot points out in *The Criterion* (1922), and as such he probes beneath the surfaces of life in Dublin in his quest for a way to express himself artistically. Like Joyce, Wolfe reveals in his work that he is deeply interested in the possibility of reviving and renewing his own life and the lives of others, first in Asheville and then in New York. He learned from Joyce that one could explore the psychic and sexual frustrations of one's hometown and, after facing and recording it all, still find in it hidden aspects of beauty and love. Wolfe died before the publication of *Finnegans Wake*, the work that records Joyce's own vision of cultural revival, but from his encounters with Asheville and New York he achieved a vision of revival all his own—a vision that came late in his short, unhappy life and one that has caught the imagination of many readers in both America and Europe.

Wolfe did not concentrate on a single American city because he felt he needed to portray the interaction between the cultures of the North and the South. He also believed that the twentieth-century megalopolis as he knew it offered no resting place. In his last book, *You Can't Go Home Again*, he gives us a vision of a renewed America, offering the possibility of new life for cities and towns. Wolfe is the only southern writer of international importance, other than Conrad Aiken, who wrote in detail about the cultures of both the North and the South and who showed the interaction between them. However, Aiken's best work is not about America as a whole but, rather, cities like Savannah. Aiken was eventually able to go home to Savannah, but Wolfe was too alienated from Asheville ever to accept it as anything but a town that seemed to stifle his best creative impulses. Yet he never found a satisfying life of artistic expression in New York, either. Finally, like Whitman, he endeavored to reach beyond his own time and place for a vision of a new America that offered wider opportunities for artistic expression.

In his novel *The Web and the Rock* Wolfe settled upon two symbols that for him summed up aspects of his life in Asheville and New York. The web, as critics like Johnson have noted, symbolized both the family and the cultural entanglements that held Wolfe in their grip and kept him from living creatively when he was in Asheville. The rock does not usually symbolize New York itself but, rather, certain aspects of the stabilizing effects of culture in New York as represented by the editor character Foxhall Edwards. At other times the lack of emotional warmth in New York is symbolized by the hardness of the rock. The failures of the great city (as Wolfe saw them) drove him back to his hometown, where he found that he could not function as an artist. He eventually returned to New York, but he did not live long enough to develop the understanding of American culture that he was seeking. Out of his struggles with the southern web and the northern rock he did evolve a vision of

cultural revival; to understand that vision we must briefly retrace
his footsteps as a young man awakening in his southern hometown
and then examine his love-hate relationship with the giant of American cities, New York.

Wolfe's descriptions of Asheville in his first two novels, *Look
Homeward, Angel* and *Of Time and the River,* might well remind readers of hometowns in other American regions. Many readers feel
that Wolfe captured the quintessential quality of life in a small
American town early in this century. Yet much in Wolfe's description of Asheville in these novels indicates that it is not a small town
at all. Sometimes he seems to see Asheville as a relatively small city,
at other times an emerging city of the New South that eventually
will have no place for him. Asheville represents a part of southern
culture that is at once attractive and repellent to him. In fact,
Wolfe's views of the small city he remembered are deeply colored in
his novels by his sense of southern history and the contemporary
southern scene of his childhood and youth in the first decades of
the century. It is Wolfe's encounter with a new city like Asheville,
which grew out of the modern commercial development of the
South, that gives his work much of its originality. No southern
writer has struggled harder against declining cultural values anchored in the southern reverence for the past than Wolfe, and yet
at the same time no southern writer so effectively satirizes the Babbittry associated with the New South's commercialism. In his descriptions of the "booster" spirit of Asheville in *You Can't Go Home
Again,* Wolfe equals Sinclair Lewis at his best.

Hugh Holman tells us that Wolfe associated himself with the New
South, but that he "was keenly aware that industrial progress and
things associated with it could have damaging effects on American
and Southern culture."[2] Holman reminds us that when Wolfe was
growing up in Asheville, the town was becoming a tourist resort.
The influx of tourists from the North plays a big part in the life of
young Gant in the first two novels and helps to give him, largely
through his association with his mother's boarders, a kind of sophistication that small-town boys in the South seldom acquired in that
era. A decade before Wolfe's birth Asheville was already well known
as the site of one of the greatest mansions ever built by northern
capitalists, the Biltmore house. The enormous Vanderbilt estate, including so much land that part of it eventually became Pisgah National Forest, made a deep impression on the imaginations of Ashe-
villians. It was a reminder that northern money was beginning to

flow freely in a town that was rapidly becoming different from
most other economically depressed southern towns and cities. Although in his novels Wolfe shows an awareness of the dangers of
great wealth, wealthy northerners also suggested to him the possibility of a new life in the Northeast, where he might find artistic
freedom unavailable to him in his hometown.

Wolfe's protagonists in his four novels, who always speak his
point of view, yearn for a region where both love and artistic creativity can be united. In thinking about such a place, Wolfe inevitably looked to the North, originally his father's home. The South for
Wolfe was connected with his mother's possessive ways; Holman reminds us that he saw the South as feminine, maternal, and inhibiting.[3] Like his father, he tended to see the culture around him in
terms of the women in his life, all of whom stood for the communal
spirit that underlies much of southern life, supportive but sometimes inhibiting. He makes use of this tradition when he shows his
protagonist George Webber and other young southerners being
dominated by, in Wolfe's poetic phrase, "the dark, ruined Helen."[4]
This dark Helen in the blood of southerners sprang, the reader
learns, from an earlier culture.

Wolfe wrote in *The Web and the Rock* that the older South was not a
tangible part of "George Webber's life, nor of the lives of his con-
temporaries—that was the South they did not know but that all of
them somehow remembered."[5] For Webber this South is "something stricken, lost, and far, and long ago." But his generation,
born at the beginning of the twentieth century, had come "into a
kind of sunlight of another century."[6] Although Wolfe celebrates
the emergence of the sunlight, he is also caught up in a yearning
for the very past that seems to inhibit him. *Look Homeward, Angel*
records his sense of some great and unexplained loss in the refrain
"Oh lost and by the wind grieved, Ghost come back again." This
lyrical cry reveals Wolfe's belief that even as he was moving away
from a dying southern culture into a new century he was leaving
behind some vital element of his life, contained in the few positive
qualities that still remained in his native culture.

The missing element was probably the joy that he had found in
the southern community. As Wolfe's protagonists grow up, they
come to believe that they should go away to find the good life in
another region. But when Wolfe wrote *Look Homeward, Angel*, after
having lived for a time in the North and having visited Europe, he
felt nostalgic for the old communal existence of Asheville and no

doubt keenly felt its loss, a loss he regrets in some of his most poetic statements. Like many southerners who move to other areas, Wolfe oscillated between love and hate for the region and its decaying culture; and those protagonists in his novels who most resemble the author often brood fitfully on the southern scene even when removed from it. No other southern writer except Faulkner reveals such a strong love-hate relationship with the South. However, Faulkner retains a kind of skepticism that makes him doubt that a good life is available anywhere. The real parallel with Wolfe in American literature is F. Scott Fitzgerald. Both grew up in provincial cities; Fitzgerald's St. Paul, Minnesota, was like Asheville very impressed by the riches of the Northeast. Both writers possessed the kind of romantic, narcissistic temperaments that made them want more from life than it could ever give them. Both evolved in their work visions of the development of renewed American values, but even at the end of their lives their personal and literary narcissism was so great that some scholars find it hard to believe their vision of American renewal was genuine. Yet there is evidence that both sought to escape the collective narcissism of their provincial communities in order to find not only what they thought of as success but also a chance to develop themselves and their literary talents.

Wolfe's protagonists, like Fitzgerald's character Jay Gatsby, go to New York to realize an enormous dream. As Fitzgerald says of Gatsby, "his dream must have seemed so close that he could hardly fail to grasp it."[7] In *Of Time and the River*, we see Wolfe's record of his own feelings that, at certain moments in New York and elsewhere in the Northeast, he was actually about to achieve his dream. Yet Wolfe, like Gatsby, finally sees that at least part of what he has been seeking is his past. He finds in the Northeast the means to develop both his literary talents and his dream of a revived America, but he finds no substitute for the joys of a home community. Similarly, Fitzgerald says of Gatsby, a romantic protagonist who represents the author's own concept of himself as literary hero, that his dream of a better America is already behind him, "somewhere back in the obscurity beyond the city, where the dark fields of the republic rolled on under the night."[8] The concept of the dream existing in the republic as a whole, which is by no means uniquely Fitzgerald's, became fundamental to Wolfe's search for a vision of cultural revival for the nation.

Wolfe's greatest problem with the feminine possessiveness he found in southern culture was that it stifled his dreams of an artistic life. The possessiveness of his mother and the other figures (mostly female) who seemed to dominate his hometown grew in part out of a strong attachment to southern history, a past that always seemed more important than the future. Western North Carolina, though removed geographically from such centers of southern culture as Richmond and Charleston, was nevertheless spiritually tied to these fountainheads of the region's traditions. Wolfe's longing to escape the web of his culture is shown in George Webber's sneer at the chief cultural center of the Carolinas: "Charleston produced nothing and yet it pretended to so much."[9] At other times George is filled with admiration for the exploits of early southern heroes; for example, when he visits Richmond to attend a football game, George's southernness floods his consciousness as he imagines that he sees the Confederate army caught up in the fury of war on the playing field before him. Although George despises Charleston at the beginning of the book, in Richmond he eventually finds himself overcome by feelings of southern pride. Like his character George Webber, Wolfe is often ambivalent about southern history; though he denounces those who glorify the past, he is sometimes entranced by that past himself.

Emphasis on women as inspirers of the community is tied closely to Wolfe's deep concern with history. The loss of men in the Civil War put women in a strong position in the South of Wolfe's day. Southern women were a major influence in his life, beginning with his mother and continuing in Asheville with a schoolteacher, Mrs. J. M. Roberts (Margaret Leonard in *Look Homeward, Angel*). Pamela Johnson describes Mrs. Roberts as the most important of all the influences on the young Wolfe, calling her "the prototype of all the women with whom he [Eugene Gant] will fall deeply in love."[10] As various critics have pointed out, Wolfe felt a lifelong attraction to strong women, though he was always leaving these women to find a new life somewhere else. Both his mother and Mrs. Roberts pushed him to search for a cultural atmosphere beyond the boundaries of the South, which they both felt was in the throes of cultural decline; Mrs. Roberts in particular urged him to go to the University of North Carolina and then to Harvard for graduate study.

Wolfe benefited from his need for strong women to direct his life but at the same time often chafed under their dominating influence. His symbol of the southern web is drawn in part from what he conceived to be the sometimes overpowering influence of women on creative men. The web is a complex symbol, usually connected not only with southern history and southern women but also with a kind of overall possessiveness—of his family in particular and of the decaying communalism of the small southern city in general.

Also in Wolfe's novels we find the theme of greed—in particular, the lust for money in new commercial cities like Asheville early in the twentieth century. In *Look Homeward, Angel* Wolfe's mother appears as Eliza Gant, a woman who is gradually caught up in a quest for more and more money. Louis D. Rubin, Jr., has written that in this book "there is no more moving episode than that in which Eliza Gant rents out her home as a boardinghouse and begins speculating in real estate. To her family, it constitutes a betrayal of her femininity." [11] The boardinghouse itself becomes a kind of web that strangles some of her children and holds others in captivity; Eliza herself finally becomes almost completely obsessed with real estate speculation. In *You Can't Go Home Again,* when George Webber returns to his hometown for the last time, he finds its inhabitants devoted primarily to acquiring money and completely uninterested in his questioning of their new values.

From his first to his last novel Wolfe continues to suggest that Asheville, the hometown that is becoming a city of the New South, exists under a kind of curse as its dying culture gradually collapses before a rampant commercialism. Eliza Gant's greatness stems from the fact that she is complex and intelligent enough to realize, in part at least, what is happening to her community as well as herself. She wants her son to seek a new life, represented by his quest for higher education, which earlier was denied to members of her family because of their poverty.

Wolfe also felt ensnared by the characteristics of Appalachia that he inherited through one side of his mother's family. Richard Chase, writing about George Webber, sees this entanglement in terms of the protagonist's mother's family, the Joyners, hill people with "whom George associates words like *puritan, hard-bitten, lost, stricken, superstitious, dark, melancholy.*" [12] To leave these attitudes behind him is a major task of the Wolfe protagonist as he seeks first the life of the university and then the life of the great city. Wolfe's attitude toward Appalachia, like his attitude toward southern culture and the great city, is ambivalent. Part of him clings to the Appalachian viewpoint while another part seeks to cast it off.

Evidence abounds in Wolfe's novels and letters that, through education and contact with both university and northern urban culture, he did manage to lose at least some of the puritanism and melancholy inherited from Appalachian forebears. But he also inherited a kind of exuberant primitivism from Appalachia that he retained to the end. Some northerners see the South only in terms of powerful primitive energies and many of them envision it as a handful of decadent planters, a mob of primitive whites, and a collection of persecuted blacks. Wolfe encountered this attitude, and thereafter he distrusted most northern views of the South. Moreover, he clung to aspects of his inherited primitivism as a defense against what he felt was an overcivilized atmosphere in certain quarters of New York.

To understand the dark and melancholy side of Wolfe as well as the primitive side (which expressed itself both in exuberant energy and in eruptions of violence), it is necessary to know something about Appalachia. Even one of the most thorough Wolfe scholars, Paschal Reeves, is confused about the differences between life in Asheville and life in Appalachia; he observes that the city of Wolfe's origins is set "in the majestic mountains of the Piedmont." [13] The cities of the Piedmont (which is a plateau)—Greenville and Atlanta, for instance—are based solidly in southern culture, which historically has emphasized the inherited social hierarchy, one in which women often had powerful roles. For instance, the southern gentleman and lady were essentially the same whether in Charleston or Atlanta, or even in Asheville.

Among the subregions that deviated from the mainstream of southern culture is Appalachia. There are other such subregions, some small and some rather large, that dot the South; Appalachia, however, is the largest. These subregions became the stronghold of pioneers, many of whom wanted to live apart from the dominant southern culture. They desired to remain as free as possible, to roam without excess material possessions or cultural baggage, sometimes including family ties. They eventually evolved a way of life that differed from the prevailing southern life-style, particularly as that life-style began to involve agribusiness and slavery. For this reason many Appalachians found themselves joining the northern armies to fight against the South, and others openly sympathized with the North; as a result Appalachia after Reconstruction suffered persecution at the hands of southern politicians.

When Wolfe was growing up, the Appalachian family structure was different in many ways from that of mainstream southern culture. For instance, the Appalachian family centered around males.

Women were often oppressed by husbands who spent more time in the woods, hunting and making whiskey, than at home. By contrast, the dying southern culture in which Wolfe grew up provided many ways—like real estate speculation—for southern women to become even more powerful than they were when the South had been primarily agrarian. The female-dominated society in Wolfe's first two novels plays a large role in thwarting the masculinity and artistic strivings of old Gant. Wolfe clung to certain of his Appalachian traits because of his need to counteract some of the communal aspects of southern culture that he felt inhibited him. Among these traits were an appreciation of the abundance of nature, a healthy skepticism about civilization, and a wild lyricism of the spirit summed up in what George Webber calls his "goat-cry." This lyricism is one of the chief characteristics of Wolfe's novels, another being a generous acceptance of all of America that is not found in most southern writers. Comparisons have been made between Wolfe's lyricism and that of James Agee, who came from the Knoxville area, on the other side of the mountains from Asheville. Knoxville, like Asheville, was influenced by hill culture and, to a lesser degree, southern culture. There is a deep-seated connection between certain Appalachian viewpoints and the ideas of writers like Wolfe and Agee who grew up conditioned by both southern culture and mountain attitudes.

Wolfe also acquired undesirable qualities from his Appalachian forebears—superstition and xenophobia chief among them—and when he left Asheville for the University of North Carolina, he was seeking escape from these influences as well as from the smothering web of his family and of the community in general. A common character in Wolfe's novels is the young literary artist longing to escape from a hill culture that has become a kind of prison. He first seeks out the university, then the great northern city.

The University of North Carolina at Chapel Hill, described as Pulpit Hill in *Look Homeward, Angel* and as Pine Rock College in *The Web and the Rock*, is not portrayed as a place of great cultural sophistication. Wolfe satirizes the small university he knew, showing that it had much in common with his hometown of Asheville. Pine Rock College, in particular, is in a southern community that often stifles the artist. Pulpit Hill, however, is often a place of release and inspiration for the young Eugene Gant. Above all, it is a place where he finds a few people who recognize his artistic and intellectual abilities. In one of the book's best scenes a professor tells him that he must go on to Harvard: "It doesn't matter about the others. They're ready now. But a mind like yours must not be pulled green. You give it a chance to ripen. There you will find yourself." For Eugene, Harvard "was not the name of a university—it was rich magic, wealth, elegance, joy, proud loneliness, rich books and golden housing; it was an enchanted name like Cairo and Damascus." [14]

When Eugene finally goes to Harvard, it is far from being the marvelous place that he has imagined. Richard Chase and others have noted Wolfe's "excesses of elation and depression" and his use of the worn-out modern myth of the city as the hoped-for fulfillment of the provincial's golden dream. Going to Harvard was for Wolfe and his protagonist Eugene Gant an acting out of this myth. As a graduate student at Harvard, Wolfe first became acquainted with the urban educational complex that was later called a university city; he also encountered the sophistication of Boston and, on brief trips, New York. Harvard was a far cry from the small country university, enshrouded in idealism, that he had known at Chapel Hill. He was introduced to what Lewis P. Simpson calls the Third Realm—"the autonomous order of mind, the Republic of Letters, a Third Realm, being made manifest as never before in Western civilization by the advanced technology of printing." [15] When Wolfe arrived there in 1920, Harvard's arts and sciences program was undergoing a cultural revolution in which the creative arts were finding a place in the curriculum. The best example of this in 1920 was George Pierce Baker's famous Workshop 47, which Eugene O'Neill attended in 1914–15 and which, according to Robert Spiller, had "confirmed his ambition and laid the foundation to his art." [16] Swept up in the spirit of this revival of the arts in general and literature in particular, Wolfe for the first time experienced a communal artistic effort. In Baker he found the kind of masculine "rock" that had been missing in his own artistic efforts in North Carolina, where his encouragement had been chiefly feminine, with one exception. He had received valuable help in Frederick Koch's writing classes at the University of North Carolina. Of Koch's influence Andrew Turnbull says: "his enthusiasm launched Wolfe on the course which . . . he pursued for the next eight years, not without profit." [17]

At Harvard, Wolfe was able for the first time to look with a degree of objectivity at the declining southern culture he had left behind, which seemed for a time to lose its powerful influence on the young artist. In *Of Time and the River* he used his experiences at

Harvard to show the joy he felt at finding a creative milieu and friends who took education and the arts seriously. Yet in the same novel he reveals feelings of uncertainty about his life at Harvard. He sees his new environment as having the values of the "rock," but he also begins to detect a lack of emotion in New England culture generally as well as in the people he meets in Cambridge. In Wolfe's work the symbol of the rock often means masculine strength, but in this book and in certain of his New York experiences described in *The Web and the Rock,* it can also refer to emotional poverty. His literary reaction to this emotional poverty included the development of his gift for satire, which began to emerge in *Look Homeward, Angel* and is evident in some of his best scenes in *Of Time and the River.* In these scenes young Gant finds himself in a creative milieu under the guidance of a master, but many of the students are so caught up in their egocentric drive for literary success that they are hardly aware of the cultural implications of their work.

Critics generally agree that the most moving sections in *Of Time and the River* are devoted to young Gant's return to Asheville. In these scenes Wolfe probably reached the emotional peak of his literary art, especially in his description of the death of the elder Gant. Clearly in this book Wolfe looked back in pain at his culturally deprived life in Asheville, but he also looked back in longing at the powerful emotions he had felt there. His return trips to Asheville show the depth of his emotional attachments and his depictions of encounters with his family stand in contrast to the emotional deprivation he felt in Cambridge.

Another way in which Wolfe dealt with this aspect of the northern university town was through his experiences with a young Harvard instructor. The character Francis Starwick is a northerner of sensitivity, learning, and culture; yet he proves incapable of the emotional friendship that Gant seeks. Wolfe has often been criticized for his inaccurate presentation of the man that Starwick was modeled on; but Starwick should be seen primarily as a symbol of the failure of love between friends, which Wolfe came to associate with urban life in the North and the South. The failure of the Starwick friendship foreshadows George Webber's failed relationship with Foxhall Edwards in the later novels.

The revival of the arts in the decade of the twenties, in part spearheaded by Baker's other famous pupil, Eugene O'Neill, provided a forum for exploring human relationships in America. Inspired by the psychology of Freud, O'Neill demonstrated that

American life was bound by a narrow puritanism that repressed the emotional and sexual components of individuals. In some of O'Neill's best plays, this repression was shown to be one of the causes of the breakup of families as well as other human relationships. Although Wolfe never became a successful dramatist like O'Neill, he nevertheless followed in the footsteps of both O'Neill and James Joyce by showing that the breakdown of cultural values was in part a result of the moral and religious puritanism that was one of the legacies from the previous century's Victorianism. Unlike O'Neill, but like Joyce, Wolfe turned to the metropolitan center for answers to the problems of cultural renewal; his graduate career at Harvard led him directly to New York. Like Joyce in Zurich and Paris, Wolfe gradually developed a view of modern experience that led to that affirmation of life we find in the later fiction of both writers.

Harvard by 1920, as I have suggested, had become the center of a new kind of urban educational complex that included institutions in the Boston area like M.I.T. and Boston University. Unlike the University of North Carolina and other American universities that were still caught up in the sleepy idealism of the past century, Harvard had become oriented to the needs of a new urban civilization. Baker's Workshop 47 is an example of a university's effort to meet the immediate demands of a megalopolis like New York, which had joined London and Paris as a culture capital, producing plays and novels that were both effectively presented and intellectually respectable by European standards. Thus Wolfe found that his Harvard education was indeed a door to the great city. It was a door, he hoped, that would lead him to new cultural values.

Unlike Sherwood Anderson and Robert Frost, who rejected cities, Wolfe maintained his belief in the importance of the city as a place for cultural development as well as cultural revival. Richard Chase, more than any other Wolfe critic, has been aware of this fact: "It is important that, unlike novelists of the present generation, Wolfe has an effective image of the city." Chase points out Wolfe's ambivalent attitudes toward the megalopolis as manifested in the juxtaposition of his admiration for New York with his "fundamentalist, Ezekiel-like tirades against the city," [18] in the words of George Webber. Many critics have seen only the narrow and immature side of Wolfe, overlooking the fact that *The Web and the Rock* and *You Can't Go Home Again* are stories of the maturation of a literary artist in the great city and the revelation of that artist's insights into the cultural development and cultural failures of that city. Read as bildungsromans, Wolfe's novels are major literary statements about the American urban experience.

Wolfe is often seen by critics as no more than a provincial writer come to New York, never entirely free from his narrow past. It is true that in certain ways he always remained a provincial who was looking for a father. In order to appreciate and understand *The Web and the Rock* and *You Can't Go Home Again*, it is necessary to know that Wolfe and his protagonists find in New York, at least for a time, the guiding hand of a father figure and an environment where an artistic career can be pursued. Wolfe had the help of Baker at Harvard in shaping the inchoate materials of his life for dramatic presentation. In New York, after he wrote his first novel, Wolfe found another masculine "rock" in one of the greatest American editors, Maxwell Perkins, the model for the character of Foxhall Edwards. Perkins saw in Wolfe's gargantuan literary output an underlying theme of the artist's search for a father and for a place to practice his art. By helping him to shape his often rich, sometimes immature literary outpourings, Perkins became in fact a father figure and a stabilizing force in the young writer's life. Because of Perkins and other friends he met in New York, Wolfe felt at last that he was done with the narrow provincialism of Asheville and with the constricting web of southern matriarchy.

In New York Wolfe also found a woman who could provide artistic guidance without smothering or inhibiting him. Correspondingly, George Webber finds Esther Jack in *You Can't Go Home Again;* she is at once a companion, lover, and mentor. Webber describes Esther (Aline Bernstein in Wolfe's real life) in this manner: "The Woman had, in fact, begun to give a kind of frame, design, purpose to his life that it had never had before. . . . It was not merely that he was in love with her. In addition to that, through his association with her, it seemed to him now at last he had begun to 'know the city'. . . . To him she was the city." [19] Thus Esther became, as Bernstein did for Wolfe, an inspirer who helped her lover and friend to celebrate the city. Esther, like Foxhall Edwards, was also a rock. Webber, in fact, thinks of Esther as "the rock of life." On the other hand, their relationship also becomes entangling, and George comes to see that it too has its own weblike qualities. But because Wolfe did risk himself with a woman, as he never had before, he was able to describe in depth a relationship that, as Richard Chase suggests, has cultural implications: "[Wolfe] has given an authentic account of the web of circumstance and commitment George and Esther have woven about themselves—or rather, as George increasingly sees it, the web in which she has ensnared him and from which he must escape."[20] Chase rightly sees Wolfe's handling of this particular aspect of his life as "a classic statement of the manifold ambivalence of the gentile provincial who finds himself among urban Jews, for Esther Jack, who for a time is his mentor in the arts of civilization, is Jewish."[21] As Chase suggests, Wolfe does grow out of some of his provincialism, enough to become "a determined practitioner" of "cultural analysis." Indeed, Wolfe presents Webber's "tortured love affair . . . as a cultural phenomenon."[22]

George Webber finally breaks off with Esther Jack for reasons not entirely related to personal disillusionment; in the end he understands that both of them have been selfish. He also finds that the culture of New York, for all its artistic vitality, cannot appreciate his fictional vision of America. His dissatisfaction with Esther Jack's way of life is expressed in the long section of *You Can't Go Home Again* called "The World That Jack Built." The section describes a party of rich and cultured members of New York society on the eve of the Great Depression. What Webber sees at the heart of this social gathering is emotional emptiness, selfishness, and greed. Webber perceives that the malign influence that has weakened the cultural values of America is, more than anything else, a narcissism that ignores the rightful claims of others. He also sees this selfishness in his own life, and like Wolfe he realizes that the angels of adoration and fame are not enough for him. The city and its culture, though they are like a rock giving support and guidance to his artistic efforts, lack the healing waters of human concern—the kind of symbolic rock Eliot often refers to in *The Waste Land*. Webber in *You Can't Go Home Again* cries out: "Was no love living in the wilderness, and was there nothing but the snarl and jungle of the streets, the rasp and driven fury of the town? No love? Was no love living in the wilderness?"[23]

While he is with Esther, Webber suddenly sees himself as a drunken beggar on horseback. Esther sees "his face grow twisted" as he tries to speak to her of his vision and cannot: "He wanted to say to her that we are all savage, foolish, violent, and mistaken, that, full of our fear and convulsion, we walk in ignorance upon the living and beautiful earth, breathing young, vital air and bathing in the light of morning, seeing it not because of the murder in our hearts."[24] Wolfe never lost his belief in the artistic vitality of New

York, but, like many other artists of his time, he became deeply aware of the jungle both in the city and in himself. His method of dealing with this wilderness, as he calls it, was to plunge into its depths. Specifically, he left Manhattan and moved to Brooklyn, a move that marked the beginning of his vision of cultural revival.

Paschal Reeves, a critic who has shown great sensitivity to Wolfe's late maturing, says that the author, "like George Webber, reached maturity late" as "the center of his interest shifted near the end of his life from the individual to the society which shapes the individual." [25] Seeing in both Wolfe and Webber a growing humanitarianism, Reeves traces this awareness back to Wolfe's new life in Brooklyn, a time when he encountered the wilderness of the streets and experienced a collective suffering such as he had never before known. Reeves writes: "The greatest single influence on the awakening of Wolfe's social concern was the depression years he spent in Brooklyn. It was the intense suffering he witnessed that caused him more and more to feel an intense and passionate concern for the interests and designs of his fellow man and of all humanity." [26] In the late thirties Wolfe visited Germany, a nation he had loved in earlier visits, to find it had turned into a place of suspicion and hate, where cultural values were rapidly collapsing. In *You Can't Go Home Again* we find a subtle indictment of the Nazis and of those Europeans who slept while Western culture everywhere was betraying itself. In this book he also reveals, through Webber's visit to his hometown turned commercial city, what he believed to be the malignant element devouring southern culture in Asheville: personal selfishness, in himself as well as others, which made it impossible to take into real account the collective cultural and social concerns of the nation.

In Wolfe's later writings there are many indications of his revolt against the rampant individualism of the twenties. In many ways Wolfe and his work were very much a part of the revival of social consciousness that occurred during the thirties. He came to see that the cultural values of art and education, to which he had diligently devoted himself since his youth, could collapse if political values were neglected. And for politics to be creative it was necessary for there to be a loving concern for others. His encounter with New York taught him what he had begun to learn in Asheville: for cities to flourish on a social basis, concern with individual needs alone was not enough. It was a lesson that America had to learn as it began to overcome the terrible social effects of the Great Depression and faced the prospect of involvement in another world war. Wolfe did not live long enough to become actively involved in the New Deal politics of the thirties, but as *You Can't Go Home Again* indicates, he did begin work on a philosophy that would account for the possibility of authentic cultural revival and America's recovery of national unity.

Wolfe's philosophical struggles, recorded primarily in *You Can't Go Home Again*, were directed against a literary naturalism that he had inherited from earlier writers of the century, like Dreiser, and against a Calvinistic fatalism that he inherited from his mountain forebears. This fatalism is summed up best in the epigraph for *You Can't Go Home Again:* "There came to him an image of man's whole life upon earth. It seemed to him that all man's life was like a tiny spurt of flame that blazed out briefly in an illimitable and terrifying darkness." Wolfe also struggled against Maxwell Perkins's "resigned fatalism," which denied the possibility of hope for the rebirth of cultural values in America.

Pamela Johnson rightly says that the poetic power of Wolfe's prose "derives from Whitman."[27] However, unlike Whitman, he never explored the dimensions of his own psyche. Under the influence of Emerson, Whitman as transcendentalist evolved a vision of the unified individual. Wolfe, who did not concern himself very deeply with religious values, never was able to resolve his hunger for love, which was often expressed as a physical hunger for food and drink: "His mania for food gives a cannibalistic slant to his love-making."[28] But he did share Whitman's hope that cultural renewal in America would bring with it a renewal of human relationships.

Wolfe's seeming awareness of his own approaching death, evident in prose written for *I Have a Thing to Tell You* but placed by editor Edward Aswell at the end of *You Can't Go Home Again*, seemed to stimulate visions of new birth. In powerful and often-quoted passages Wolfe tells us of losing "the earth you know, for greater knowing; to lose the life you have, for greater life; to leave the friends you loved, for greater loving, to find a land more kind than home, more large than earth. . . . I believe that we are lost here in America, but I believe we shall be found." The enemy, he tells us, is "Single selfishness and compulsive greed."[29] But in spite of and even because of the destruction of earlier cultural values by these malignant forces, Americans will once again search their souls, and this search will lead to cultural rebirth in the nation: "I think the true discovery of America is before us. I think the true fulfillment of our spirit, of our people, of our mighty and immortal land, is yet to come. I think the true discovery of our democracy is still before us."[30] Part of what Wolfe was forecasting in *You Can't Go Home Again* was already coming about in the late thirties and early forties as America sought a new unity that would enable the nation to overcome its lingering financial depression and wartime enemies.

Wolfe also seems to approach the possibility of worldwide cultural renewal with his portrayal of the death of an old way of life and the birth of new values. His popularity in foreign countries, particularly in Germany, is based in part on his affirmation of life in the twentieth century, his belief that modern humanity's urban problems could eventually be overcome. As I have sought to show, his encounter with the modern city did yield the fruit of significant visions.

Wolfe's encounter with various cities must be emphasized in order to understand and appreciate much of what is good in his fiction, particularly that written after 1930. Certainly few important American writers have needed understanding and appreciation more than Wolfe. No major writer of this century has been so ridiculed by critics and intellectuals. Many critics, in fact, place Wolfe alongside Theodore Dreiser, as a writer who lacked form; Norman Mailer calls him "the novelist as giant" who "labored like a Titan" and was "the greatest five-year-old who ever lived."[31] Pamela Johnson's *The Art of Thomas Wolfe* is one of the few books that examines Wolfe's work without patronizing the author, and even she suggests that no critical method yet exists for analyzing his powerful but uneven genius. But for the past thirty years critical and scholarly efforts have illuminated Wolfe's strength as a literary artist. Hugh Holman has demonstrated that Wolfe's style, so often criticized for its uneven, sometimes immature qualities, is in the tradition of southern writing, in which a mixture of styles is not uncommon. Floyd Watkins has demonstrated how Wolfe fits into the tradition of southern rhetoric.[32] Holman, Watkins, and other southern critics have shown how rich Wolfe's portrayal of the southern life of his day is. Louis D. Rubin, Jr., has suggested that the form of Wolfe's novels, with the exception of the first one, was the result of unnecessary editorial interference with his work. "The result," Rubin writes, "was less than fortunate, for what was written as confessional was made to seem as autobiographical boasting behind the facade of supposed third-person 'objectivity'."[33] Wolfe's novelistic form, however, will never satisfy most contemporary critics, because these critics are formalist in their viewpoint and see the novel in the context of the tight fictional structure first created by Flaubert, the father of the modern novel.

In the end, those who admire Wolfe will simply have to accept the weak writing along with the strong. Wolfe might best be seen as a poet writing in novelistic form, a poet with good and bad passages. Richard Chase suggests as much when he writes that every Wolfe reader "will have his favorite passages" and that "what Wolfe loses by his uneven and faultful way of writing, he makes up in fecundity and variety."[34] Yet I insist that Wolfe not be viewed simply as a writer of great passages. Wolfe's energy and vision, in fact, lend an organic unity to his work, and an understanding of his theme of the artist's encounter with the city gives the reader a deep insight into both the meaning and essential unity of his best fiction.

Finally, I think we have lacked a way of classifying Wolfe's work. I would like to suggest a classification by taking a cue from Chase's word, "fecundity." There is in Wolfe's best work a richness and energy that make him—along with Eugene O'Neill, Hart Crane, Tennessee Williams, and James Dickey—a Dionysian writer. The Dionysians wanted to affirm the human spirit's search for a better way of life. The first modern Dionysians were Nietzsche and Strindberg. O'Neill, who studied under the same teacher as Wolfe, drew deep inspiration from Strindberg and helped develop a new kind of drama in America. Like O'Neill, Wolfe's best work foreshadows a literary vision not yet fully realized. Above all, Wolfe, like Whitman, seized upon the American city in its beauty and agonizingly rapid growth and brought forth affirmative visions of its renewed culture. Also like Whitman, Wolfe in affirming the American experience came to see that the cultures of the North and the South would in time flow into a larger American culture that would be greater than the sum of both. More than Whitman, Wolfe saw that the old American cultural values were dying, but as a mythical writer he also saw the possibility of the revival of new values that would lead to new cultural unity and a deeper explanation of the meaning of American life.

6

Tennessee Williams
Desire and Impotence in New Orleans

When Tennessee Williams died early in 1983, his stature as a major American playwright was confirmed. Even the popular press seemed to grasp the fact that Williams was far more than a writer whose primary aim was to shock audiences with his portrayals of the seamiest side of southern decadence. *Time,* for instance, called Williams a "moral symbolist," stating that "the shocking surface was never the substance in Williams" and that he had achieved a "catharsis of self-transcendence": "In breaking out of the imprisoning cycle of self-concern, the playwright and his characters evoke a line from *Ecclesiastes:* 'To him that is joined to all the living there is hope'." [1]

Although Williams often wrote about the plantations and towns of the upland South, he spent most of his life in cities. He grew up in St. Louis and presented his first dramas there before moving to New York to help launch a new period of southern and American literature after 1945. No work announced the postwar period of the nation's literature more propitiously than Williams's *The Glass Menagerie;* presented first in Chicago and then in New York in 1945, it was a major event in American theatrical history. With this play, Williams's first to succeed in New York, Eugene O'Neill had a worthy successor. Two years later came *A Streetcar Named Desire,* and with successful productions of this play in London and New York

Williams found himself an international figure. In the history of southern literature the period after World War II is sometimes called post-Renaissance because it follows the more highly regarded period of the Southern Renaissance. It is still a period without a proper name, but it may yet prove to be as significant as the period that preceded it.

Williams brought to the American theater a rich Chekhovian atmosphere and a poetic language that haunted playgoers long after they had left the theater. He also created some of the most memorable figures of the modern stage—Amanda Wingfield, Blanche DuBois, and Big Daddy, among others. Williams's poetry and his exploitation of human emotions have overshadowed his spiritual quest and his moral vision. For Williams the values that held together the family and the community had suffered a severe eclipse, but he believed that these values could be renewed by an effort of humans to make loving contact with other humans. Man's only redemption, he once said, was when "one puts himself aside to feel deeply for another person." He sought a way of life that had a central place for beauty, love, and justice. Even while exposing the many failures of southern culture, this scion of the genteel South believed that one city above all others in the South still contained elements of an earlier, richer culture: New Orleans. The play thought to be his most characteristic, though not necessarily his best (*The Glass Menagerie* probably deserves that honor) is his work about New Orleans, *A Streetcar Named Desire*. Though he depicts it populated with impotent, narcissistic, destructive personalities, Williams continued to believe that the Crescent City still contained elements of true community. Up to his death he maintained a residence in New Orleans, where he said he hoped to die. He died in New York, however, the city where he first found a large audience for his plays.

The Glass Menagerie and *Streetcar* announce the two great Williams themes, the destructiveness of runaway sexual desire and the need to seek the open road in search of a life-style that overcomes puritanism and narcissism. Tom Wingfield in *The Glass Menagerie* is the symbol of man on the open road, searching for something undefinable and pursued by guilt for having fled duties at hand. Wingfield is a mask for Williams himself; the character's determination to dissociate himself from the decadent and narcissistic aspects of southern culture is reminiscent of a remark Arthur Miller made about Williams at the time of his death: "He chose a hard life that required the skin of an alligator and the heart of a poet. To his everlasting honor he persevered and bore all of us toward glory."[2]

Williams succeeded where Wolfe failed in dealing effectively with the greatest of Walt Whitman's themes, which, according to D. H. Lawrence, is the American's search for fulfillment and comradeship on the open road. Williams continued to develop this theme until 1969; then, in *The Night of the Iguana*, he created characters who are able to grasp the meaning of the life of the open road and who are capable of sustaining, with difficulty, a loving relationship. In two earlier plays, *Camino Real* and *Orpheus Descending*, Williams presents characters he called romantic nonconformists, people who are seeking a new comradeship and creativity, both personal and social. He shows the defeat of the protagonists in these two plays, but in doing so he defines the problems of personal and cultural renewal. And in *The Night of the Iguana*, as well as in a later and very difficult play, *The Milk Train Doesn't Stop Here Anymore*, he details some of the attitudes that make individual and cultural revival possible.

The theme of personal revival appears consistently in Williams's work, though efforts to achieve this revival often meet with frustration. From *The Glass Menagerie* onward Williams used mythic themes to point to the possibility of cultural renewal in our time. Joseph K. Davis discusses Williams's use of the Orpheus motif as "one of the consistent mythopoeic themes in Williams' work," foreshadowed in Tom Wingfield's "affirmation of man's beastlike aspects."[3] Davis identifies the meaning of this Orphean quest in Williams as a search "for unification of man's animal and intellectual dimensions through artistic means."[4] In other words, Williams deals with the problem of the Cartesian split that Allen Tate, Conrad Aiken, and Walker Percy explore in their work. Humans are fragmented, Williams tells us, and they seek at least a measure of inner reconciliation to keep from being destroyed by the opposites at war within themselves. If they do not seek inner reconciliation, they are torn to pieces. Orpheus himself suffers dismemberment, as do a host of other mythic heroes, and Williams sometimes shows the artist being torn to pieces by barbarians. Yet in some of his best plays he portrays artists as survivors who have learned to renew themselves. The poet Nono in *The Night of the Iguana* may represent the ability certain artists have to let go of their old selves to find new selves. The great mythic theme, as Mircea Eliade reminds us, is death and rebirth, a theme that Williams often echoes.

Because so many people look at his artistic origins in the context of a sometimes brilliant dramaturgy that is partly original and partly borrowed (as techniques in the hands of great artists usually are), and because some critics still do not take Williams seriously as a result of his New York–Hollywood successes, the real source of his mythic vision is seldom understood. As I have suggested, Williams was involved with Whitman's great task of "creating an art for democratic people," as Esther M. Jackson puts it in her analysis of the relationship between Whitman and Williams.[5] And we know that Williams was deeply involved with celebrating the idea of the unity of body and soul, so important to Whitman and Lawrence. His admiration for Lawrence was so great, in fact, that he wrote a play praising his genius, *I Rise in Flame, Cried the Phoenix.* Yet the central mythic development of Williams is tied up with the urban and mythic vison of James Joyce, which is at once tragic and epic. On the surface at least Williams appears to be more under the influence of Eliot than Joyce, and we find few deliberate uses of Joycean techniques; but the spirit of Joyce permeates his work.

In his first important play and first great success, *The Glass Menagerie,* Williams brings up several of the great Joycean themes. Tom Wingfield, like Stephen Dedalus, confronts a world in paralysis in a middle-sized American city, St. Louis. He is caught up in a family and religion that he must leave if he is to find himself. For Williams, St. Louis was representative of the kind of American provincial city that trapped and frustrated the true artist. Of Tom Wingfield he says, "His nature is not remorseless, but to escape from a trap he has to act without pity."[6] Wingfield's break with his mother causes him much guilt and pain. But the Williams and Joyce protagonists do not know how to kill the spider at the center of the family web; they only know that they must leave and not return if they are to go on living. Yet after they leave, they are always haunted by the past, by a "familiar bit of music," as Williams says at the end of the play. These protagonists go forth to find an urban jungle, but they have developed a defense against this jungle, and that defense is their art. Amanda, Tom's mother, accuses him as he prepares to leave of "manufactur[ing] illusions," but Tom has already told us at the beginning of the play that he is the opposite of the stage magician who "gives you illusion that has the appearance of truth." Instead, he says, "I give you truth in the pleasant disguise of illusion."[7] Amanda, of course, is the narcissist who creates an unreal world, whereas Tom is a searcher for truth.

Tom does not leave his mother with disgust or horror or rage but with pain and love. He is not capable of much love, psychically wounded as he is, but he seeks to cultivate what he is capable of as he moves out onto the open road, passing through "cities that swept by me like dead leaves."[8] Because he continues to believe in love, Williams's protagonist is capable of what Joyce called the epiphany, a moment of spiritual or psychic insight involving tenderness or love. Williams once said that the premise underlying his entire artistic life "has been the need for understanding and tenderness and fortitude among individuals trapped by circumstance."[9] And so Tom remembers his mother not with loathing but with dismay for what has gone wrong in her life. The spider at the center of the family web then is not the mother but rather her hunger, a hunger so uncontrollable it has caused her to spin a crippling psychic web around her daughter Laura. Tom knows he must leave before it cripples him too.

Williams, like Joyce (as he showed in *A Portrait of the Artist as a Young Man*), loved his family, but he knew that he could realize himself artistically only by first separating himself from them and then by exploring their dimensions. Also like Joyce, Williams wandered through cities that he was never a part of, always living in exile; but he carried in his heart his family, much of his inherited religion (his mother was the daughter of an Episcopal priest), and his native southern culture. One of the chief differences between Williams and Joyce is that Joyce knew early in his career what his artistic role would be, whereas Williams only knew that he had to make a journey into his native region and culture, carrying with him certain problems that had to be solved artistically. By the end of his major creative phase, Williams had pointed to solutions that are in some ways like Joyce's, though never achieving their visionary power. This second great American playwright of our century, whose dramas are equaled only by those of O'Neill, embodied in his work the insights of both Freud and Jung; he brought us, as Joyce did, an artistic rendering of the pain involved in modern life and a hope for the renewal of love and the fulfillment of human sexuality.

Williams's first successful work offers a dramatic economy and lyricism not found in the work of any other American playwright. His examination of his background begins with his own mother, characterized as Amanda Wingfield in *The Glass Menagerie*. Like Wolfe, he shows us a southern cultural heritage held tightly in the grip of women with ravenous appetites for money and success and control over their environment. The father of the family is mostly absent, and the son takes his place for a time; there is, however, no way to satisfy that hungry spider within the masterful woman, the true hierarch in the Williams family. Amanda defines her own nature in two statements. First, sobbing, she tells her two children: "My devotion has made me a witch and so I make myself hateful to my children!" [10] Having lost the sense of harmony possessed by the creative hierarch, she resorts to a form of psychic witchcraft to hold her family together. Control, not leadership, is her watchword, though she makes everyone deny this painful fact. She says she has had to resort to "Spartan endurance." In her role as secular leader she is a Spartan, but in her role as religious and cultural leader she is, of course, a modern puritan. When Tom tells her that man "is by instinct a lover, a hunter, a fighter," she answers: "Instinct is something that people have got away from! It belongs to animals! Christian adults don't want it!" [11] Tom, the son, rebels violently against the puritanism of his mother. Williams himself defined freedom from puritanism as one of his chief values, saying: "I was brought up puritanically. I try to outrage that puritanism." [12] He shows in his plays that puritanism is a source of human impotence because it springs from the inability to love. The puritan is unable to express himself either spiritually or instinctively.

In Williams's major works this split between instinct and the spiritual life, created by American puritanism, is a prevailing theme. A genius, F. Scott Fitzgerald said, is one who can hold two opposite ideas in tension. Williams holds in tension the ideas of his mother and those of Tom, refusing to let either go and always seeking that moment of epiphany when the two are momentarily one. When Tom asks Amanda what Christian adults do want, she says, "Superior things! Things of the mind and the spirit!" [13] Williams never ceases to believe in the importance of spiritual values, but he rejects Amanda's dictum that "only animals have to satisfy instincts." The true cultural leader, he says in several of his plays, is the one who renews life, creates a life-style that allows the mind, the spirit, and the instincts to work, at least some of the time, in harmony. When the play opens, Tom Wingfield does not yet fully realize this truth, but as a prototype of Williams's protagonists he searches for and finds, if only momentarily, this vision of renewal. Williams in his plays digs into the layers of southern culture past and present, eventually finding his way back to the Latin culture that formed the basis for much of the original communal life of the Gulf coast and the Mississippi uplands.

Williams's deepest exploration into both the life and the death of southern culture occurred in 1947 (two years after *The Glass Menagerie*) with his most famous play, *A Streetcar Named Desire*, and with another play, less famous and less well understood, *Summer and Smoke*, which was first produced in 1948. The latter deals with the failure of culture in a Mississippi upland town like Columbus, where Williams was born and lived for a short time before his father took the family to St. Louis. (Columbus, Mississippi, represents a segment of the South that I will discuss later.) *Summer and Smoke* tells us that culture is dying in the uplands and that those who would renew themselves must turn to the southern city or to New York to find in the urban cultural center the meaning of the lost values that undergird all cultural activity. The central figure in the play is named Alma; in keeping with the semiallegorical nature of the work, she reminds her friends that *alma* in Spanish means "soul." Like Amanda in *The Glass Menagerie* she tends to deny her instinctual desire to develop her soul, but when she falls in love with a young doctor she has to face her own instincts. The end of the play sees her moving beyond the life of the town in order to try to develop these instincts, but in spite of her efforts, as the play ends she is losing her grip on her meager spiritual values.

Blanche DuBois in *Streetcar* is an older Alma. For Blanche the soul is of great importance, as Leonard Quirino emphasizes in an excellent essay: "The soul, for Williams in this play, seems to be that entity which produces and is sustained by culture but is not synonymous with it."[14] Williams makes this clear in his introduction to *Streetcar;* in the last paragraph he asks what "good" is and answers: "the obsessive interest in human affairs, plus a certain amount of compassion and moral conviction, that first made the experience of living something that must be translated into pigment or music or bodily movement or poetry or prose or anything that's dynamic and expressive—that's what's good for you if you're at all serious in your aims."[15] He ends by saying that "purity of heart is the one success worth having, the only thing that will beat the 'monosyllable of the clock'," which is "Loss, Loss, Loss."[16] Heart or soul—the terms are the same: they refer to the spiritual principle in people that culture nourishes and that, when operative, unites all of the human's warring elements—mind and instinct, body and soul.

Blanche is a tragic heroine, Williams's greatest. She has struggled against the warring opposites in herself and has lost, yet she has retained some shreds of goodness, some fragments of her inherited cultural values and her original innocence; but she cannot stand up against the destructive power of Stan Kowalski, her nemesis. Jacob H. Adler defines her situation thus: "in Blanche, who is involved with both real and ideal and cannot reconcile them, nymphomania and prudery, love of the past and hatred of the past, genuine culture and pretentious fakery exist at the same time."[17] Blanche is destroyed by a tragic flaw. In contrast, Alma at the end of *Summer and Smoke,* as Adler points out in his analysis of this neglected play, has made an adjustment to life.[18] Though she is tragic, she is not necessarily doomed. But for Blanche it is too late. Her tragic flaw is her excessive desire and the rage that she feels when it is not satisfied. As Williams has explained, she must pay a price for having caused the suicide of her homosexual husband in her tempestuous earlier life. She knows that no man can ever sexually satisfy her and that, consequently, all her affairs will lead only to despair and hatred.

If we see *Streetcar* as a tragedy and New Orleans as the tragic scene, we can begin to understand Williams's view of the decay of southern culture. In the opening lyrical description of the French Quarter the audience is given a hint of an undying musical spirit that will in time bring forth new life. Williams says in his stage directions for Scene 1: "In this part of New Orleans you are practically always just around the corner, or a few doors down the street, from a tinny piano being played with the infatuated fluency of brown fingers. This 'Blue Piano' expresses the spirit of the life which goes on here."[19] The New Orleans described in this first scene is still a cultural center or, as Williams puts it, "A cosmopolitan city where there is a relatively warm and easy intermingling of races in the old part of town."[20] This section is named "Elysian Fields," suggesting the hope of a new life in the South in which the harmony of music is always present and the races meet on an equal basis.

The central action in the play is Williams's statement about the life and death of both the old southern culture and the American megalopolis, which for Williams is nothing more than a meaningless urban sprawl. As the play opens, Blanche has just arrived in the city from her home in Laurel, Mississippi. Her family home is one of those symbolic white mansions of southern pseudo-myth, a plantation house called Belle Reve, "a great big place with white columns." It has been lost, as Blanche explains later, because "our improvident grandfathers and uncles and brothers exchanged the land for their epic fornications—to put it plainly."[21] Like Amanda Wingfield, she clings to the official puritanical line that desire in itself is bad, to be repressed if possible; yet she herself is caught up in uncontrollable desire. Her desire has destroyed her husband and freed her to pursue other men. She appears on stage dressed in white, described as looking like a moth; and, like a moth, she is being drawn to the flame of a final desire that will destroy her.

Williams in his best work is far closer to Greek tragedy than many have imagined. His tragic characters are destroyed because they are swept up in a hubris that is accompanied by overpowering desires. Nemesis inevitably follows and dispatches them. What has kept so many people from seeing the best of Williams's plays in this context is the easy identification viewers often make with important central characters. A. Alan Chesler has examined some of the many interpretations of Stanley Kowalski, for example, and has found that important critics of culture and drama like Robert Brustein and Eric Bentley actually think of Kowalski as a hero. This attitude has even found its way into literature textbooks: Louis D. Rubin, Jr., writes in *The Literary South* (1979) that Blanche's "decadence, snobbery, and frustrated malaise are contrasted with what is portrayed as the virile, healthy, profane vulgarity of Stanley Kowalski."[22] Rather deceptively, Williams at the beginning of the play introduces Stanley as a robust, seemingly healthy character, and Blanche herself thinks it might have been a good idea for her sister to marry this rough-hewn man to get some new blood in the family. But Stanley proves to be a rapist who lives by the principle of brute force.

Part of the reason for so much misinterpretation of his character is the engaging way in which Marlon Brando played the role on Broadway and in the cinematic version of the play. But Brando misinterpreted the role and played a rapist the way many people imagine a rapist to be, a man of strong sexual powers who gives women what they "really want." Since the play was written, it has been shown in many studies that a rapist generally attacks a woman not with strong sexual desire but with cold, impotent fury and the intent to degrade his victim. The rapist behaves as he does because he is psychologically impotent.

Williams carefully reveals Stanley's true nature: he distrusts weakness, as well as any kind of superiority that is not based on brute strength alone. He is an autocrat, always attempting to control others, yet creating chaos around himself. In the character of Stanley, Williams gives us his own view of the destructive side of the modern megalopolis. Jacob Adler has written about power and culture in Williams's plays, and these concepts are indeed central to all of his best work.[23] When power is cut loose from culture, Williams tells us, it becomes destructive, even when it wears the masks of virility and jocularity. Rape is its goal, and the psychic destruction of the victim is the desire of the rapist. Behind the rapist's forcefulness lies the impotence of one who wields personal power but can know neither love nor joy. For Williams true impotence grows out of the inability to love, and from impotence springs both desire (like Blanche's) and rage (like Stanley's).

Williams was New Orleans's greatest poet at a time when Louis Armstrong was its greatest musician, and the old New Orleans that Williams evokes at the beginning of the play is haunted by the music of the blues, which laments love's loss and yet still hopes for a love to come. This New Orleans is an old southern cultural center, down at the heels but still living. The New Orleans that Stan Kowalski belongs to is, psychologically speaking, the megalopolis that always dominates in a time of collapsing culture. Its impotence, however, presages its ultimate collapse, whereas the lyricism emanating from the French Quarter of New Orleans in Williams's play proclaims its ability to rise from its own ashes.

Thomas J. Richardson has described what he calls Williams's romance with and absorption into the city of night, a city of music and freedom. Williams himself said of the city, "My happiest years were there," and "I found the kind of freedom I had always needed. And the shock of it against the puritanism of my nature gave me a subject, a theme, which I have never ceased exploiting."[24] Williams found what for him was creative in southern culture contained in the communal life of the inner city of New Orleans; his youth in St. Louis hardly seems to have counted for anything in his imaginative vision. In *The Glass Menagerie* St. Louis is presented as a dreary city to be avoided. But in the New Orleans of *Streetcar*, despite the impotent desire of the two leading characters, there is a community based on life rather than death.

A cursory examination of *Streetcar* might lead one to believe that Stanley Kowalski is a symbol of the northern invader who has come to destroy southern culture, but this would be an oversimplification. Southern culture, in effect, is self-destructive, as Williams tells us in his other important play about New Orleans, *Suddenly Last Summer*. Written in the late fifties, this play goes to the heart of the southern hierarchy's self-destructive tendencies in order to examine the mad desire of leaders of a culture in its death throes. In some ways it is Williams's most frightening work because it depicts the degeneration of desire into a need not only to rape and to be raped but also to be devoured physically. Williams's story "Desire and the Black Masseur," in which a man invites and receives mutilation at the hands of his masseur, prepared the way for this play about a religion that sees God as a cannibal and man as a creature to be cannibalized. Yet Williams makes the point that desire gone mad and impotence turned to castration represent a human attempt to break through the walls of the narcissistic prison and that the end of desire, as he poignantly demonstrates in *Streetcar* with its two streetcars named Desire and Cemeteries, is always death. Hot desire and its opposite, the cold impotence caused by puritanism, are everywhere destroying the cultures of the world, Williams tells us. New Orleans for him is two cities: one city is always destroying and being destroyed and the other is a night city of music and love, a place where remnants of culture remain, presaging the possibility of true revival.

Music is Williams's greatest symbol of a love based not on desire but, rather, on a concern for the beloved. He undoubtedly had to descend to the morbid depths of *Suddenly Last Summer* to prepare himself for *The Night of the Iguana,* his last play to speak to large audiences. In this play Williams suggests the possibility of a continuing love that is founded on a concern for others. In a sense he had been preparing to write this play all his creative life. His first play, which was a failure called *Battle of Angels*, shows the crucifixion of a modern Christ figure, whose loving presence provokes the cold, impotent fury of puritanical, castrating powers. But in *The Night of the Iguana* he shows several ordinary mortals moving toward moments of love and toward a union based on mutual concern rather than consuming desire. Fittingly for Williams, the play is set in Mexico and the characters are Americans on the road— travelers who still have hope of renewing their lives. The love that Shannon and Maxine find in *Iguana* springs from Shannon's realization that his concept of God and the cosmos was always wrong, was in fact based on the puritanism of his southern past. Shannon's God denies the love of man and nature, and when Shannon discovers the puritan in himself and sees God at work everywhere in the world, he can stop and live in one place. He has had to go on the road to flee puritanism, which created in him a mad desire and a fear of a threatening God, the same puritanical God that Sebastian in *Suddenly Last Summer* sees as all-devouring. But when Shannon accepts a God who cares about everybody and everything, he can stop running.

Williams, like Wolfe, often talks about humans shut up in a psychic prison, unable to relate to other humans. His plays make it clear that such a prison causes people to be narcissistic, to have a strong desire to possess others, and to rage at their own psychic impotence. In his best plays there are characters, such as Hannah Jelkes in *Iguana*, who are able to step out of the prison and relate to others.

By the time Williams wrote *Iguana* he knew that the kind of protagonist he created in *Battle of Angels,* the modern Christ figure, had to be crucified for dramatic purposes. The protagonist in *Battle of Angels* is conceived as a hero, but, like Joyce when he changed his first protagonist's name from Stephen Hero to Stephen Dedalus, Williams knew that certain disguises and strategies would be necessary to continue that cultural development in the arts that would be necessary to bring about a new age. And in two masterpieces, *Streetcar* and *Iguana*, Williams reveals his deepest vision of personal and cultural revival.

Between *Streetcar* and *Iguana* Williams wrote two basic types of drama: modern Chekhovian, lyrical tragedies like *Sweet Bird of Youth* and *Suddenly Last Summer,* and expressionistic dramas like *Camino Real,* in which he makes enigmatic statements about human development. Sometimes we see the two styles combined in one play. Regardless of which style he uses, his major theme in his best work is always the need for loving concern for others. Two plays that deal successfully with a developing character who has this loving concern and can therefore bring new life to wounded individuals are *Summer and Smoke* and *Cat on a Hot Tin Roof*. Williams chose to set both plays in an urban-rural continuum in which the presence of a city (New Orleans and Memphis) is felt but where small-town and country life is also of vital importance—an area of the South like that surrounding Columbus, Mississippi, where he spent much of his early life. In this setting he worked out dramatically many aspects of the problems of the old southern hierarchy and community.

In both plays he shows the failure of the male hierarchy and of southern aristocracy, a failure that brings with it puritanism and the loss of true community and reduces society to a collection of warring individuals. The failure of true community inevitably means the rise of the southern "bosses" so often satirized. In *Sweet Bird of Youth* and *Orpheus Descending* the bosses manipulate large numbers of people and try to overpower Orphean individuals who are attempting to bring love back into people's lives. But our time, Williams tells us, is that of the dismemberment of Orpheus. And in such a time women, like Isis, must arise to gather up the mythic hero's scattered parts and to prepare for a new age of heroism by preserving elements of culture. In *Summer and Smoke* and *Cat* Williams depicts the making of two such heroines. By the end of the two plays they are still developing their powers for doing good, and it is not clear whether they will eventually become Isis figures or not. The audience is left with the idea that there is at least the hope of such a development.

Summer and Smoke makes it clear that the problem of culture is the problem of the human soul, seat of the ability to love and show concern. In this semiallegorical play, Alma Winemiller carries the burden of "soul-life" in a town that denies the importance of the soul. Like many other Williams heroines, she shrinks from the body and the instincts. In contrast, the man she is drawn to, a young doctor, avoids knowledge of the soul, declaring that he believes only in the brain, the stomach, and the sexual organs. By the end of the play he realizes that his life without Alma, and the loving concern that she offers, will be wretched. Alma herself by the end of the play is seeking a way for her soul to relate to her body and her instincts, both of which her puritanical parents have taught her to deny. Only by achieving some sort of harmony between body and soul (one of the great Whitman-Lawrence-Williams teachings) can she discover her true powers. Only by leaving the doctor can she eventually return as Isis to preserve his mutilated life. The ending is ambiguous; Alma could possibly go the way of Blanche. Earlier Williams created a precursor of this character, another Alma, the heroine of his story "The Yellowbird," who goes to New Orleans and achieves a measure of freedom and creativity. Her name (which means "soul," as mentioned earlier) is a talisman, protecting her from puritanism's castrating powers.

Cat on a Hot Tin Roof, one of Williams's most popular plays, opens on an urban-rural plantation with all the trappings of money, power, sex, and, above all, an authentic boss, Big Daddy Pollitt. Big Daddy is not so much a castrating hierarch as a benevolent despot who is trying to stop time and turn his Delta plantation into an enchanted illusion, only to find his power reduced to impotence by cancer. His son Brick, athletic and boyish, is also impotent, trapped in his latent homosexuality and the memory of schoolboy friendships. He reacts to his impotence with cold fury, which he directs against himself rather than others. His wife, Maggie, the cat with nine lives, fights for life and love. She is the model of all Williams women who learn to deny illusion, no matter how beautiful that illusion might seem, and can thus overcome both impotence and lust in order to find love and a mastery of life. Maggie knows that southern culture has almost disintegrated and that its only hope is the revival of life through loving concern. Serafina in *The Rose Tattoo* is a woman like Maggie, and even Big Daddy's wife, Big Mama, is by the end of *Cat* becoming a woman who lives beyond illusion, seeking a new life based on her own inner creativity instead of on a plantation way of life that worships the past.

Maggie, Serafina, and Big Mama are all characters who foreshadow Maxine in *Iguana*, the woman who has found within herself the powers of Isis, which enable her to begin the spiritual rehabilitation of Shannon. Together, Maxine and Shannon represent the possibilities of the kind of human relationship that will eventually restore true community. The other creative woman in the play, Hannah Jelkes, is a middle-aged Alma who has learned the wisdom of the East while serving her grandfather, an aged poet who, before he dies, completes his last and best poem in praise of courage and the beauty of nature. Thus one woman preserves the wounded poet and his wisdom and courage. The other woman preserves Shannon, the wounded priest who ultimately has a vision of a God who unconditionally loves all of his creatures and every aspect of their humanity. Williams demonstrates in *Iguana* that love becomes a lasting possibility only when humans have the courage to relate to the cosmos and to a power that is all-loving. The answer in Williams's work to the problems of desire and impotence is a visionary relationship to the interrelatedness of all life.

Williams is often presented as a playwright who wallows in a Freudian morass, who dramatizes only the psychological disasters of modern life. In fact, he deals with the kinds of problems Freud explored, and knowledge of Freudian concepts like narcissism and the Oedipus complex is essential to understand much of what Wil-

liams wrote. But the concern of the popular press as well as his audiences is usually with the decadence and not with the therapeutic
vision in Williams's best work. Freud himself wrote that his own
work was concerned with the total love life of the individual and
that the attainment of a mature sexuality was part of the development of this love life. Williams's plays depict both the psychological
morass modern humanity has fallen into and the possibility of moving beyond that morass, and they contain a power and love that are
the result of Williams's own psychic growth. If there had been no
growth, he would have gone the way of Wolfe and many other
American writers, into bitter agony and early creative death.

Williams himself records in his *Memoirs* much of his own troubled life that went into the plays, the poetry, and the fiction. In analyzing this work Victor Kramer rightly says that "Williams' odyssey
has been a progression into and through madness."[25] In interviews
after 1970 Williams described his descent into drug addiction for
nearly the entire decade of the sixties and his subsequent reentry
into society. In his *Memoirs* he speaks of his solitary life, while in his
plays he talks about man's imprisonment. The *Memoirs* and the plays
are full of the people and relationships he has known. As the *Memoirs* tell us, the plays are made out of the life of the poet and playwright.

But Williams is a Joycean artist and could have survived only as
such. By this I mean that he did not borrow Joycean techniques as
Wolfe did or plunge into the myths of foreign societies as Lawrence
did; instead he mastered the mythic method that both Joyce and
Eliot used in their best work, relating the meaning of mythic figures to modern life. Williams's own life provides the final proof of
the Joycean influence. Lawrence isolated himself and died before
his time, and Williams may have written his play about Lawrence's
death to help free himself from his own similar tendencies toward
withdrawal. To the end, Williams continued to interact with the
various literary figures of his day and to try to reach a mass audience, believing, as Whitman did, that language at its best is a carrier
of love.

Although the public press has stood in the way of our understanding Williams, ironically it has also provided excellent masks
for him to wear. The post–World War II writers who were his followers learned this lesson of disguise through use of masks. Truman
Capote is an excellent example; Carson McCullers is another. Nei-

ther of them shared his Joycean view of the modern world; but if Williams is to be understood in his southern context, his relationship with Capote and McCullers must be taken into account. All three came from the upland part of the Deep South: Columbus, Georgia; Troy, Alabama; and Columbus, Mississippi. This area—along with urban centers like Macon, Augusta, Columbia, Montgomery, Jackson, and Vicksburg—believed in the destiny of the Cotton Kingdom more than the rest of the South, devoted itself more doggedly to its victory in 1861, and, in the period from 1865 to 1940, felt its failure more deeply. Since 1945 the life of the upland areas has vastly changed, becoming fully modernized by new agricultural techniques and more attuned than the rest of the South to the contemporary demands of industry. Even so, certain writers from these areas showed in their work the physical and psychic hunger that the South was experiencing in this difficult period.

Erskine Caldwell's *Tobacco Road,* published as a novel in 1932 and subsequently made into a Broadway play and a motion picture, set the tone for new works about suffering in the South. As Robert D. Jacobs has explained in his studies of Caldwell, *Tobacco Road* should be seen as part of a tradition of folk humor in the South going back to A. B. Longstreet. Though Jeeter Lester bears little resemblance to the poor whites of the South, in him Caldwell has created, Jacobs tells us, "a character myth for the twentieth century." [26] When the play began its record run on Broadway, it became apparent that Caldwell had also created in Jeeter and his relatives powerful symbols of psychic hunger. The way was prepared for McCullers, Capote, Williams, and many lesser figures, even for one of the greatest novels in southern fiction, Robert Penn Warren's *All the King's Men.* Warren's Willie Stark is the wounded South's perennially hungry man who devours the remnants of his dying culture until a bullet ends his career.

It remained for a genius like Williams, who knew the theme of hunger well and who also possessed a Joycean detachment and had immersed himself in both Christian and Greek myth, to lift it to such a pinnacle of modern drama that he had to be compared with the greatest modern European dramatists; in modern southern literature only William Faulkner is greater. Williams wrote so powerfully about desire and impotence that many critics think he only wrote about individual and cultural collapse. But it is now widely acknowledged that the playwright pointed the way toward a vision of creativity beyond desire. Williams's plays confirm the fact that he had something important to say about the revival of communal life. He himself had no doubt of the value of his own life-giving vision. As he made clear in comments about his life, Williams went through periods of madness that sprang from his own overpowering desires and the puritanism that brought them into being. But time and again he recovered by finding the two threads that make his work great: poetic language and a loving concern for others. He is at last being seen as a major figure in American arts, and his work is a monument to the continuing revival of American culture.

7

Ralph Ellison
Black Artist in Tuskegee and New York

A new southern generation and a new southern fiction appeared in 1940 with the publication of Carson McCullers's *The Heart Is a Lonely Hunter.* This novel achieved a certain popular success and McCullers, expanding her efforts with *Reflections in a Golden Eye* and *Member of the Wedding,* began to look like the leader of the new southern literature. But in 1951 William Styron published *Lie Down in Darkness,* and some critics thought that he would be a new Faulkner. At the same time a new kind of novel began to capture the attention of serious readers. The most significant of these novels were Ralph Ellison's *Invisible Man* and Flannery O'Connor's *Wise Blood,* both of which appeared in 1952. Ellison's novel in time came to be recognized as the most important work of fiction by an American black in this century. Critics in a 1965 *Book Week* poll, for example, selected *Invisible Man* as the most distinguished work of fiction to appear after World War II.

Norman Mailer wrote in 1964 that after the war "the important art in America became the art of the absurd."[1] Ralph Ellison and Flannery O'Connor seemed in their first important works to have mastered that art, and great things were expected of them. But Ellison never produced another completed novel and O'Connor did most of her best work in the short story; there was to be no new Faulkner. However, they both mastered techniques taught by

Hemingway, Joyce, and the French dramatists of the absurd, and they faced squarely what their region and their respective communities had to teach them about a dying culture. Their deep personal awareness of the struggles of two southern communities—the blacks and the poor whites—led them to throw off the style of psychological realism that dominated southern fiction after 1940. McCullers and Styron had effectively used this style, as had an even greater novelist, Robert Penn Warren, whose *Night Rider* in 1939 and *All the King's Men* in 1946 became important landmarks in postwar southern fiction. But psychological realism, with its emphasis on the agnostic existentialist trapped in a society obsessed by history, was a style that was clearly entering a period of decline after World War II. Second-rate writers continued to employ the style, but Mailer was proven correct: writers like Ellison and O'Connor captured the attention of serious readers by using absurdist techniques that mirrored their awareness of the collapse of cultural values.

In psychological realism time is still an orderly, if oppressive, process. In the fiction and drama of the absurd, time is frequently collapsed; consequently, anything becomes possible and nothing is predictable. In the literature of psychological realism, cultural decay is omnipresent and a few people desperately try to hold onto old values. For writers from James and Conrad to Warren and Styron the vision of culture reflected by the style of psychological realism has been so widespread that new styles like absurdism were at first misunderstood. But with the help of sensitive critics like Mailer, Martin Esslin, and Ihab Hassan, we have gradually begun to understand the style of absurdism in drama. For the absurdist, culture is declining because many values of European civilization have all but vanished. The result of this loss of values is that the absurdist protagonist lives in a chaotic world into which he must fling himself in order to find a life-sustaining vision. Above all, he must learn to cope with the major fact of the world in the postwar period: the rapid and chaotic growth of urbanization.

Ellison and O'Connor, as I have suggested, were emotionally involved in the struggles of oppressed peoples—Ellison with the black minority in America and O'Connor with the children of the ruined yeoman class of southerners cast off the land by widespread urbanization. Ellison and O'Connor reveal a full awareness of the sufferings of blacks and poor whites, but their chief topic is neither this suffering nor the communities of these two groups (which are in fact subcultures within the South, erected as defenses against groups with greater political and economic strength). Their real subject is the effect of the great city on members of these groups who have become separated from their traditional communities. O'Connor depicts protagonists such as Hazel Motes in *Wise Blood* struggling against postwar urbanization by recalling memories of the prophetic, evangelical Protestantism that once sustained the yeomanry of the South. Ellison's *Invisible Man* shows the black artist's quest for new cultural values in the modern city.

Ellison believes that the black artist in America, engaged in a serious quest for his identity, is treated as if he were invisible. Both whites and blacks often deny the visibility of the serious black artist because, according to Ellison, they are afraid that if they disagree they too might be considered invisible by others. The individual who is treated in this way must eventually view most of what happens to him as essentially absurd. In explaining absurdist art and the role of blacks in American life, Esther Merle Jackson says that the black man has become in this century a symbol of "the total condition of man in the twentieth century"[2] and that this condition can "be traced to the tension arising from the collision between the ethic of power and the idea of moral law."[3] As the ethic of power increases, she says, moral law declines, and the individual often finds himself in the absurd position of attempting to exist as a member of a culture that honors morality but that expects him to act as if he is no more than a cog in a machine, to be manipulated according to someone's whim. For blacks, of course, the failure of moral law was more devastating than it was for whites, and this failure was protested by Richard Wright in *Native Son*. But although Ellison was in full sympathy with Wright's work and in fact was aided by Wright in his early artistic efforts, he could not use Wright's naturalistic style. Because he felt so deeply the absurdity of the black's position in America, he had to seek, as Thomas D. Jarrett tells us, an artistic approach "which would attempt to capture the truth about the human condition."[4] To accomplish this task he felt the need to move beyond naturalism and attempt some of the artistic feats of the absurdist writers of France in the period after World War II.

Ellison's best-known work of short fiction employing techniques of absurdist writing is the story "Battle Royal," which is also chapter 1 of *Invisible Man*. A truly absurdist work of literature deals with a situation in which individuals come to see that their behavior is essentially meaningless and, therefore, destructive to life. In "Battle

Royal" black boys are expected to act according to the community's cultural values, which grow out of religious and legal traditions that call for a shared communal life in which everyone's individuality is respected. However, these same boys are also expected to engage in a mock fight as part of a show put on for a group of the city's white leaders. The boys want to please the elders of the city, believing that they can eventually have a meaningful place in the city's social structure. But as they participate in the show, they begin to feel that they are being treated like trained animals, as if they have no dignity or wills of their own. On one hand they are asked to be "good" boys according to the city's cultural values and on the other they are required to act for the amusement of others. In the process of degrading themselves they come to sense, by the end of the story, their own invisibility. They begin to see that they will be accepted in society only as ciphers in a power relationship that negates the values they have been taught in the cultural institutions of the family, the school, and the church. This story thus serves as a kind of prelude to *Invisible Man*, adumbrating as it does the many double binds in which young blacks find themselves as they grow up. Ellison is saying that it is absurd to pretend that there are living cultural values when individuals are continually asked to act as if none of these values exist.

Although in "Battle Royal" Ellison suggests that after World War I communal relationships in cities were being supplanted by relationships based primarily on power, his native Oklahoma City, where he grew to maturity between 1914 and 1933, was not by any means bereft of cultural values. The state of Oklahoma was during Ellison's time—and still is in many ways—too diverse to classify, being western and southern and even a little northern. The society that the young Ellison knew was segregated and the social structure was southern, but blacks were not crushed by an insensitive power structure. Ellison has said in an interview that Oklahoma "had no tradition of slavery, and while it was segregated, relationships between the races were more fluid and thus more human than in the old slave states."[5] His parents, he says, had come to Oklahoma "like most of the other Negroes, . . . looking for a broader freedom, and had never stopped pushing against the barriers."[6] Throughout his work Ellison reflects a healthiness and strength that seemed to belong to the black community of Oklahoma City, as well as a feeling of hopefulness that barriers eventually would come down and that any individual might become the modern Renaissance man, as Ellison himself hoped to be. He did in fact realize some of his dreams, learning to express himself effectively in at least two art forms, literature and music, and enjoying a rich intellectual life as a teacher and thinker.

In some ways Ellison is similar to Wolfe in his progress and background, but he is less caught up in the agony of the past. His work is not as poetic as Wolfe's, but one finds in his essays and his novel passages of visionary power. Like Wolfe he believed in the rebirth of America: "Out of this conflict a type truly great enough to possess the greatness of the land, a delicately poised unity of divergencies—is slowly being born."[7] Whereas Wolfe's vision of the rebirth of American culture concerns the future, Ellison sees the process of renewal occurring beneath the surfaces of society during our own century.

Ellison resembles Wolfe, more than any other important southern writer, in his early beginnings in a small city that was mainly southern (though much less so than Asheville), situated very near a geographical area most of whose people rejected southern culture (Appalachia on one hand and the American West on the other). Both were greatly influenced by their college environments. Both writers felt oppressed by many aspects of southern culture but were deeply drawn to other aspects, particularly those having to do with family and group rituals. Both were musical—Ellison being influenced by native black music and the rhetoric of the southern black preacher, Wolfe by the verbal music of southern oratory. Above all else, both authors went to New York in search of a culture more resilient than the one they had known in the South. Wolfe penetrated the inner artistic circles of the city but discovered that he would have to search further for a larger vision of America. Ellison found himself shut out from white culture in New York and unable to live comfortably with black culture in Harlem.

Ellison did benefit from the work of the Harlem Renaissance and that of the first important black novelist, Richard Wright. However, he denied that Wright was a major influence: "Wright was no spiritual father of mine, certainly in no sense I recognize—nor did he pretend to be, since he felt that I had started writing too late."[8] On another occasion Ellison said: "He [Wright] was generously helpful in sharing his ideas and information, but I needed instruction in other values and I found them in the works of other writers— Hemingway was one of them, T. S. Eliot initiated the search."[9] Ellison and Wright are most similar in their ability to use materials from their own lives and at the same time to go beyond fictional autobiography in order to achieve objectivity concerning the black experience in America.

For the black artist, more than for most artists in other ethnic groups, it has been necessary to find in art a means of rising above personal suffering to obtain a larger vision of humanity. If Wright, like Zola, sees his art as a passionate cry for justice, as well as a way of overcoming suffering, then Ellison sees his own work primarily as a quest for creativity, aided by Eliot and Joyce. Ellison is most like Wolfe—and most unlike Wright—in his major theme, based on his own life's quest: the artist's search for self-expression. Unlike Wolfe, Ellison turned to other writers—Hemingway, Eliot, and Joyce—for technical knowlege about how he could use his experience as a black for artistic purposes without being overcome by the powerful emotions that grew out of this experience. Wolfe's emotionalism often offends readers, but Ellison's artistic control, learned so well from his mentors, enables him to examine with an artist's detachment the black experience in a world of collapsing cultural values.

Ellison's quest for artistic self-expression began in Oklahoma City. Although he was born in an urban environment, he was aware of the rural past of his own family and black people generally. He says in "That Same Pain, That Same Pleasure: An Interview" that though his mother came from a Georgia farm she was "of the city." During the cotton-picking season he would encounter other black youths from his school who worked on farms; from them he discovered some of his material:

> Just the same, those trips to the cotton patch seemed to me an enviable experience because the kids came back with such wonderful stories. And it wasn't hard work which they stressed, but the communion, the playing, the eating, the dancing and the singing. And they brought back jokes, our Negro jokes—not those told about Negroes by whites—and they always returned with Negro folk stories which I'd never heard before and which couldn't be found in any books I knew about. This was something to affirm and I felt there was a richness in it. I didn't think much about it, but what my schoolmates shared in the country and what I felt in their accounts of it—it seemed much more real to me than the Negro middle-class values which were taught in school.[10]

This participation in the black American folk background is paralleled by James Weldon Johnson's experience in 1918 of hearing an old-fashioned black American sermon and feeling something "primordial" stirring in him.

Ellison went from Oklahoma City to Tuskegee Institute, an Alabama educational center for blacks made internationally famous by Booker T. Washington. Washington, who had support from wealthy magnates like John D. Rockefeller and Andrew Carnegie, was thought to be moving toward a solution to the race problem in America. But the protagonist in *Invisible Man*, whose progress represents Ellison's own struggle to get an education, is not nearly as interested in social problems as he is in the problem of the serious modern literary artist. One of the most moving passages in the book is a description of a class at a college like Tuskegee in which Woodridge, the professor who most inspires the protagonist, is lecturing about Joyce:

> I could see him vividly, half-drunk on words and full of contempt and exaltation, pacing before the blackboard chalked with quotations from Joyce and Yeats and Sean O'Casey, thin, nervous, neat, pacing as though he walked a high wire of meaning upon which no one of us would dare venture. I could hear him: "Stephen's problem, like ours, was not actually one of creating the uncreated conscience of his race, but of creating the uncreated features of his face. Our task is that of making ourselves individuals. The conscience of a race is the fight of its individuals who see, evaluate, record. . . . We create the race by creating ourselves and then to our great astonishment we will have created a culture. Why waste time creating a conscience for something that doesn't exist? For, you see, blood and skin do not think!" [11]

The importance of the above passage as an account of Ellison's development cannot be overstated. In it we see the black leader calling on other blacks to use intellect and art to create an individual who can bring forth a revived culture. The appeal is presented with great intensity because the black artist knows that he has had to struggle harder to be both an individual and an artist than anyone else in America. But, as Ellison suggests throughout *Invisible Man*, it is this very struggle that gives the black artist his profound understanding of the need for a new culture in America that will benefit all ethnic groups.

Before examining the artist's struggle and his vision of the possibility of new values as seen in *Invisible Man,* the artistic qualities of the book as well as some of the many literary influences on it should be examined. In one sense *Invisible Man* is Wolfe's *Look Homeward, Angel* and *Of Time and the River* rolled into one, but because the work is not essentially autobiography—though some of it closely parallels Ellison's life—it is unlike anything Wolfe ever wrote. Artistically, Ellison disapproved of the sort of fiction Wolfe wrote, and once said in an interview: "Real characters are just a limitation. It's like the turning of your own life into fiction: you have to be hindered by chronology and fact." [12] He maintained that the two most important characters in the book, Ras and Rinehart, "just jumped out," as did several other characters in the book. Ras, whom he described as "the personification of chaos," [13] is a key character in the part of the book that Ellison wrote in an absurdist, or expressionistic, style. He described the parts of the book set in the South as "naturalistic," though I think the word *realistic* would be more accurate because *naturalism* suggests a philosophy and a viewpoint not found in the novel. Though stylistically influenced by Hemingway, Ellison was never a purist; he used a mixture of styles in his fiction. In his realism he drew on southern folk language and on his own observation. He borrowed his absurdism in part from the French but was driven by his own dreamlike imagination. It is the method of the drama of the absurd—one form of expressionism—that dominates the book; with this method Ellison hoped to go beyond an autobiographical statement to explore the inner meaning of the black artist's experiences in the modern city.

An important part of the book's style, as Hassan noted some years ago in his seminal study *Radical Innocence,* is the use of humor and music: Ellison, Hassan says, draws upon "the healing powers of the American joke and Negro blues." [14] He goes on to say that "the joke and the blues . . . find their common ground in the attempt to reconcile opposites." [15] And the book is essentially about reconciling opposites. Through the agony and the surrealistic madness taking place against the background of the South and the North, the book records an epic, or mythic, progress that ends with several monsters slain and several chimeras passed successfully, and with acceptance of what the modern knight of faith must go through to remain alive and to grow in spirit. Ellison's use of music as a symbol of reconciliation is basic to his mythic vision in *Invisible Man*. As a musician himself, Ellison sees the continuation of black music as a sign of the possibility of the cultural rebirth of both the black community and of America itself.

Excessive interest in *Invisible Man* as the work of a black writer has obscured its acknowledged chief literary source, Eliot's *The Waste Land*, a work Ellison first read in 1935. After reading it, Ellison asked himself why a black man had not written a work like it. *Invisible Man* is no doubt Ellison's answer to his own question; but instead of calling on the myths of the distant past as Eliot did, Ellison calls on the folklore of his own people and of America generally. In his task he had help from Stanley Edgar Hyman and Kenneth Burke; because these two thinkers have put great emphasis on the relationship between myth and ritual, Ellison continually raises the question of whether true ritual is alive in the modern world and how true myth can function again in the lives of modern people.

The international influences on Ellison's novel, however, should not blind the reader to the hero's involvement with the continuing intellectual struggle among blacks between the forces represented by Booker T. Washington on the one hand and W. E. B. Du Bois on the other. The college in the book is modeled on Tuskegee, and its founder is like Washington. The protagonist continually responds to the founder's portrait in various ways, finally with disillusionment. Washington felt it necessary for blacks to accommodate the white power structure and to accept an inferior social position in the hope of achieving something better in the future. At first, W. E. B. Du Bois went along with this "gospel of work and money," but eventually came to consider it too costly. He began to oppose Washington's views, calling for blacks to take a more radical stand for full equality. The figure in *Invisible Man* who represents the radical black view is the protagonist's grandfather, who dies believing that he should never have put down his weapons after the Civil War and should have demanded at that time full equality in American life for blacks. He tells the hero a riddle, or problem, that is not solved until the end of the book. His grandfather's sphinxlike question must be answered before the protagonist can be at peace as a black man and an American. The resolution of the problem lies in part in the protagonist's identification with Frederick Douglass at the book's end, not because this black leader is famous but because he maintained a personal integrity in all his actions.

Invisible Man also must be seen as a part of modern southern literature that—like the works of Faulkner and Wolfe—deals with the problems of hierarchy and community, the two dominant aspects of southern culture. Although black people were placed in a caste and separated from the white gentry on the one hand and the white working class on the other, the problems of hierarchy and community are just as important to blacks as they are to whites in the South. Southern black society itself has always had a gentry and a working class, the one descended from house servants and artisans (who were often related by blood to their owners) and the other descended largely from field hands. Ellison in his novel and essays makes us aware of the hierarchal nature of black society in both the North and the South. Because of its strong attachment in the past to religious leaders, black society often seems even more hierarchal than white society. More than any other black writer, Ellison has helped us to understand the black view of northern and southern cultures, which have shaped black life and have excluded blacks from full participation in both regional and national society. *Invisible Man* begins with the most important facts of black society, exclusion and oppression. Like Faulkner and Wolfe, Ellison shows the complete social repression of blacks in the South before 1970, and expresses his belief that cultural revival in America must be accompanied by a full emancipation of blacks.

The hero of *Invisible Man,* who is nameless, is first shown as a promising boy orator in a southern community. He is praised by the members of the white power structure, but he is also forced to take part in a show, staged for the entertainment of whites, in which he and other half-naked, blindfolded blacks pretend to fight each other; in another part of the show, they are required to pick up coins from an electrified blanket. When the protagonist speaks of social equality, he is forced to recant. Unable to develop his talents in his community, he sets his sights on going to New York and becoming an artist, but first attends college to prepare himself for this task. At the small-town college he chooses, he is fortunate, like Wolfe, in finding a sensitive professor, Woodridge, who gives him Joyce as a model to follow in his life's quest.

At college the protagonist sees instinctively that art alone is not enough to provide a way of life. What he needs, in order to appreciate the arts and to practice them, is a true culture and leaders who work within the cultural framework. He encounters some of the rituals of southern blacks, particularly in the realm of music and oratory, that have sustained the black community during antebellum and postbellum repression. At the same time that he participates in the creative rituals of black culture and is introduced to the heritage of Western literature by Professor Woodridge, he is also drawn to the communal life of the rural black people who live outside the little town where the college is situated. He finds that he is diverted from his relationship with these people by the attention that he is forced to pay to the college's president, Dr. Bledsoe. This awesome hierarch is intent on entering the newly developing black middle class and is gradually losing contact with the rich communal life of the rural blacks. Eventually the protagonist rejects Dr. Bledsoe because he finally sees him in his true light, as a self-serving hypocrite who deceives blacks and whites alike in order to use power for his own gain. The meaning of the rites of Horatio Alger, enacted by Dr. Bledsoe at chapel exercises, becomes clear: "Here upon this stage the black rite of Horatio Alger was performed to God's own acting script, with millionaires come down to portray themselves; not merely acting out the myth of their goodness and wealth and success and power and benevolence and authority in cardboard masks, but themselves, these virtues concretely!"[16]

Even though the protagonist is repelled by the Horatio Alger ritual, which consists of parading northern millionaires before the students, he nevertheless decides that he must go to New York to join the ranks of those who represent a true hierarchy in American life. Dr. Bledsoe gives him a letter of introduction to one of these northern leaders, a Mr. Emerson, who represents Ralph Waldo Emerson (for whom Ellison was named). He has already met one of the college's benefactors, a Mr. Norton, who represents the great Harvard humanist Charles Eliot Norton. Norton and Emerson stand for the failure of northern culture and northern idealism to provide for blacks their rightful place in American life. In New York the protagonist is unable even to meet Emerson but finally encounters Emerson's son and tells him that he would simply like to talk with the great man; the son informs him that Emerson does not talk *with* people but *to* people. Thus the hero finds himself once again in a world where there can be no community between the rulers and the ruled—or even between father and son, when the father is one of society's hierarchs.

By now the Joycean theme of the search for a father has emerged. This problem is resolved when the hero finally understands what a mad doctor has told him early in the book: "Be your own father, young man. And remember, the world is possibility if only you'll

discover it." [17] The development of the hero's individual psyche is
the only solution to the problem of the development of creativity,
the protagonist discovers. He also learns that he must accept life in
a cultureless world of underground invisibility. Such a life brings
with it, however, a sense of true individuality; and the protagonist
also finds satisfaction in being recognized by others who have not
lost their individuality. One of these people is his Harlem landlady,
Mary, whom he rejects at first, but to whom he keeps returning.

Before the protagonist can find his individuality, he must struggle
with certain modern urban organizations. He works for a time in a
New York factory and then drifts into a left-wing political party, the
Brotherhood, which Ellison tells us is not meant to be the Commu-
nist party, but stands for any ideological organization in which the
individual is subordinated to collectivism. In this group the protagonist can use his oratorical talents, but he discovers that its hierarchs want little or no real human intercourse with him; the women
in the group seek him out only as a sex object or as an object of pity
because he is black. His leader, Brother Jack, tells him that he was
not paid to think and that the way followers must be handled is not
to ask them what they think but to tell them what to think. This
rejection finally causes the protagonist to repudiate the Brotherhood and all other urban organizations.

The absurdist techniques the author uses are well suited to the
section of the book dealing with New York because Ellison is doing
what all good absurdist dramatists have done since Charlie Chap-
lin's early motion pictures: he shows the forgotten little man of society trying to find a place for his individuality amidst the overpowering social and industrial machinery of the modern world.
Not until he leaves the Brotherhood does Ellison's hero realize that
he must accept his life of invisibility. In New York the protagonist
does not have a community of black people, fellow sufferers, to fall
back on. Still he knows that he cannot go back, that he can learn
only by going forward. In accepting his invisibility he learns that as
a black man he has certain inherited advantages that others do not
have: a history of being able to survive while his individuality is constantly denied. He at last sees that only by accepting a life of invisibility can he begin to affirm and discover his own individuality.
And he learns that, in Hassan's words, "ideologies, whether radical,
literal or reactionary, betray the human quest for self-definition." [18]
For Ellison this is what causes invisibility: the refusal of social organizations to tolerate the individual. The human being is seen by

them as a function, a cog in a machine, or an animal. Most people, Ellison's hero learns, are invisible but do not yet know it.

By accepting fully the underground life of invisibility, the hero can also begin to understand the wisdom of his grandfather. "Agree 'em to death and destruction," his grandfather had said. Those who deny individuality are "their own death and destruction except as the principle lived in them and in us." [19] The principle he refers to, which was denied in the mock battle between young blacks back in the hero's hometown, is that there is a basic humanity in all people. New England prophets like Emerson and Charles Eliot Norton had proclaimed this principle. The proclamation had gone out with the stamp of governmental authority to the newly freed blacks after the Civil War, but it was being denied in the twentieth century. Those denying it were too powerful for anyone to overcome directly, and only those who continued inwardly to affirm their own individuality and the common humanity of others would survive.

I have said that *Invisible Man* is a mythic work. What the grandfather recommends and what the hero does is to dive into the "belly of the whale," as mythologist Joseph Campbell calls it when the questing hero descends for a time into darkness to learn certain lessons before emerging to continue his journey to full humanity. [20] The hero is removed for a time from the ordinary world of so-called reality: "Step outside the narrow borders of what men call reality and you step into chaos . . . or imagination. That too I've learned in the cellar, and not by deadening my sense of perception; I'm invisible, not blind." [21] By accepting his invisibility the protagonist begins to discover the vision needed to become aware of the element in himself and others that makes full humanity possible. In Campbell's terms, he discovers the boon of life that exists at the core of all creatures.

Having thus become sensitive to both his inner humanity and his imagination, the protagonist can take up the task of nineteenth-century prophets like Emerson and Whitman who announce the coming of the true America. "Our fate," the protagonist sees, "is to become one, and yet many—This is not prophecy but description." [22] The failure of race relations in America then can be seen both as a joke and a challenge: "Thus one of the greatest jokes in the world is the spectacle of the whites busy escaping blackness and becoming blacks every day, and the blacks striving toward whiteness, becoming quite dull and gray. None of us seems to know who he is or where he is going."[23] The great question, the protagonist learns, is about identity—about the loss of humanity when all people, blacks and whites, try to escape themselves and thereby become invisible to each other.

The protagonist ultimately understands that his grandfather has preserved more of his own humanity than most people, black or white, despite a system that (according to Ellison in one of his interviews) was worse *after* the Civil War than before. He knows that his grandfather has initiated him into the quest for creativity and individuality and that he at last, with his grandfather in mind, is discovering the true father in himself. Thus he finds that the recovery of one's full humanity means a reconciliation of seemingly opposing internal powers: "I condemn and affirm, say no and say yes, say yes and say no." He condemns his persecutors because "though implicated and partially responsible, I have been hurt to the point of abysmal pain, hurt to the point of invisibility."[24] But he can still love. In fact, his renewed vision of his own and others' humanity has increased the flow of love in him. He has been victimized and forced to be a cog in educational, industrial, and political machines, has struggled with destructive black nationalists, and has witnessed a friend sell out his humanity and die in the streets. All these experiences have made him see that the quest for full humanity is the one thing of value in his life because it perpetuates the ability to be concerned with others. All that has happened to him has only clarified his ability to see and love: "And I defend because in spite of all I find that I love. . . . Perhaps that makes me a little bit as human as my grandfather."[25]

Invisible Man ends in much the same way as *The Waste Land,* with the journey not completed but with the quester moving in the direction of a new life. Eliot's quester clings to the artistic forms left to him in the wreckage of the world's cultures. Ellison's hero takes with him the music of Louis Armstrong and the life history of Frederick Douglass, among other things. He knows that soon he will be emerging from underground to seek to live out the harmonies of Armstrong and the values of Douglass, the black leader who rose above the conflict represented by Washington and Du Bois. Values, Ellison says, are discovered underground and the imagination is thus activated, but one must keep moving to discover new life: "The hibernation is over. I must shake off the old skin and come up for breath."[26]

In announcing his rebirth, the protagonist can also proclaim his return to communal life. As an artist he has had to separate himself from others in order to face fully the suffering caused by his invisibility. Only after separation can he begin to make use of the values of his past and relate them to his own artistic stirrings. What Ellison has accomplished in his absurdist presentation of his hero's life in New York is what Martin Esslin tells us the drama of the absurd has regularly sought to do: "The challenge to make sense out of what appears as a senseless and fragmented action, the recognition that the modern world has lost its unifying principle is the source of its bewildering and soul-destroying quality; it is therefore more than a mere intellectual exercise, it has a therapeutic effect."[27] Ellison, like other practitioners of absurdist techniques, hopes to free blacks and others from their sense of isolation in what sometimes seems a meaningless world and to set them on the quest for a cultural unity that will in time result in both personal and social revival. What seems like despair in the work of Ellison and other absurdists is actually the acceptance of the chaos of modern urbanized life. As Esslin says, "a phenomenon like the Theatre of the Absurd does not reflect despair or a return to dark irrational forces but expresses modern man's endeavor to come to terms with the world in which he lives."[28]

In his career Ellison has continued to present a hopeful view of the possibilities of modern man's revival of culture. Of his many prophetic descriptions in *Invisible Man,* one of the most significant is the prediction of the return of thousands of northern blacks to the South after 1965—to "that 'heart of darkness' across the Mason-Dixon line," as Ellison calls the South before the Supreme Court decisions of the sixties. In the seventies we have seen such a movement, and the protagonist in *Invisible Man* speaks for some of these people: "Sometimes I feel the need to reaffirm all of it, the whole unhappy territory and all the things loved and unlovable in it, for all of it is part of me."[29]

In his essay "Harlem is Nowhere" Ellison reflects upon the history of the migration of American blacks to the North, where they were not accepted as cultural equals: "like the legend of some tragic people out of mythology, a people which aspired to escape from its own unhappy homeland to the apparent peace of a distant mountain; but which, in migrating, made some fatal error of judgment and fell into a great chasm of mazelike passages that promise ever to lead to the mountain but end ever against a wall."[30] This statement sums up one of the fundamental themes of *Invisible Man.* The black person is not worse off in the North than in the South "but . . . in the North he surrenders and does not replace certain important supports to his personality." Ellison thinks of the black person in terms of culture, of "the psychological functions" of institutions, which protect the citizen against "the irrational, incalculable forces that hover about the edges of human life like cosmic destruction lurking within an atomic stockpile."[31] Working against these destructive forces are the psychological forces within the soul—the individual and the collective soul—where culture begins and ends and where its failure is most evident.

Ellison speaks both as a black artist and as a man of culture who happens to be black. As a black artist he seeks ways of carrying on the spirit of black musicians like Louis Armstrong and black writers like Langston Hughes and James Weldon Johnson, who cultivated in their work the values of the black community and at the same time assimilated the sophisticated culture of the great cities of the world.

Since 1960 Ellison himself has emerged as a literary hierarch. In 1970 he accepted the Albert Schweitzer Professorship in the humanities at New York University, becoming like his namesake, Ralph Waldo Emerson, an American thinker and prophet honored in his own time. His writing is increasingly being seen in relationship to the best existential fiction of the last two hundred years—not so much that of the French writers as the German novelist Hermann Hesse and the Russian writers Fyodor Dostoevski and Alexander Solzhenitsyn. All three suffered at the hands of their countrymen but continued to love and praise the essential goodness at the heart of their nation's cultures. Like them, Ellison paid a high price in suffering and emerged with poetic and prophetic statements about America and the South. He speaks as strongly as Wolfe for the revival of American culture, though not from a sense of his own death as Wolfe does in *You Can't Go Home Again.* He continues the tradition of Emerson and Whitman, seeing the whole of America, and has taken up Faulkner's role of interpreting the burden of the South's agony. At the same time he has accomplished something he felt from the start was needed in American literature—a black man's version of Eliot's *The Waste Land.* More than any other southern writer, Ellison chose Eliot and Joyce to emulate, and his emulation has proved exceedingly fruitful. He may eventually be seen as a leader in the mold of Frederick Douglass, one of his guides into the life of the new America.

8

Flannery O'Connor
Prophetic Pilgrimage to Atlanta

Since her first book's appearance in 1952 Flannery O'Connor has generally been thought of as an author who wrote chiefly about southern grotesques obsessed with Christ. In her stories and novels religious fanatics often seem to burn themselves out in explosions of violence and self-inflicted pain. Indeed, most of her characters—the wild grotesques as well as the placid Babbitts—are caught up in a violent reaction to the general decline of cultural values. O'Connor chose for her typical protagonist the figure of the backwoods prophet. With this figure she challenges cultural decline by addressing the new secular cities—symbolized for her by Atlanta—with a vision of renewed religious life, which O'Connor believed was the only way cultural values would be renewed. As a serious Catholic she had formed her ideas concerning the death and rebirth of culture after an extensive reading of modern Catholic theologians like Guardini, Adam, and Maritain, as well as philosophers like Eric Voegelin and religious existentialists such as Martin Buber. But it was her imaginative power that enabled her to create those memorable fanatics like Hazel Motes who stalk the city searching for new religious and social values that will turn it into a true community again. These characters bring the message that it is not by remembering the past but by seeking new visions that cultural life will be revived.

In 1980 Lewis P. Simpson wrote that Flannery O'Connor had "refocused the southern fictional imperative" by "rejecting the mode of remembering" and by embracing "the mode of revelation."[1] Southern storytelling in the past has been based principally on the uses of memory, but O'Connor's work suggests that with the decline of cultural values memory becomes radically dissipated. Thus, she claims, a new basis for serious fiction must be sought. Simpson writes: "The debasement of memory in Miss O'Connor is directed toward preparing the way to assume the vocation to prophecy."[2] O'Connor was not herself a prophet; in fact, her fiction seldom reflects many details of her personal life, with the exception of descriptions of her mother's large dairy farm near Milledgeville, Georgia, where she lived after 1950 and where she did most of her writing.

Her death at thirty-nine ended a career that seemed to be only beginning; yet she made a major fictional statement in what amounts to a small collection of stories. Even her two novels, *Wise Blood* and *The Violent Bear It Away,* are more like long stories than novels in the usual sense. In many ways she was simply a hardworking professional writer whose chief concern was getting on with what she considered to be her one vocation—story writing. However, her recently published letters indicate that her quest for a new beginning of culture based on new visions of God was central in her thought.

O'Connor's letters, which tell us much about the activities of her daily life, stand in much the same relationship to her fiction as Ralph Ellison's essays and interviews do to his fiction. Both writers were intensely concerned with problems of new stylistic techniques for postwar fiction, and both were searching for new cultural beginnings in their fiction and nonfiction. Both are often seen as spokespersons not of their race or sex, or of southern life, but, rather, of their times. Some will argue that, judged strictly from a literary standpoint, neither Ellison nor O'Connor has written enough to receive major consideration; but people seek a voice that will continue to haunt them, and Ellison and O'Connor both have voices that cannot be ignored by anyone who takes literature or culture seriously.

Southern literature after 1945 seemed to move in the direction of psychological realism, not religious existentialism. When her first novel, *Wise Blood,* appeared in 1952, O'Connor received recognition; in 1955 with the appearance of her short story collection, *A*

Good Man Is Hard To Find, it was clear to critical observers that an important "talent" was on the scene. However, she was generally perceived as only a minor presence. Robert Penn Warren with *All the King's Men* in 1946 seemed to be showing the direction serious southern, if not American, fiction would be taking; but he peaked with that novel. William Styron, born the same year as O'Connor, promised much with his brilliant first novel, *Lie Down in Darkness,* but *Set This House on Fire* and *The Confessions of Nat Turner,* which followed, did not offer any new directions to the rising generation of southern novelists. In the work of Warren and Styron are powerful visions of southern culture in its death throes, and both are concerned with religious problems; but, with the exception of *Lie Down in Darkness,* there is no sign of the possibility of religious or cultural rebirth in their chief works.

O'Connor's central vision, on the other hand, is one of renewal, but, like Joyce and Eliot, she conceals it behind her portrayals of the terrible agony of people divested of all cultural values. Like Carson McCullers she *seems* to write about the end of humanity. But her rural Georgia grotesques do not reflect the stark horror we find in McCullers's fiction; in fact, O'Connor's grotesques sometimes revel in a kind of humor all their own, reminiscent of some of Erskine Caldwell's better characters. Unlike Caldwell's characters in *Tobacco Road* and *God's Little Acre,* O'Connor's characters do not suffer physical deprivation but instead sometimes exhibit a terrifying psychic deprivation that drives them into cold violence and perverse expressions of backwoods, hellfire religion. O'Connor captures the spiritual groping of the displaced white working class better than any other writer of the South.

McCullers in her first book, *The Heart Is a Lonely Hunter,* sought to picture southern society as a whole: the white gentry, the white yeomanry (or working class), the black community. However, she found she could do her best work writing about the lonely seeker in more concentrated fiction like *Reflections in a Golden Eye* and *Member of the Wedding.* O'Connor, on the other hand, gives us throughout her work a view of the whole society, though seen in miniature: the South that she saw in the forties and fifties. Her wasteland vision, which encompasses all three communities of southern culture, reveals a society in its death throes.

For O'Connor the central crisis of modern culture was the rapid decline of religious and family values. For her the modern city was a place where most people found it impossible to live by religious values; for many of these people science was the key to a good life. But O'Connor believed that science could not provide the authentic means of communication that she found missing in modern cultural institutions. And, although the southern city lacked religious values, the southern countryside offered no answer either, because it had fallen prey to a dangerous fanaticism, which grew out of a quest for identity through religion. Cultist perversions of Christianity, accompanied by the sharp, deceptive ways of the city, could be found among rural people everywhere, as, for example, in "Good Country People" and "The Life You Save May Be Your Own." No story in O'Connor's canon is so terrible as "The River," in which she writes about two of her favorite subjects: the breakup of the family and the destructiveness of fanatical religion. A neglected child from a wrecked family reaches out for the love denied him by seeking a literal baptism at the hands of a fanatical young preacher; at the end of the story he drowns. O'Connor demonstrates that a fanatical attachment to the letter of religion, separated from the vision of spirit that is basic to all sacrament, can lead to death. Yet she has a certain sympathy for her fanatical characters because she sees that religion is their way of maintaining their identity.

O'Connor's brilliant handling of religious fanaticism as a major aspect of cultural collapse has led many of her co-religionists, as well as many others, to question the real meaning of religious belief. As her letters reveal, her ideas and beliefs were based on orthodox Catholic tradition. Yet her orthodox practices, which included reading Aquinas every night, did not stand in the way of her acceptance of a variety of religious insights from various traditions. The complexity of her writing often amazes those critics who have either a simplistic view of religion or none at all. An *Atlantic* review of her letters sums up much commentary about her: she was "puzzling to the critics."[3] This is probably a result of the fact that the religious views underlying her work seem quite foreign to most critics.

O'Connor was not herself ever rigid or fanatical. In fact she was always ready to receive help or advice from those she considered her literary peers; yet she also kept her own literary counsel. She merited the high praise of John Crowe Ransom, Allen Tate, and Caroline Gordon, but she was not a part of their Agrarian tradition and in some ways might even be called a rebel against it. One mark of her early genius was her ability to draw inspiration from certain writers without being overwhelmed by their brilliance. Two of these

authors were Nathanael West and William Faulkner. Robert Fitzgerald's introduction to her second short story collection includes
an anecdote about O'Connor, in her mid-twenties, urging Fitzgerald to read West's *Miss Lonelyhearts* and Faulkner's *As I Lay Dying.*[4]
Both books had seized her imagination—West's book inspiring her
with its mordant wit and its vision of cultural decay in the cities,
Faulkner's novel speaking to her of the agony of a family going to
pieces in the rural South, a theme that became central to her own
work.

The complexity of O'Connor's religious insights owes much to
her interest in two of the most profound and disturbing religious
writers of the twentieth century, T. S. Eliot and James Joyce. Of the
two Joyce meant more to her, as she suggests in those letters in
which she refers to the influence on her work of *Dubliners* in general and "The Dead" in particular. Her most telling statement
about Joyce is in her letters; after speaking of the influence of
Catholic writers like Bloy, Bernanos, Mauriac, and Greene on her
work, she says that "at some point reading them reaches the place
of diminishing returns and you get more benefit reading someone
like Hemingway, where there is apparently a hunger for a Catholic
completeness in life, or Joyce who can't get rid of it no matter what
he does." And her next statement sums up her view of Joyce as well
as her own literary method at its best—the method, that is, of the
Joycean epiphany: "It may be a matter of recognizing the Holy
Ghost in fiction by the way he chooses to conceal himself."[5] From
Joyce, more than any other writer, O'Connor learned to create
characters who were Christians in spite of themselves (Hazel Motes
in *Wise Blood*), individuals who "can't get rid of it" no matter what
they do, and who, because of the very persistence of Christ's presence in their psyches, inevitably encounter the hidden Holy Ghost
in moments of epiphany.

For O'Connor's fanatical protagonist the encounter with the city
brings forth the repressed Christ in the unconscious mind, planted
there by early religious training. O'Connor's first work, *Wise Blood*,
a novel she rewrote and revised many times, deals with a protagonist who feels called to a great secular city of the south. The city in
the book is called Taulkinham, but clearly she had in mind Atlanta,
for her the prototype of the chaotic modern city. Born and reared
in a little Tennessee town mired in cultural and religious decay,
Haze has been in the army and has fully accepted secular modernism. He believes that if one has a good car, he does not need reli-

gion. Yet Haze, unlike most of the other people around him, cannot accept the modern urban search for power and pleasure, its separation from what O'Connor considered the basis of all true culture: the cultivation of the soul through encounter with the sacraments. Haze instinctively—through what O'Connor calls "wise blood"—feels the need for some kind of religious foundation; he sees at last that his car cannot fulfill the function of a sacrament.

O'Connor makes it clear that Haze has come from a rural family whose Protestantism had turned to fanaticism. As a result of his family's ferocity, Haze hates the very name of Jesus, and he feels called to preach a new religion without Jesus. O'Connor once said that for her, Haze represented Protestantism carried to absurdity; one of her most memorable remarks was that the South, though not Christ-centered, was Christ-haunted. A haunted individual can be dangerous, and Haze's psyche includes the characteristics of a psychotic killer. A similar protagonist in this respect is the Misfit in "A Good Man Is Hard To Find." Referring to Yeats's poem "The Second Coming," O'Connor wrote: "I believe that there are many rough beasts slouching toward Bethlehem to be born and that I have reported the progress of a few of them."[6] The rough beast in Haze, once it has confronted the great city, must manifest itself in violence.

After his service in the army, Haze goes to megalopolitan Atlanta feeling unable to return to his hometown. The great city seems to him the only place he can go: "Where you came from is gone, where you thought you were going never was there, and where you are is no good unless you can get away from it."[7] His automobile is an instrument for coping with the unstable life of the city, where he discovers that preaching is his real occupation. However, he cannot abide the false prophets he finds preaching everywhere in the city. The beast in him surfaces and, in a rage, he kills one of these preachers. This murder, along with the loss of his car, marks the turning point in the book and in Haze's life. The hidden Christ in Haze struggles against his conscious rage. This rage is experienced by many young people in O'Connor's fiction, people who are deprived of cultural values and unable to live a meaningful or satisfying life in a world dominated by megalopolises. Haze reacts to his rage with a series of penitential acts, but, reverting to the fanatic Protestant teachings of his childhood, he turns his violence on himself, puts out his eyes with quicklime, and eventually dies an early death.

Seen from one angle, Haze's is the senseless death of one caught up in the letter of the law with no knowledge of its spirit. Haze is imitating what he believes to be a Christian penitence, unaware that the sacrament of penance is not based on imitation but on an encounter with grace given to one who seeks it in humility.

In the life of Hazel Motes, O'Connor explains how fanaticism is the result of a religion cut off from a sustained rational Christian teaching, to which she believed the pilgrim must devote himself daily (as she did). She also created in Haze an individual gradually working his way back to God, helped by a young friend called Enoch Emery, who proclaims that he has "wise blood." O'Conner thought of Enoch as an archetypal figure in her own life; he was for her the young innocent who helps to guide the wounded soul back to God. Haze's tragedy is that he can never fully free himself from fanaticism based on literalism and imitation rather than on a daily encounter with grace. The key to understanding Haze's career is to see it in connection with the city he confronts, first as a man leading a modern life of pleasure-seeking and then as a prophet who challenges urban disorder with a religious vision of unity. The chief reason he preaches the church without Jesus is that when he was a child the name of Jesus was always invoked in an unloving manner. The innocent "wise blood" in him demands that the city bring forth a love that is real, for without this love the city is no more than a wasteland.

In the second phase of Haze's career, the phase of repentance, O'Connor introduces another of her basic characters and, with that character, another attitude toward urban chaos and lovelessness. This character is Mrs. Flood, a middle-aged woman who owns the boardinghouse where Haze stays and who looks after him. Mrs. Flood, like other women in O'Connor's stories, maintains a superficial religion in her life that denies the living presence of Jesus and, in the midst of urban cultural collapse, seeks to build an orderly way of life based on a well-run farm that is thoroughly mechanized and urban. Mrs. Flood is drawn to Haze, but she is a thoroughgoing modernist and his efforts at penitence appall her. "It's not natural . . . it's not normal . . . it's something that people have quit doing."[8] But Haze has rejected modernism and intends the rest of his life to be one long penance in preparation for the time when he will become a true prophet. Although that time never comes, his last days are a silent statement directed against a city that cannot accept a religious prophecy. One final irony (among many) in the book is that as Haze is about to die Mrs. Flood realizes she really does love him. In several of O'Connor's best stories, love and reconciliation, those missing elements that O'Connor believed would restore the cultural foundation of the city, burst forth under the pressure of death, but always too late. The isolation of the middle-aged woman and the young seeker seems to be the last word in a story that is at once comic and tragic.

Flannery O'Connor was born in Savannah, only a few blocks from the birthplace of Conrad Aiken. On both sides of her family were Irish Catholics, many of whom were prominent in Georgia even before the Civil War. The well-to-do Irish Catholics were a powerful force in the life of Savannah, which in 1925 (O'Connor's birthdate) was still considered by many to be Georgia's only city in the European sense; as one of the early ports in the South, it had close connections with Europe. O'Connor always retained in her work that wit and sense of manners characteristic of writers like Ellen Glasgow who have their roots in the Tidewater area. When she was thirteen, however, her father contracted lupus and the family moved to her mother's family home in Milledgeville, Georgia. It was not quite a move to the country; this antebellum town had once been the capital of Georgia and still thought of itself as an urban cultural center. But by the time O'Connor graduated from the Georgia State College for Women in Milledgeville, she could not easily identify with its small-town ways. Believing that her destiny was to be a serious author, she, like many other southerners, decided that in the North she would find a culture more conducive to fulfilling her ambitions. O'Connor always disdained the work of fellow Georgian Carson McCullers, and McCullers is recorded as making one slighting reference to O'Connor, but they had in common the urge to leave behind the dying southern culture and experience the urban culture of the North. McCullers went straight to New York City, while O'Connor went first to the school of creative writing at the State University of Iowa; afterward she went on to New York to pursue her literary ambitions. However, in 1950 her life took a drastic turn: she contracted lupus and was forced to live the rest of her life on her mother's farm.

Southerners like O'Connor and McCullers, as well as Wolfe or Ellison or even Tate, always felt a sense of literary isolation in the South. The North seemed to abound with possibilities of meeting people who would point them properly in the direction of their ambitions. In O'Connor's case the northern experience was apparently essential to her career. At Yaddo, a Saratoga Springs, New York, retreat for artists, she met Robert Lowell, who became both a friend and an advisor. Through Lowell she then met in New York City possibly the two most important people in her literary career, Sally and Robert Fitzgerald. Like O'Connor the Fitzgeralds were Catholics, and when they moved to a Connecticut farm in 1949, O'Connor went with them, happy to be out of the city. Even then O'Connor associated the Enoch Emery type of character in *Wise Blood* with an aspect of herself, and she later wrote: "Enoch didn't care so much for New York. He said there wasn't any privacy there. Every time he went to sit in the bushes there was already somebody ahead of him."[9]

O'Connor considered New York, like Atlanta, to be primarily a megalopolis where individualism seemed to disappear. Her story "Judgement Day," based on her memories of New York, presents this view of the city. She appreciated New York as a cultural center, where various pratitioners of the arts could meet and develop their ideas. But she also knew that, after World War II, culture everywhere in the world was dying and that the city, lacking the order and creativity of the old culture, represented an urban sprawl that was culturally chaotic. Faulkner, who influenced O'Connor greatly, had said as much in *Sanctuary;* for him, Memphis in the thirties symbolized the cultureless aspect of great cities. O'Connor believed that, of the city's many problems, the most destuctive element was the breakup of the family and the neglect of children. She never married or had children, but her emotional attitude toward young children is strikingly evident in her work. For O'Connor the answer to the problem of megalopolitan civilization was a prophet who would go directly to the center of the city and, like Jonah, prophesy against wickedness in the hope that, like Nineveh, the city would repent. It was an old-fashioned view of both religion and the city, but O'Connor had an old-fashioned religious sensibility.

By the end of 1950, just after completing the first draft of *Wise Blood,* O'Connor began to experience the first symptoms of the same type of lupus that had killed her father in 1944. The following year she moved to her mother's dairy farm, called Andalusia, a few miles outside Milledgeville. There, in the fifties, she did most of her writing. After 1960 her health deteriorated rapidly and she died in 1964. On her deathbed she completed her last story, "Parker's Back," which appeared in her second volume of stories,

Everything that Rises Must Converge, published posthumously in 1965. O'Connor always insisted that she was primarily a storyteller, and these stories together with those of her first volume, *A Good Man Is Hard To Find,* have, more than her two novels, stamped her work on the minds of readers all over the world.

By 1980 O'Connor was considered by many critics to be second in importance only to William Faulkner as a modern southern writer who plumbed the heart of southern culture. Both captured the imaginations of serious readers in many countries partly because of the complexity of their personalities and their work. Their work is open to numerous interpretations; as in that of many great modern writers, ambiguity abounds. Analyzed by any number of critics, the mystery in their best writing somehow remains, along with a seriousness of both philosophical and artistic purpose. Like Faulkner, O'Connor surveyed the South from the vantage point of the country, the small town, and the city; also like him, she was aware of the collapse of religion and family. Unlike him, O'Connor wrote much of her best fiction in the last decade containing a semblance of unified culture in America—the fifties—and she saw with startling clarity what the succeeding decades of shattered cultural unity would be like. She saw in the fifties—that relatively quiet decade to which the seventies sought to return—that all attempts to create an artificial stasis were failing, that young people were beginning to reject the solutions of their elders, and that violence and crime were growing in intensity. Living until 1964, she saw the beginnings of a decade marked by sexual revolution, the decline of the nuclear family, the loss of any real sense of community, and the rise of religious cults that brought with them a dark and terrible fanaticism. Finally, she foresaw that urban sprawl would embrace even small towns and the countryside itself, where eventually only a handful of people would still be living in the agrarian past.

It must be understood that O'Connor was not a recluse hidden away on a farm, as suggested by *Time* magazine in a review of her letters. She often visited universities, for example, to give lectures and read her stories. Like some of her best characters, she went to meet the city; she knew there could be no retreat from urbanization.

But she was opposed to the idea generated by the modern social sciences that knowledge without grace could create a true culture. She herself had majored in social science as an undergraduate, but her conservative religious viewpoint constantly asserted itself in her best fiction. This viewpoint manifested itself in young fanatics like Hazel Motes who admit their own rage against life but cannot free themselves from a profound concern with Christian grace. Hazel Motes in *Wise Blood* is followed in the stories of *A Good Man Is Hard To Find* and *Everything that Rises Must Converge* by a succession of similar half-mad grotesques, young people who cannot shake off their awareness of the possibility of grace. In these characters O'Connor simultaneously reveals her acceptance of the death of the old southern culture and her awareness of the possibility of the revival of new religious and communal life. Her Nashville Agrarian mentors and their followers (with the exception of Allen Tate) had, in one sense, gone in another direction. They clung for the most part to the fragments of the old culture, which O'Connor in her brief role as a woman of letters often honored. Some southerners followed Warren into northern culture and wrote increasingly about the triumph of time over the dying cultures of the world. But for O'Connor, as for Joyce, Eliot, Mann, and other major international authors, death and rebirth are deeply interconnected.

O'Connor's own favorite story in *A Good Man Is Hard To Find* was "The Artificial Nigger." It is possibly her strongest depiction of the appearance of grace in ordinary life, and, fittingly, the epiphany happens in Atlanta. The subject of the story is the challenge offered by a trip to Atlanta for two characters who together sum up modern man: Mr. Head and a little boy named Nelson. Mr. Head, who represents for O'Connor the mind creating its own world, takes the boy to Atlanta; in keeping with his name (he is one of several semiallegorial characters in O'Connor's fiction), he has a view of the city (and particularly of the blacks in it) that is based on a false set of ideas. His error is that he lives according to his intellectual processes alone and tries to deny his emotions. The result of his mental abstraction is that he becomes emotionally separated from Nelson. When he encounters living instead of abstract blacks, he literally deserts the boy because of his mental confusion, which springs from perceiving the differences between actual black people and the ones in his mind, created by racist thinking. When he observes the communal life of the blacks he is forced to encounter, the result is a soul-searching that leads to a moment of grace, which reunites him with the boy and with his own emotional self, hitherto repressed.

For O'Connor, Atlanta is sometimes a symbol of the possibilities latent in new cities seeking a cultural revival. In the title story of her second volume, *Everything that Rises Must Converge,* Atlanta is the megalopolitan setting in which a mother and son struggle with the problems of living in a city they cannot understand or comfortably accept. Their very discomfort drives them to seek the correct solution: human reconciliation, O'Connor's great theme. In a few of her stories, "The Artificial Nigger" being the best, she depicts the discovery through grace of a reconciliation that puts aside the threat of destruction. But more often in her best stories reconciliation comes too late; consequently tragedy occurs, as in "Everything that Rises Must Converge," because the central characters have put off their spiritual development until it is too late. In such stories she depicts an emotional release we associate with tragic catharsis as defined by Aristotle; indeed, Thomas Merton has compared her to Sophocles. Tragedy is an art form that also reminds us that comedy in the true sense is possible, that a lasting reconciliation can be attained by those who surmount the flaws within their nature.

Of O'Connor's fiction, that which is most admired throughout the world begins with comedy and ends with tragedy. The theme of reconciliation and rebirth after tragedy is prominent in her works, many of which deal with modern, cultureless man moving beyond an age of tragedy. When cultures collapse, tragedy is inevitable, but a countermovement toward lasting reconciliation often parallels this collapse. This movement toward the comic myth was symbolized for her by the pilgrimage of a backwoods Protestant prophet, more sinful than the sinners he condemns, to the new Atlanta, symbolic of all the world's cities separated from their old cultural centers. The character of the prophet appears in her first novel, *Wise Blood,* and in her second, *The Violent Bear It Away.* He also appears, as I have suggested, in some of her most successful stories and in her novella, *The Lame Shall Enter First.* In the latter this character admits that the fanaticism of his prophecy results from his attachment to the ways of the devil and that his mission cannot continue until he is actually "saved," that is, until he accepts the grace of God given through the figure who has haunted him all his life, Jesus Christ. O'Connor was not finished with this theme, as can be seen in a fragment of a novel entitled *Why Do the Heathen Rage?* and published in *Esquire* near the end of her life. The critic Sally Fitzgerald best sums up the movement of characters like Hazel, cut off from the mainstream of religious tradition, who can neither separate themselves from their belief in Christ nor accept his salvation. Fitzgerald says, of the anagogical level of O'Connor's stories:

> She meant to show the good under construction. . . . The grotesqueness, the ugliness of her characters and their actions were part of the evolutionary course of human destiny. Haze's spiritual journey was the working out of his preservation, his salvation if you will. That is the agony of the novel, built on Flannery's absolute belief in the reality of Christ and the struggle on earth in which He is the determining factor.[10]

Many readers have asked why O'Connor, a devout Catholic, chose a Protestant fundamentalist for her chief character. Stanley Edgar Hyman calls it a "brilliant choice" because it "gave her imagery that is naturally dramatistic" and "forced her from the constraints of good taste."[11] In her hands the backwoods prophet becomes the twentieth-century Everyman, cultureless and suffering but still reaching out for the reconciliation between humans that is necessary for an age of true comedy to come into being. As she grew older, O'Connor leaned more and more on the vision of Teilhard de Chardin, and she borrowed his words, "Everything that rises must converge," for her second story collection. These words express one of her most basic beliefs—that those who sincerely struggle to rise spiritually will be drawn by the grace of God toward the inevitable convergence of reconciliation. For O'Connor, as for mystics in many cultures, grace can appear on all levels of existence and in many different forms, making possible moments of reconciliation and illumination that point toward the ultimate reunion of God and man.

Many commentators have noted O'Connor's habit of setting characters with opposing traits in opposition to each other. Her sense of opposites sometimes seems so strong that Stanley Edgar Hyman refers to her "Christian dualism."[12] Her dualism must be seen, however, in the context of her Christian rationalism. Many find it unlikely that an important modern writer would read Thomas Aquinas most of the nights of her life. But it was her intimate knowledge of both medieval and modern Catholic theology that led her into rationalism and into the use of allegory with a sacramental vision at its center. This vision is manifested in fictional descriptions of occasional moments of emerging grace, moments that

point to the reconciliation of opposites. These moments of reconciliation—Joycean epiphanies—are what give some of her most
painful stories their great power. In "A Good Man Is Hard To
Find" the grandmother suddenly recognizes her opposite, the
criminally insane Misfit, as "one of my own boys." Momentarily he
is reconciled with a woman who he realizes is his mother, but this
reconciliation comes too late; his murderous ego, unpurged by
grace, drives him to kill her. He cries out to her: "He [Jesus] thown
everything off balance." He tells her that, since he was not present
at the precise historical moment of Jesus' life, he cannot believe.[13]
Cut off from all sacraments and the faith they require, he must play
the role of one who flees God but who also longs for reconciliation
with both God and humanity.

Flannery O'Connor once told me that she received some of her
best letters from prisoners. Few writers have understood criminal
psychology as well as she. The criminal *must* try to overthrow the
established order because of his hatred of the world he grew up in.
The opposition of characters in O'Connor's fiction is usually based
on two types—smug insiders who have created balance in their
lives and angry misfits ready to destroy this balance. The misfit is
often a hellfire preacher or a raging prophet, not always because he
believes in God but because he wants to tear down the old order.
He is often aware of his own hypocrisy and wishes he could believe.
The influence of Nathanael West's *Miss Lonelyhearts* was never more
apparent than in O'Connor's depiction, in most of her stories and
in her two novels, of the madness of modern cults and their raging
"prophets," all part of the throng of destructive people living in societies whose cultures are dying. In the fifties O'Connor's fiction
foresaw the coming of the cults of the sixties and seventies whose
religious orientation was not toward life but, rather, death. Her
story "The River" is about a group of people who think they are
creating a counterculture but are in fact moving toward the death
of all cultural values.

O'Connor is similar to Dostoevski in that she has sympathy for all
who are caught up either in the web of criminal fanaticism or in the
boredom of organized "stability." In her best work both types are
capable of moving toward an acceptance of the grace that makes
new cultural values possible. In the story "Revelation" Mrs. Turpin,
one of O'Connor's self-satisfied women who own land and have social status, is challenged by a young woman who is a misfit. The
girl, a stranger to Mrs. Turpin, suddenly calls her a "wart hog from

hell," and Mrs. Turpin actually begins an inner struggle with this concept of her own hellishness. She prays for help, and in one of O'Connor's most successful depictions of an epiphany, the answer to her prayer comes in the form of a vision of the City of God, which moves upward toward convergence: "A visionary light settled in her eyes. She saw the streak as a vast swinging bridge upward from the earth through a field of living fire. Upon it a vast horde of souls were rambling toward heaven." [14] Mrs. Turpin sees the souls of all those she has thought beneath her socially, as well as those of herself and her husband. It is one of O'Connor's great visions of reconciliation, and it is a statement in the Augustinian tradition of a spiritual city that moves toward heaven, the city hidden within all material cities of the world. Mrs. Turpin receives a vision of true community by acknowledging the diabolic side of herself and praying for insight into how the devil can be overcome.

Much in O'Connor's fiction points toward the need for the recognition of diabolic influence and the possibility of grace. Through grace, O'Connor tells us, cultural values can be renewed. The realization of the death of the old Christian culture of the South pervades her work, but many of the characters deeply concerned with that death are drawn to the city (nearly always Atlanta) to work out a drama of religious and cultural rebirth. Typically, a test of strength is present at the center of a struggle: a misfit and a smug insider fight over a third figure, often symbolized by a child or one who is vulnerable to the collapse of traditional family values.

In some of O'Connor's earliest stories a pseudo-prophet struggles against the insider, represented by a prosperous woman seeking to maintain the status quo. But by the time she came to write her second novel, *The Violent Bear It Away* (1960), O'Connor had progressed to the creation of a figure that had long fascinated her, the psychologist and secular humanitarian who, she believed, was in some ways the leader of the modern urban world. She was not an enemy of either modern psychology or of humanitarianism; rather, she attacked the idea that psychology and good intentions alone can create the values of culture. Her psychologist in *The Violent Bear It Away*, Rayber, is a cold fanatic who sees himself as a high priest in the march of scientific and technical progress. His antagonist, Tarwater, is a hot fanatic who is tempted and physically raped by a "stranger," who is in fact the devil. Both characters represent O'Connor's allegorical presentation of the problem of hierarchy and community. Inspired by his great-uncle, an older backwoods preacher, Tarwater sees his mission as leading the child of his uncle, Bishop, into the ways of faith. Thus the child becomes the center of a struggle between two ways of life: the old religion, which has become violent and destructive in Tarwater's own life, and the new psychology, which cannot feed the hunger of the soul and can never bring about human reconciliation. All the psychologist's knowledge and reasoning cannot stop Tarwater from destroying Bishop. In his rage against Rayber he cries out: "You can't say NO. . . . You got to do NO." [15] Tarwater represents a violent, cultureless world that cannot be brought to order by Rayber's "science" and "progress." Yet even as he is drowning Bishop, Tarwater finds himself reciting the words of baptism. The role of prophet clings to him despite his nihilism, and when he returns to his native Powderhead, Tennessee, he sees in a vision his great-uncle, who had sent him forth, being fed on the true food of the spirit. He then hears the charge to warn the "CHILDREN OF GOD OF THE TERRIBLE SPEED OF MERCY." [16] His last act in the book is to set his face "toward the dark city, where the children of God lay sleeping." [17]

The Violent Bear It Away is O'Connor's most accomplished piece of expressionistic fiction, possibly her most painful, and certainly her most difficult. She never wrote again from such profound depths, but she found a greater light and clarity in certain stories to follow. Her novella, The Lame Shall Enter First, is the centerpiece of her second volume of stories, though it was first published in the Sewanee Review in 1962, two years after The Violent Bear It Away, which has the same theme. The Lame Shall Enter First uses an expressionistic method similar to that of The Violent Bear It Away, but the work is bathed in a more sober light. Moving from Wise Blood to The Violent Bear It Away to The Lame Shall Enter First, O'Connor had a clear-cut sense of where she was headed with her vision of the prophet seeking the city. In her last stories O'Connor showed an awareness of the possibility of the prophet finding his own salvation and helping others to find theirs. The Lame Shall Enter First is an excellent example of the author's awareness of the role of a religious prophet in the modern city. [18]

In The Lame Shall Enter First Sheppard, a psychologist, is symbolic of the modern psychologist who is the urban shepherd of souls. His antagonist, Johnson (son of John, the most devoted of Christ's disciples), represents the old Protestantism, like Tarwater. Johnson must also express the violence in his nature, and again the psychologist who has taken him in charge cannot change this. "I lie and steal because I'm good at it," Johnson says. The two struggle over the soul of Sheppard's son until the boy is driven to suicide.[19] Johnson admits his own diabolism but says that in time he will give himself wholly to his mission of serving Christ. Sheppard at last sees that he too has been in the grip of a diabolic force. O'Connor treats Sheppard sympathetically, even tragically, by depicting him as one who has sought reconciliation with his son through good deeds and has never known the grace that makes lasting love possible: "He had stuffed his own emptiness with good works like a glutton. He had ignored his own child to feed his vision of himself. He saw the clear-eyed Devil, the sounder of hearts, leering at him from the eyes of Johnson."[20] Sheppard has no way of overcoming diabolical powers because knowledge alone cannot enable him to summon the powers of grace to combat evil. O'Connor thus voices Allen Tate's old attack on the abstractions of modern thought.

Robert Drake says that the great city in O'Connor "usually appears as a modern Sodom or Nineveh."[21] This is generally not true, because for O'Connor the city lacks the psychic wildness of the country. Actually she shows the modern megalopolis drawing everyone into itself, engulfing all the smaller towns and cities. But the city *is* the place where evil must be fought and where there is a possibility for the conversion of people fallen from grace. The city is reflected throughout *Everything That Rises Must Converge*, particularly in the first story, set in Atlanta, and the last, set in New York. Both stories deal with relations between the races, and both suggest the emergence of a new egalitarianism. O'Connor seldom probes the minds of black people because, as she once said, she did not know their inner lives; nevertheless, she does have an intuitive understanding of the black community and its importance as a harbinger of new cultural life. Both stories have some of the qualities of O'Connor's own favorite, "The Artificial Nigger," and both are concerned with reconciliation between blacks and whites as well as between young and old. Unlike most modern fiction dealing with these two difficult subjects, O'Connor's stories create a sense of reconciliation—even if it arrives too late—that is both personal and cultural. O'Connor's point is that the death of culture brings with it the need for reconciliation that will make a true community possible in the future. This reconciliation exacts a price. People pay through suffering so that life can go on. This is her vision in "The Artificial Nigger," as Sally Fitzgerald reveals in her introduction to O'Connor's letters, quoting the author: "What I had in mind to sug-

gest with the artificial nigger was the redemptive quality of the
Negro's suffering for us all." Fitzgerald goes on to say that "The Artificial Nigger" is a work that "contains the germ of a final enlarge-
ment of understanding for Flannery O'Connor."[22]

The need for an experience of reconciliation between people in
conflict achieved through suffering and psychic pain: this is
O'Connor's vision, so often hidden beneath her comic and hard
surfaces. It is as if these painful facts must not be often exposed
because to do so would be to dissipate the sense of mystery that sur-
rounds them; for her the mystery is a necessary part of those rec-
onciliations that lead to new cultural formations. But what has
confused readers and critics even more than O'Connor's view of
mystery and reconciliation are her criminally fanatic "prophets."
Some reviews of her work have said that she was making cruel fun
of fundamentalist prophets, and a few have even thought that she
approved of religious fanaticism.

The quest for God's grace, which, if sincere, is rewarded by moments of spiritual power and by brief revelations, is O'Connor's
great theme. As a person and an author she pursued this subject
tenaciously. Her commitment to it made it possible for her to write
about the "rough beasts" of the contemporary world without fall-
ing under their spell. Her knowledge of grace gave her the confi-
dence to believe that culture could and would be renewed in the
South and elsewhere. She believed that when those called to prophecy receive the grace of God they will be revealed as the hierarchs
("sacred leaders") of new cultural communities.

That O'Connor herself had the qualities of a true hierarch can be
seen in Sally Fitzgerald's collection of the O'Connor letters, *The
Habit of Being*. Fitzgerald was closer to O'Connor in matters of literature than any other woman except Caroline Gordon, and she
shows in her introduction an understanding of O'Connor found in
no other book about her. The letters reveal her philosophical concern for the renewal of religious faith and of a culture based on
faith. And the letters prove that she believed that the spiritual vision that effects reconciliation and communal renewal was a gift
that would be given to those who sincerely searched for it. The
terms of her search have thrown off certain readers because, as
Robert Drake has put it, "she apprehends man's predicament in
terms of classical Christian theology; and she uses the traditional
terms without flinching: *sin, grace, redemption, Heaven, Hell,* and all
the rest. Furthermore, she often seems to regard her function as
prophetic or evangelistic and no bones about it."[23]

With the decline of traditional Christianity one would think that the terminology that O'Connor uses would alienate most readers; yet her work is well received. Her imaginative power doubtless has much to do with this; also, the uncompromising nature of her mental and emotional outlook, which allows us to see humanity in extreme situations, is fascinating. One of the most famous of these situations is the moment in "A Good Man Is Hard To Find" when the homicidal young man called the Misfit faces the family he is about to kill:

> Jesus was the only One that ever raised the dead . . . and He shouldn't have done it. He thown everything off balance. If He did what He said then it's nothing for you to do but throw away everything and follow Him, and if He didn't, then it's nothing for you to do but enjoy the few minutes you got left the best way you can—by killing somebody or burning down his house or doing some other meanness to him. No pleasure but meanness . . . .[24]

Young people in particular respond to the power and meaning in this passage, which presents life as what Kierkegaard, speaking of faith, called an either/or proposition. For many people nearing the end of the twentieth century, this proposition can be stated as a choice between urban chaos and the growth of new cultural values based on a vision of transcendence.

Walter Sullivan in two books, *Death by Melancholy* and *A Requiem for the Renascence*, points to Flannery O'Connor as the one writer since World War II who has achieved a vision of transcendence. In *Death by Melancholy* he makes the point that contemporary writers die of melancholy because of their failure to find support from expiring cultures. The answer, he suggests, is for the writer to develop new cultural values out of his own soul. Although the writer is seldom up to the task of being his own visionary, O'Connor did believe that the writer could help to prepare the way toward cultural revival by communicating a heightened awareness of those values necessary for meaningful existence. O'Connor is not the only contemporary writer to have this view. Walker Percy, whose religious vision differs in many ways from O'Connor's, also believes that the writer of fiction can depict new cultural values. O'Connor believed that in encountering the city, the individual who feels called to prophecy can bring forth new visions of the old Christian apocalypse. Percy, on the other hand, sees the suburbs as the new urban scene where most people will be living by the end of the century. The work of the religious individual for Percy is not apocalyptic but, rather, an unobtrusive ministry. What Percy and O'Connor have in common, despite their many differences, is their Catholicism and their belief that theology and philosophy have a role to play in our contemporary cultural crisis. Both proclaim the end of a unified southern culture, and yet both suggest the possibility of cultural revival growing out of the renewal of old southern values.

Lewis P. Simpson has suggested that the southern writer still retains many of the older values such as "love of the land, dependence on manners, a penchant for the concrete as opposed to the abstract, and an 'innate sense' of the mystery of existence."[25] For O'Connor and Percy the mystery is closely related to one of the great southern concerns—religion. Both authors are aware of the dangers of religion, but, like many southerners before them, they believe that a creative religion is needed to make family and community meaningful. On religious matters O'Connor and Percy are conservative, but, as Simpson has pointed out, both proclaim that a transcendent vision is needed in order to survive cultural collapse and to begin the work of cultural renewal, a vision accompanied by the act of putting the past behind one. Visionary activity is likely to come only to those who can accept the agony of cultural death. The South, as O'Connor said, is Christ-haunted if not Christ-centered; her best fiction is about the Christ-haunted fanatic seeking to become Christ-centered. In her best fictional moments she suggests that this event will occur and with it will come a new life in the South.

The most amazing aspect of O'Connor's life and work is that she could take what many regard as a forgotten aspect of human vision, the apocalyptic, make it central to her work, and gain both critical acclaim and a wide readership. Furthermore, she could do it with a strange mixture of tragedy and laughter. Frederick Asals, in his insightful study of her work, speaks of "the frightening presences of the divine and the demonic that are the ultimate poles of her universe" and shows that her best work evokes "simultaneously laughter and fear."[26] Although her work seems old-fashioned when compared with, for example, Percy's, O'Connor has made a profound mark on the imaginations of many sensitive readers. Who can say that what Asals calls her vision of the "transfiguration of consciousness" will not in time prefigure the renewal of family life and religion, for O'Connor the two most basic of human activities?

9

Walker Percy
A Postmodernist's Quest in the Suburbs

For Walker Percy the encounter with the modern city engenders a quest for a new life. Percy emerged in the late seventies as a nationally significant man of letters, one who had gained approval not only from critics but also from a large number of readers. Nonetheless, for most of his life Percy has felt himself to be an outsider on the American scene, never fully at home in the North or South.

The most fundamental question Percy and his fictional protagonists face is how to overcome a despair that expresses itself in apathy or violence. Although all of Percy's protagonists are caught up in the general narcissism of the sixties and seventies that Christopher Lasch and others have analyzed at great length, narcissism is not presented as the individual's chief problem. The malign element for the Percy protagonist is the despair that results from narcissism. In each of Percy's five novels we find the protagonist awaking to his need to move beyond despair. In all but one of the novels (*Lancelot*, in which the protagonist's efforts to escape despair only cause him to sink deeper into it), the central figure confronts his own narcissistic past and that of the dying southern culture he has inherited. But remembering the past is only a secondary activity for the protagonist. He is chiefly engaged in searching for a revelation that will help to free him from his narcissistic despair. Thus Lewis

175

P. Simpson rightly places Percy with O'Connor as a writer who, "rejecting the mode of remembering, . . . embraced the mode of revelation."[1]

To understand the nature of the revelations in Percy's work one must examine his existential philosophy as well as his use of Joyce's concept of the epiphany in presenting characters whose lives are circumscribed by the contemporary American suburb. Percy shows how, by a series of small spiritual revelations, modern individuals can break through the loneliness and despair created by their narcissism and begin communicating with others. Through this communication, Percy suggests, contemporary individuals can join with others in an authentic revival of cultural values based on creative personal development. Above all, Percy claims that modern man can overcome his tendency to lose himself and his past, which is caused by wallowing in a consumer-oriented modern suburban existence.

Percy has himself suffered the effects of the southern past, and few writers have explored so thoroughly the world of suburbs and shopping centers, where the past sometimes seems to disappear. Percy in his fiction shows that the late modernist individual, at the end of a period of overwhelming industrial and technological expansion, is a person who consciously chooses a suburban way of life and continually tries to turn it into a static "paradise" in an attempt to slough off his past altogether. By the sixties, when Percy emerged as an important American novelist, the great city centers were already being seen as violent places, either avoided or visited only occasionally. The countryside, on the other hand, was left to the handful of mechanized farms necessary to grow crops. In between were the suburbs, an increasingly desirable place in which to live out the "American Dream" and to be free from the many problems of the past and from the urgent need to create new cultural values. Percy shows not only the despair of those who refuse to face the problems of the past but also, through the "mode of revelation," how some of them move beyond despair and its resulting violence to find a meaningful life in suburban America. For Percy, revelation must grow out of a philosophical quest that often begins with an individual's choice to seek a mythic existence involving psychic death and rebirth.

As a quester and an artist-intellectual, Walker Percy might be expected to rail against suburban materialism, but instead in his novels and essays he generally smiles at the foibles of suburbanites. His satire—sometimes inspired by John Cheever and John Updike—is relatively gentle and no doubt accounts in part for his large readership. Percy himself has lived most of his creative life in a suburban town—or "exurb" as some sociologists have called the settlements located near great cities—where he has described himself as spending his days like many other Americans: working during the day and at night watching television and drinking. Living in Covington, Louisiana, twenty-five miles from the heart of New Orleans, Percy has pursued his career with growing success, yet he has not cut himself off from his surroundings, nor has he lost interest in great city centers like neighboring New Orleans, Atlanta, and New York, where he once attended medical school. In the eighties Percy appears as a man of letters who has come to terms both with his suburban surroundings and with the old split between northern and southern cultures. Not knowing his work well, one might even conclude that he has accepted suburbanism as the dominant American life-style and has forgotten the South of the past. Such a view, however, would be wrong.

For Percy, life in the suburbs is based primarily on avoiding the problem of dying cultural values. He holds the view that modern people cannot simply vegetate in suburban "paradises" because the collapse of culture is happening there as well as everywhere else. The violence that is a result of this collapse must be faced both in oneself and in others if the quest for new ways of life is to continue. Percy is acutely aware of the fact that facing the decline of old cultural values is painful, but he is also aware that restoring the cultural framework is necessary to make civilized existence possible. His work tells us that new values will evolve slowly through the efforts of seekers who struggle to slough off the past and seek a basis for the renewing of such values.

Discussing Percy's first novel, *The Moviegoer*, Simpson identifies Percy's way of handling the quester's journey. The book's hero, Binx Bolling, Simpson says, "knows southern ghosts when he sees them and would like to yield himself to them. But he resists them and becomes a laconic prophet of the self's redemption through the Kierkegaardian leap into faith."[2] Percy's fifth and, as this is written, most recent novel, *The Second Coming*, also deals with the "self's redemption" and sums up many of Percy's themes. Artistically, *The Second Coming* is not as imaginatively powerful or as intellectually complex as *The Last Gentleman* or *Lancelot*, but it incorporates themes that run through all of the author's work and points to solutions of

problems raised in his earlier fiction and essays. But before examining this book and the other novels, I will examine Percy's own
personal quest as reflected in his essays.

Percy carries on the tradition of the religious quest as we see it in
Kierkegaard and other religious existentialists. Kierkegaard was
the first strong influence on Percy; the thesis of *The Moviegoer* is
contained in an epigraph that is a passage from Kierkegaard's *The
Sickness Unto Death*, which states that a psychic illness called despair
is destroying individual lives as well as culture itself. For Kierkegaard the only cure for this disease, which often masquerades as
melancholia (our contemporary "depression") or as a vague, unre-
mitting anxiety, was a "leap of faith." Although this is a vague term
and generally misunderstood, Kierkegaard does define it in his description of the "Knight of Faith," a simple individual who turns his
daily life into a search for God, a search that is rewarded by occasional religious insights which point to ordinary services performed
in "faith" for the good of others. Percy uses the term *pilgrim* instead
of "Knight of Faith" but means by it much the same thing. Of his
protagonist in *The Last Gentleman* Percy says that "the reader is free
to see him as a sick man among healthy businessmen or as a sane
pilgrim in a mad world."[3] He also says of this protagonist that "he is
what Gabriel Marcel calls a *wayfarer*—like an old-fashioned pilgrim
on a serious quest. He is not merely content to do what everybody
else does—be satisfied with a consumer's paradise."[4] No statement
better sums up Percy's life quest, and the goals of his protagonists as
well. Percy does not disparage the suburbs as such, but he believes
that only through the life of pilgrimage, as his mentor Kierkegaard
demonstrates, can one experience the creative joy necessary for
cultural revival. In *The Second Coming*, Percy depicts the development of the pilgrim's social nature, but he arrived at this vision only
in his sixties. For most of his creative life he has worked with the
character as an existential quester who withdraws from mainstream
views of life in order to search for ways of overcoming his despair.

The word *existentialist* is as much a cliché as Kierkegaard's "leap of
faith," but Percy brings new meaning to it. Kierkegaard, who is
generally considered the founder of existentialism, taught Percy
the meaning of despair as well as the concept of the knight of faith.
But first he taught him that man's subjective nature must be taken
into consideration. This revelation from Kierkegaard came at a key
moment in Percy's life. From the time he matriculated as a fresh-
man at the University of North Carolina until he contracted tuber-

culosis as an intern at New York's Bellevue Hospital, Percy was primarily caught up in the objective view of life inculcated in him by
his prolonged study of the natural sciences. Forced into the long
rest cure that was necessary for his recovery from tuberculosis, he
undertook an extensive reading program in philosophy and literature; gradually he discovered his own despair and that of others as
he slowly began to accept the importance of his subjective, or inner,
life. Unlike Kierkegaard, he did not reject science and objective
thinking. Instead he moved on to other, more congenial thinkers;
chief among these was Gabriel Marcel, a twentieth-century French
Catholic existentialist. For Marcel the important act for the existentialist wayfarer is to accept not only his own subjectivity but also the
subjectivity of others on the pilgrimage. Marcel used the term *intersubjectivity* to describe relationships among wayfarers. Thus Marcel
and Percy would reject Kierkegaard's doctrine of the "single one,"
that individual who accepts no binding relationship with another
person. In both his life and his work Percy made the acceptance of
others, especially in the male-female relationship, an essential in-
gredient in his own philosophy.

To what extent Percy works within the tradition of Catholic existentialism that Marcel helped to initiate can be determined by examining his encounter with the modern city. Like so many southerners in this century Percy went to New York in part to search for a
cultural existence larger than that defined by the limitations of a
dying southern culture. In the mid-thirties, he entered the University of North Carolina, no longer the remote country institution
that Wolfe had known earlier but a growing university center that
had achieved national recognition. By choosing to study chemistry,
mathematics, German, and medicine, Percy seemed to be embracing the concepts of the New South, whose program called for a
strong emphasis on science and technology and for new cities modeled more or less on New York's example. He then gravitated toward New York and Columbia University, but the shock of living in
America's greatest city unsettled him; he engaged in long bouts of
moviegoing, to the extent that he began a series of regular sessions
with a psychiatrist. As a firm believer in Freud, Percy accepted
these sessions as any resident of New York might—necessary
therapy to overcome the inevitable shocks of modern urban existence. He became an intern at New York's Bellevue Hospital in 1941
and seemed well on his way to becoming one of modern society's
brightest ornaments, an established medical doctor. But the pro-

cess of recovery in the tuberculosis sanitorium in upstate New York led him to become something quite different—an existentialist philosopher.

Percy came to existentialism by way of Kierkegaard largely as a result of his encounter with New York. Kierkegaard had been all but forgotten until the translation of his works into English in the thirties, when suddenly he was viewed as an important "new" thinker in major intellectual centers like New York, London, and Paris. The subject of existentialism remained generally unknown to most Americans until the movement was popularized by Sartre and Camus after World War II. But in the early forties, in the sanitorium, Percy began to read Kierkegaard, Dostoevski, and other figures prominent in the existentialist movement.

Percy never practiced medicine but instead, with the help of an independent income, began a pilgrimage of his own, later using his experiences in his startling novels of the sixties and seventies. For a time he devoted himself to extensive reading, not neglecting the sciences, but supplementing his knowledge with independent study in literature, history, and philosophy. In 1954 he published his first article, "Symbol as Need," in a small philosophical journal; with this and similar articles he established himself as a professional philosopher. Essentially he remained an existential wayfarer who followed not in the footsteps of his original mentor, Kierkegaard, but in those of his second, Marcel. This shift of emphasis paralleled Percy's return from New York to live in the South.

Unlike Wolfe, who could not leave New York to go home again to the South, Percy found that home was the only place he could go in order to carry out the kind of pilgrimage he felt awaited him. Robert Coles, in his book *Walker Percy: An American Search,* traces Percy's quest and his involvement with existential philosophy.[5] Coles treats Percy's creative and intellectual life in both the North and the South, but I think he misses Simpson's point about the author's encounters with "southern ghosts" in *The Moviegoer.* Percy's return to the South was essentially an effort to face old ghosts, particularly the ghost of his own father, who had committed suicide in a Birmingham suburb. His father's fate is connected with the violence that Percy showed in his novels to be the essential element in the death of southern culture.

How should one face one's own violence as well as the violence of others? This was Percy's first great question. Marcel gave him the answer in his definition of his term *intersubjectivity:* with grace and love. Shortly after World War II, after returning to the South, Percy took two major steps on his pilgrimage: he married a Mississippian named Mary Bernice Townsend, and he became a Roman Catholic. Both steps were later recorded in the lives of his protagonists as representative acts of the individual who sought to go to the heart of cultural decay and defeat the enemy that had brought about the decline of culture.

According to Kierkegaard, despair was destroying cultures. But what caused despair? Percy asked himself while writing his early essays. The answer he tentatively reached, as early as his first published essay, "Symbol as Need," was that despair is caused by the inability to truly communicate, or, in Marcel's terminology, to engage in meaningful intersubjective relationships. In "Symbol as Need" Percy links his studies of modern philosophers like Cassirer and Langer to his Catholic viewpoint as expressed by St. Thomas: "It is apparently Saint Thomas and not Mrs. Langer or Cassirer who had the first inkling of the mysterious analogy between the form of beauty and the pattern of inner life."[6] This thought became a constant in Percy's work: the symbols by which artistic beauty is expressed are linked with "the pattern of the inner life." Subjectivity for Percy thus has a pattern, as does the universe itself. Following Aquinas, Percy posits the ancient concept of the microcosm and the macrocosm: man is a little cosmos, or harmonious design, existing in the larger cosmos that is the surrounding universe. By calling upon the inner and the outer harmony of these two, which Percy sees as the unseen God expressing himself in time, humans receive the grace that enables moments of love and true communication to occur.

Like Marcel, Percy is working in the tradition of the spiritual pragmatism of William James as stated in "The Will to Believe." In fact, Jay Telotte shows close parallels between Percy's approach to language and communication and that of one of the men who most deeply influenced James, C. S. Peirce. Telotte writes that "relative value might be found in an intersubjective 'knowledge,' that is, within the commitment to a community of . . . questioners (a community which the linguistic theories of both Percy and Peirce stipulate as absolutely essential for all truly human communication)."[7] The community of questioners consists of those who accept the religious role of wayfarer, or pilgrim. The pilgrimage can only be continued by a series of "leaps of faith" based on choosing to relate oneself to the harmonious pattern. This leap of faith based on choice is what Telotte means by "'metaphysical' abduction" in his description of the nature of Percy's fictional protagonists' successful communication: "All of Percy's protagonists take a least a tentative step toward such a 'metaphysical' abduction, and by so doing they break out of their alienation and fashion a new possibility of life for themselves and others. In attaining this sense of harmony with their world—'their father, nature,' as Peirce would say—they strike a comfortingly hopeful note for Percy's broad audience."[8] "Nature" is what Peirce, following the tradition of Stoicism, chose to call the harmonious pattern that individuals relate to; but Percy, following Marcel, relates the harmony to the one divine order discussed in the philosophy of Aquinas, as well as that of Augustine, Plato, and Heraclitus.

Wayfaring, then, along with choosing to relate to divine harmony, is at the basis of the religious view expressed in Percy's essays and novels. Unlike O'Connor he rarely invokes either Christ or Catholic symbolism, though they are often present behind the scenes. The chief reason for this is that Percy believes that the old symbols now fail to work for most people. He is painfully aware of the collapse of the cultural values contained within religion, education, and the family—once potent transmitters of knowledge about the symbols and rituals needed for true communication. Therefore what is important for the protagonists of his novels is that they experience the pragmatic results of faith itself instead of what might be called "religious experience." The result is manifested in the pilgrim's gradual loss of his despair and the recovery of enough love to show a real concern, not for "mankind" in general, but simply for a handful of people met on the pilgrimage. Some religious readers wonder if Percy even deserves to be called a Catholic or Christian novelist because of his seeming failure to use many of the rituals and symbols of religion. However, in her study of ritual in Percy, Patricia Bowden shows how many ritualized activities there are in the novels. She quotes Marcel, who in effect says that one who believes may anywhere and at any time experience an "epiphany" in which one suddenly encounters "a fullness of life, the marvelous resources of a world where promises abound, where everything that exists is called to universal communion."[9] In all except *Lancelot*, where the decline of that protagonist only proves Percy's point, the novels show central characters beginning in the midst of alienation and moving on to sudden revelations of the "fullness of life." Although Percy's work might not strike some as being specifically reli-

gious, the progress of his wayfarers in four of the novels indicates
that Percy's intentions as an artist are essentially the same as Dante's.
The Italian poet says of his *Commedia:* "The whole work was undertaken not for a speculative but a practical end—the purpose of the
whole is to remove those living in this life from a state of misery,
and lead them into a state of felicity." [10] Thus Percy and Dante both
write about the original subject of comedy—the movement of the
pilgrim from misery to happiness.

Percy has said that "A novelist these days has to be an ex-suicide.
A good novel . . . is possible only after one has given up and let
go." [11] His own novels and his best essays begin with this awareness
of inner violence. To go beyond this violence, his work tells us, one
must first face it in oneself and in others. And to encounter fully
his own impulses toward self-destruction Percy knew that he would
have to spend his creative life on his native ground. After his return to the South he tried for several months to live in Sewanee,
Tennessee. This move was probably not so much a retreat to the
country as an effort to join a new university center. Sewanee was
connected with Vanderbilt University, spiritual home of Agrarians
like Ransom and Tate; it was as if Percy, having tried New South
liberalism at Chapel Hill and Yankee pragmatism at Columbia, was
now establishing a connection with the Agrarian viewpoint. As late
as 1979 he referred to Faulkner and Tate as being "as close as we
[Southerners] have come to cosmos-shaping poets." [12] For several
years during the fifties he regularly sought help from writer Caroline Gordon—Tate's wife and Flannery O'Connor's literary mentor—in his attempt to write a Catholic novel.

Because he saw his own pilgrimage as the central focus for his
fiction he began to write autobiographical fiction in the general
manner of Thomas Wolfe. But Caroline Gordon read his manu-
scripts and influenced him to change his method to one more suit-
able to Agrarian critical tenets. Autobiography disguised as fiction
was never acceptable to the Agrarians, but parts of one's life artistically shaped for aesthetic effect were. The result was that two of
his novels never got out of manuscript form but a third, *The Moviegoer,* was published in 1961. A small artistic masterpiece based
loosely on material from Percy's life, it won a National Book Award
and has since become a contemporary classic. In the tradition of
Agrarianism, it contained certain philosophical concepts unobtru-
sively woven into the story. One might have expected the author, as
a philosopher, to write a novel of ideas in which cardboard charac-

ters would expound the author's views, but Percy managed to sub-
ordinate ideas to human experience. He has never ceased being an
existentialist in the French sense, a man of letters equally comfortable with ideas and artistic creation and most at home in an urban
environment. For many years he carefully studied the works of
Kierkegaard, Dostoevski, Marcel, Buber, Heidegger, and Camus;
their basic influence on him must be kept in mind in order to
understand his vision of cultural revival in a postmodernist world.

American commentators on existentialism often fail to understand certain key concepts of the movement. For instance, Walter
Kaufmann writes that existentialism is "not a philosophy but a label
for several widely different revolts against traditional philosophy,"
whose "one essential feature" is "their perfervid individualism."[13]
Actually traditional philosophy has always been existentialist to
some degree insofar as it holds to one central concept: the essential
meaning of existence can only be understood by human beings if it
is seen in the context of lived experience; Socrates expresses this
idea in *The Apology*. Modern existentialists, however, have gone beyond this basic definition to differ about the nature of the essence
that makes existence itself possible. Some, like Sartre, have denied
that existence is related to essence. Others, like Buber and Marcel,
have been essentially religious, maintaining that the individual must
encounter the divine in order to have a meaningful existence. In
general, all existentialists are concerned with discovering authentic
existence, and all of them believe that, in order to philosophize,
one must accept the series of life crises to which humankind is heir.

F. H. Heinemann has written that the existentialist viewpoint always appears at a time of cultural crisis. At the basis of this crisis is
the individual's sense of alienation, accompanied by fears of the loss
of personal identity. The fact that modern existentialism came into
being as a reaction to Hegelianism and Marxism, Heinemann
writes, "implies that it has something in common with them, namely
the desire to overcome the alienation of man."[14] Existentialism
charges that philosophical systems like those of Hegel and Marx
can never free humankind from alienation and its resulting despair
and violence. Two nations seduced by Hegel and Marx—Germany
and Russia—attest to this; their dictators' attempts to use ideology
to banish alienation only yielded in these nations a deeper alienation followed by a profound violence. For Heinemann, then, the
"existential philosopher is one whose thought *is* action. Consequently he exists in his action-responses and in them creates him-

self and his world." Heinemann quotes Fichte's statement to illumi-
nate the essentially mythic nature of existentialism: "Philosophy is a
transformation, regeneration, and renewal of the spirit in its deepest root: the emergence of a new organ and, with it, a new world in
the flux of time." [15] The existentialist novelist like Percy, then, is
not a philosopher who writes fiction but a mythic quester who expresses philosophical concepts in literary images.

One of the most important statements of Percy's ideas is the essay
"Notes for a Novel about the End of the World," in which he acknowledges his acceptance of the end of modernism: "It might in
fact turn out that the modern era, which is perhaps three hundred
years old and has already ended, will be known as the Secular Era,
which came to an end with the catastrophes of the twentieth century." [16] This statement might well be an epigraph for *The Last
Gentleman*, Percy's second novel, which records how Percy at the age
of eleven dealt with the breakup of his family because of his father's
suicide. In his third novel, *Love in the Ruins*, Percy shows how the
crises of the century in fact involve all of society; in the other four
novels he deals not so much with social as with personal catastrophes. He continually emphasizes that only those who act creatively
in the postmodern age will successfully face the social catastrophes
of modernism.

For Percy the impulse to commit suicide, based as it is on despair,
is a major aspect of the malign element that is destroying the culture of modernism. "Everyone is about to commit suicide," King
Leopold III of Belgium said on August 22, 1939. [17] The French existentialists after World War II referred continually in their work to
Europe's cultural suicide. But in his play *The Flies* (1944), Sartre said
that the true hero can make himself into a new person by choosing
to face the violent impulses in himself and others. This concept of
choice is fundamental to Percy; as a follower of Marcel he tran-
scends Sartre's pessimism to show that the choice to go on living can
set one on a path that leads beyond alienation.

Marcel in books like *Tragic Wisdom and Beyond* and *Mystery of
Being* presents the possibility of a "joyful wisdom" (Nietzsche's
term) that lies beyond pessimism. The term is apt because for Marcel and other existentialists philosophy in its radical meaning, "love
of wisdom," is not concerned with speculation but with pragmatic
events of love and joy that result from conscious choices to become
involved with others. In "A Novel about the End of the World"
Percy speaks of the pilgrim encountering catastrophe: "When the

novelist writes of a man 'coming to himself' through some such catalyst as catastrophe or ordeal, he may be offering obscure testimony to a gross disorder of consciousness and to the need of recovering oneself as neither angel nor organism but as a wayfaring creature somewhere between." [18] Interestingly, Percy at the end of this essay does not cite Marcel as his chief inspirer but, rather, James Joyce. The Catholic novelist, Percy tells us, resembles Joyce's Stephen Dedalus, in that he "calls on every ounce of cunning, craft, and guile he can muster from the darker regions of his soul." [19] Flannery O'Connor said that the Catholic writer can learn more from Joyce, a man who left the church, than from others who remained in the church. And Joyce, the most philosophical if not in fact the most religious of modern English novelists, like Marcel evolved a concept of epiphany, or spiritual revelation.

Percy's first novel, *The Moviegoer* (1961), consists of a series of small epiphanies set in New Orleans in the fifties. In this book the protagonist, Binx Bolling, thinks he is living a life of modern pleasure until he begins to realize that he is filled with despair. In New Orleans, a city that has come to be known to many of its inhabitants as the Big Easy, the death of culture has already been tacitly accepted; in Binx's milieu nearly everyone is devoted to the pleasures of food and sex. New Orleans as a unified city hardly exists at all in Binx's mind; he relates primarily to Gentilly, his own section of the city. He is addicted to endless moviegoing, for him a kind of partial suicide, a way of losing his personality. The challenge of the city for him is whether he will gradually sink into a mental fog or seek authentic existence. He decides to seek God; in the following monologue he speaks to himself:

> What do you seek—God? you ask with a smile.
> I hesitate to answer, since all other Americans have settled the matter for themselves and to give such an answer would amount to setting myself a goal which everyone else has reached—and therefore raising a question in which no one has the slightest interest. Who wants to be dead last among one hundred and eighty million Americans? for, as everyone knows, the polls report that 98% of Americans believe in God and the remaining 2% are the atheists and agnostics—which leaves not a percentage point for a seeker. [20]

Binx encounters a failure of religious values. Others around him say that they believe in God; but once they have declared this belief, they go back to enjoying movies and other ordinary pleasures. But Binx knows that in order to live at all he must do something about the apathy that makes him want to lose himself in moviegoing: "The only possible starting point: the strange fact of one's own invincible apathy—that if the proofs were proved and God presented himself, nothing would be changed. Here is the strangest fact of all." [21] For Binx the only restoration of the cultural value of religion comes through the discovery of pragmatic energies powerful enough to overcome apathy. His choice to seek God gives him hope, which allows him to achieve an intersubjective relationship, defined by Marcel as an authentic encounter with another person, in this case a woman named Kate. Aided by this relationship, Binx marries and makes his life's work in the medical profession. Of the fruit of Binx's search Janet Hobbs writes: "At the end of *The Moviegoer* Binx seems silently to have renewed his search. Thus he has become one of Kierkegaard's men of faith. . . . Binx has learned both how to live and how to die." [22]

In many ways *The Moviegoer* is a fictional prelude that announces the chief themes of Percy's four later novels. Two themes in particular—the exorcism of ghosts from the dead southern past and the brief epiphanies achieved by the quester—are dealt with in brilliantly rendered passages. A minor character in the novel, Aunt Emily, is modeled on W. A. Percy, the first cousin of the author's father who adopted young Walker and his two brothers when their mother died in an automobile accident. Though sympathetically presented, Emily represents the stoic moral code of the old southern aristocracy, a code that is largely detached from spiritual values and provides little help for Binx. Binx finally rejects stoicism in order to search for deeper spiritual insights, which come to him gradually in a series of epiphanies.

The most finely wrought ephiphany occurs near the end of the novel when Binx watches a black man in New Orleans entering a church. Binx's thoughts about this simple event suddenly fill with deep awareness of both human and divine existence. At the same time he realizes that the New Orleans he knows, which is renowned for pleasure-seeking, represents only one aspect of a rich, diversified city. By the end of the novel, he has given up the narrow moral code of the dead past, as well as his belief in pleasure-seeking as a way of life, in order to search out the rich possibilities for intersubjective relationships in the urban life around him.

In his second novel, *The Last Gentleman* (1967), Percy again takes up the story of a young man beginning a religious quest, but his handling of this material is deeper and more complex; he draws on his earliest memories of growing up in an affluent Birmingham suburb, the son of a brilliant young lawyer who was a member of one of the South's most renowned families. When the young man in the book, Will Barrett, accepts Kierkegaard's path of the knight of faith, he finds the strength to leave New York and return to Birmingham in order to face many ghosts from the past. In one sense he is the last southern gentleman, still trapped in the coils of a dead culture. But by the end of the book his quest has led him out of the Old South and has taken him beyond the Babbittry he finds in the New South. He encounters the postmodern experience defined in the book's epigraph, a quotation from Romano Guardini, a Catholic theologian admired by both Percy and O'Connor: "We know that the modern world is coming to an end. . . . Loneliness in faith will be terrible, but the more precious will be that love that flows from one lonely person to another . . . the world to come will be filled with animosity and danger, but it will be a world open and clean." Will begins to achieve glimpses of the new world of postmodernism in his relationship with a young woman, Kitty Vaught, whom he hopes to marry.

Before Will can become involved with Kitty and her family, he must confront the memory of his father's suicide. He comes to realize that his father killed himself because he could not face the decline and death of southern culture. Remembering what happened, Will experiences an epiphany: "*Wait*, I think he was wrong and one looked in the wrong place. No, not he but the times. . . . It was the worst of times, a time of fake beauty and fake victory."[23] Having understood his father's collapse, Will can accept life as a religious pilgrim whose chief calling is to love those around him and to prepare for the coming of a new culture based on new inspiration. Eventually, he saves Sutter, one of Kitty's brothers, from suicide by showing him the falseness of his defeated idealism, which, like the failed cultural values that deceived Will's father, have only served as a prop for Sutter's sagging ego. Sutter abandons the idea of suicide and resolves to continue his work as a doctor. For another brother, Jamie, Will serves as a kind of lay priest, becoming the instrument of his salvation.[24] As Jamie is dying, his belief in Will makes faith possible for him.

In Percy's next novel, *Love in the Ruins* (1972), the author again portrays the postmodern world, in which another despairing man faced with the loss of cultural values discovers the role of wayfarer.

The protagonist, Thomas More, is at the beginning of the novel a lapsed Catholic whose marrige is ruined. By the end of the novel he has accepted life as a pilgrimage and rediscovered the values of religion and family. But before finding the path of pilgrimage he works his way through despair and a desire for suicide. He even has a vision of the devil bargaining for his soul but draws back in time to accept the sacramental life of Catholicism as the basic defense against the dark forces threatening to overwhelm humanity. Percy makes it clear that sacraments—rites that relate individuals to divinity—are necessary to preserve the sanity and the lives of those who continue on the path of pilgrimage, and that the revival of cultural values in a postmodern age grows out of the interconnected pilgrimages of many people. Those who cling either to the image of past cultural glories of the Old South or to an image of isolated suburban contentment inevitably sink into depression and violence.

Because *Love in the Ruins* concentrates on depicting a wide view of society, it lacks both the intensity of characterization and the depth of emotion of his first two novels. Percy in this third novel moves beyond religious and family values and examines those connected with politics and the professions. *Love in the Ruins* suggests that politics will continue in a time of social collapse much as it has in the earlier part of the century, with various factions struggling against each other. But people seek new values, Percy tells us, and as they find them they witness the collapse of the belief that through politics or any other single human activity all human problems can be solved. Thus *Love in the Ruins* is in part a diatribe against utopian thinking, in which Percy claims that no single activity can free man from despair. Humans, he says in the essay "The Mystery of Language," cannot save themselves from despair and suicide by science but, rather, by discovering through pilgrimage the pragmatic virtues of hope and love coupled with creative joy in meaningful work: "The existentialists have taught us that what man is cannot be grasped by the sciences of man. The case is rather that man's science is one of the things that man does, a mode of existence. Another mode is speech."[25] A human, defined by Percy according to Heidegger, is "that being in the world whose calling it is to find a name for Being, to give testimony to it, and to provide for it a clearing."[26] For Percy, as for all the religious existentialists, Being—or divine essence—underlies human existence and must be experienced if the basic philosophical and religious virtues are to be realized. Percy's greatness as an existentialist is that he can move from the language of philosophy to the fictional illustration of his ideas in the concrete terms of individuals encountering cultural collapse in modern urban environments. The protagonist in *Love in the Ruins* learns that science can be valuable rather than destructive once he learns to live as a human who regularly encounters Being and hence experiences the continuing renewal of hope and love.

Love in the Ruins, like its successor *Lancelot* (1977), is a philosophical novel in the best sense of the term in that it depicts individuals struggling with concepts and learning to incorporate those concepts into lived experience. Percy's chief concept is that of essence—what Heidegger called Being—and he puts life, as seen from the standpoint of essence, opposite the bifurcation of individual experience, which is seen as the way most modern people live. Allen Tate believed that the chief problem faced by modern man was a strong sense of separateness that, he thought, grew out of the Cartesian split—that is, Descartes' vision of a fundamental separation between body and soul, object and subject. Percy has called this split "a bisected reality, a world split between observers and data, those who know and those who behave and are 'encultured'."[27] But because science "must remain silent in the face of the true-or-false claim," humans cannot be given "values" or "culture" by behaviorists or other scientists who play God for other, "lesser" individuals. Each individual, Percy tells us, must discover basic values for himself by accepting his pilgrimage. Thus More in *Love in the Ruins* acts as a Cartesian on the assumption that with an invention he can play God and save humanity. He then has an experience in which he observes his own split personality: "a chronic angelism-bestialism that rives soul from body and sets it orbiting the great world as the spirit of abstraction, whence it takes the form of beasts, swans and bulls, werewolves, blood-suckers, Mr. Hydes or just a poor lonesome ghost locked in its own machinery."[28]

As is often the case in Percy's books, a hero must face suicide before turning around. But once More begins to confront the realm of essence existing behind phenomena, he realizes that he is neither beast nor angel but, rather, a wayfaring man somewhere in between. Only this realization, followed as it is by a series of rituals in which brief epiphanies are achieved both within the Church and in everyday life, makes it possible for More to marry again, to love his wife, to use his scientific knowledge as a doctor to help others, and to engage in the politics of a wrecked culture in an attempt to find new cultural values.

In *Lancelot* Percy continues his search for ways to revive cultural values. Lance Lamar, the book's protagonist, has views similar to those of More in *Love in the Ruins*. Pushing Lamar's utopian idealism to its inevitable limits, Percy shows the destructiveness that results. In an insightful essay, "Walker Percy and Modern Gnosticism," Cleanth Brooks (drawing heavily on the German philosopher Eric Voegelin) describes *Love in the Ruins* and *Lancelot* as Percy's statements about the modern gnostic attempt to renew culture. The "genuine gnostic ring," Brooks tells us, is found, for example, in the statement of a revolutionist in *Love in the Ruins,* who says, "We're going to build a new society right here."[29] Lance Lamar, after turning into a homicidal maniac and blowing up his ancestral New Orleans mansion—demonstrating his complete rejection of southern culture—accepts the revolutionist's view that one can by a simple act of the will build a good society on the foundation of the old one. As the book ends we see him setting out to create a new mythology on which to erect a new culture in much the same fashion that Alfred Rosenberg and other Nazis sought to erect a "myth of the twentieth century" on which to found a new "Reich." Voegelin speaks of pseudo-Christs (Hegel, Marx, Freud, for example) who arise as Western civilization begins to fragment, and Percy shows More before his conversion seeing himself in a mirror as "a dim hollow-eyed Spanish Christ." We see Lance Lamar, like More, at the end of the book ready to act out his fantasies of saving the world. Unlike More, however, he has not been converted to the concept of pilgrimage.

Many of Percy's readers felt that with *Lancelot* he had somehow lost his way. As Simpson has noted, "the story of Lancelot ends darkly."[30] But the darkness of the novel is tempered by the character of Percival, a psychiatrist-priest who humbly ministers to the needs of his parishioners. Percival says little in the novel—his main function is to listen to his friend's story—but what he says and the way he acts indicates that he is, like Binx Bolling, Will Barrett, and Thomas More, an existential pilgrim. Percival desires the revival of culture as much as Lance does, but as a priest he accepts the teaching of his faith that this revival can occur only through the slow renewal of religion and family relationships.

Religion and family, for Percy, are necessary to cultural revival, but they in turn can be renewed only through the renewal of communication. For Percy, as for Marcel, the pilgrim is one who, through faith and love, rediscovers the essentials of communication. Lancelot's story is that of one who is suffering from what Freud called a fixation. His mind is caught up in the glories of a dead culture, as he tries to build a new, utopian culture. Ironically, he lives in an exurban world that many already consider a utopia, but its inhabitants, like Lance, are unable to communicate about basic human issues and, without even knowing it, are sunk in despair. Percival, on the other hand, is the one character in the book who has overcome despair and who feels no compulsion to destroy the remnants of the dead culture. He knows that these remnants will be gradually reintegrated into new cultural patterns by those who discover the way to true communication. As a humanist and a Christian, Percy, through Percival, thus shows that revival will never spring from people who are in despair and therefore incapable of communication. The true revolutionary revival, for Percy, will be conducted by those who draw together in communicative endeavors, which must be accompanied by love and by Marcel's "joyful wisdom."

The greatness of *Lancelot* lies in the depth of Percy's psychological exploration of its protagonist. Lewis A. Lawson says that the two chief characters in *Lancelot* "personify a tradition that Percy has often treated, the southern Stoic and the Christian" and that "there can be no synthesis of these two forces." He shows how Percy drew on aspects of his own life—his knowledge of the Stoic code "transmitted to him by William Alexander Percy" and his own Christian pilgrimage growing out of a "family tradition of depression and early suicide."[31] Studies like Lawson's are necessary to understand the aspects of Percy's work that can be understood in light of Freud's work. As a young man studying medicine, Percy fell under Freud's spell, but later he satirized Freudian excesses. Percy was inevitably influenced by C. G. Jung, whom he studied in the late seventies. Jung's concept of individuation and insights into those powers of the psyche that he calls archetypes are closely related to Percy's existential concept of pilgrimage. Percy has expressed his attitude toward Jung and Freud thus: "I believe my current assessment of Jung would have to pay tribute to his great corrective to Freud by getting away from libidinal energies and into the archetypal encounter as a means of individuation." He has also acknowledged that, although he was not interested in Jung when he wrote *Lancelot*, the character's psychological condition, seen from the

Jungian viewpoint, consists of a "successive anima and shadow possession . . . which [I] was more or less aware of doing."[32] Lancelot, by Percy's own admission, is unable to be a pilgrim because he is possessed by the image of his mother (the anima, or image of woman). As is often the case, a man possessed by the image of the anima (or a woman by the animus) is seized by the powers of destruction. In the political realm into which Lancelot is projected, the shadow powers possessing him drive him to destroy his ancestral southern home, a symbol of southern culture. Then the anima reasserts itself and drives him to try to create *ex nihilo* a new culture in the image of the previous one. Percy makes clear that this effort is demonic and doomed to failure.

Percy's next novel was *The Second Coming* (1980), which he describes as dealing "rather more explicitly with Jungian individuation."[33] In fact, *The Second Coming* is a companion piece to *Lancelot*, in which Percy shows one protagonist caught up in the destructive energies of the shadow and another protagonist overcoming destructive energies by accepting the underlying oneness of being (symbolized by the Jungian archetype called the mandala). The central figure of *The Second Coming* is a middle-aged Will Barrett (from *The Last Gentleman*) who has retired to the North Carolina mountains and has strayed from the path of pilgrimage. Will finds that the affluent retirement community where he lives is not a retreat but, rather, a part of the network of American suburbs and exurbs, where everyone seeks a false paradise based on material comfort and trivial pleasures. As in Percy's other novels, the despair of several characters becomes apathy or rage as the surface glitter of their suburb is shattered by various fanaticisms.

However, because Percy's chief theme is not cultural collapse but cultural regeneration in the lives of a few people, Will begins his pilgrimage anew—or, in Jungian terms, undergoes individuation. As in Percy's earlier fiction, the pilgrim soon finds another person with whom he can continue the journey and discover the power of love that makes true communication possible. Allie, the girl Will aids in overcoming schizophrenia, speaks of the process of individuation: "I was somewhat suspended above me but I am getting down to me."[34] Will himself, after encountering the fanaticism of characters who are trying to create a new religious life by fiat, comes to see that Being cannot be separated from ordinary life in the world. He meets an old priest who instructs him in this ancient knowledge, and he experiences an epiphany at the end of the novel: "His heart leapt with a secret joy. What is it I want from her and him, he wondered, not only want but must have? Is she a gift and therefore a sign of a giver? Could it be that the Lord is here, masquerading behind this silly holy face? Am I crazy to want both her and Him? No, not want, must have. And will have."[35] Percy's insight into the relationship between Being and the individual includes his persistent belief that the individual can choose to encounter both Being and individuals in intersubjective relationships and that this choice necessitates a pilgrimage in which one continues to have epiphanies concerning the possibility of intersubjective relationships.

More than any of Percy's novels *The Second Coming* performs two services. One is that it clarifies the differences between intersubjective relationships that are caught up in destructiveness (Will and his father) and those that are creative because they are based on communication (Will and Allie). The other is that it shows how any effort to achieve individuation can have a creative effect on others and may lead to a beginning of the revival of cultural values. Will's pilgrimage has good consequences not only for his companion, Allie, but for his other friends in the community, who are led to seek both individuation and the renewal of cultural values. Whatever the literary merits of *The Second Coming* might be, the book's philosophical insights concerning pilgrimage and renewed cultural values are among Percy's best.

By the time Percy published *The Second Coming* he had become the leading essayist for both popular and serious journals on the subject of the South. In a 1979 essay for *Harper's* he maintains that the South is fully restored to the Union and that the race problem no longer dominates the region's thinking; he acknowledges that the southerner "is both southern and American, but much more like other Americans than different."[36] He has speculated in several of his popular essays that the South might be able to save the Union as the North once did: "It gives a certain satisfaction to the South having to save the Union. After all, it is our turn."[37] For Percy the great new cities of the South are symbolized by Atlanta, whose "cylinders and towers and palaces" are "perched on a hill like Zion."[38] He believes that the problem for modern humanity is the same in the contemporary South as it is anywhere else: psychological dissociation. The American novelist today is saying that "something has gone badly wrong with American life, indeed modern life, that people generally suffer a deep dislocation in their lives that has nothing to do with poverty and ignorance and discrimination." He goes on to say that it is the very people who have escaped poverty "and moved to the exurbs who have fallen victim to the malaise." The result is that the "successful grandchildren" of poverty-stricken southerners, both black and white, "are going nuts in Atlanta condominiums."[39]

The dislocation that drives suburbanites and exurbanites to frenzy is based on an inability to communicate, growing primarily out of the acceptance of the American Dream, which views the material comforts of suburban life as humanity's highest goal. This acceptance leads to an ignorance of Being, that metacultural element necessary for true communication. From this spiritual element, Percy shows, spring all the cultural values that are now in rapid decline. The way to new cultural values, he tells us, lies in accepting life as a pilgrimage in which the missing element is sought, found briefly, and then sought again, its essence being glimpsed in the moment called the epiphany. Percy's awareness of the missing element came early in life, as he grew up in an affluent Birmingham suburb. His later encounters with cities like New York, Atlanta, and New Orleans always led him back to the suburbs to face the problem of dislocation. Unlike other major southern writers, his primary concern was philosophical rather than artistic. Yet art resulted from his efforts, and in the seventies and eighties he became the leading southern spokesman for a life-style based on the spiritual quest.

Epilogue

Theodore H. White ends his autobiography, *In Search of History,* with the statement that American culture died during the sixties and that "The revolution of the Storm Decade and its aftermath would be a testing of whether the old ideas that had made America a nation could stretch far enough to keep it one; and whether a new culture could nourish a political system as strong and success-ful as the one that was passing away."[1] I have already suggested that somewhere around 1960 American culture as a unity had ceased to exist, and along with it the cultural unity of the South. But, as I have sought to demonstrate, the shattering of cultural unity has not brought with it immediate and overwhelming chaos. Many jour-nalists, critics, and cultural historians in this century have seen only the breakup of cultural unity all over the world, without seeing any underlying movement leading to cultural rebirth. They see mod-ern artists as depicting only the inevitable results of cultural decay and death without ever glimpsing their underlying visions of re-birth. One of the few exceptions, C. G. Jung, wrote in the late fifties of the vision of "world renewal" implicit in much of modern art: "The development of modern art with its seemingly nihilistic trend towards disintegration must be understood as the symptom and symbol of a mood of world destruction and world renewal that sets its mark on our age."[2]

Theodore White is an American journalist who detects both

dread and hope all around us, as the cultureless void seems to close in on modern man. The dread, usually repressed, has been there for many years; without an awareness of cultural revival, this dread must increase. Cultural death exists alongside cultural renewal, which is not always easy to detect; but Jung reminds us that the mood of death and rebirth "makes itself felt everywhere, politically, socially and philosophically."[3] In the stormy sixties, a feeling of renewal in American life was apparent in the civil rights movement and in attempts to rebuild cities and create a so-called Great Society. Americans have found that a great society cannot be created by political and economic means alone. White shows an awareness rare among journalists and historians (and among social scientists generally)—that a successful political system can grow only out of the cultural life of a nation. Many new nations have adopted constitutions like ours, but the failures of their cultures have made it impossible for them to transmit cultural values into lived experience. The greatness of the beginnings of the American experiment lies in the cultural life of the people who created it and in the American communities that supported the values of great leaders, who rose in the footsteps of lesser, now forgotten leaders. Cultural revival will emerge in unexpected places as the gradual process of death and rebirth continues. Many of our best literary artists remind us in their work that the process goes on. The most important of these artists still at work is undoubtedly Walker Percy.

Percy in his essays and novels offers new critical and imaginative insights concerning cultural revival in the decade of the eighties. He also shows us that in spite of inevitable cultural disintegration, life can go on with humor and with a rational appraisal of the human condition. The South of the seventies and eighties is a place of turbulent, painful, and sometimes ugly change; but it is also a place of cultural growth. In spite of growing illiteracy, crime, and drug addiction in the southern city, Percy sees something more happening under the surface of these events, and he has made us aware of the efforts of creative people to bring about in many small and ordinary ways a revival of both culture and community.

One proof that Percy's optimism is not unfounded is that his work is important to so many readers. Similarly, in the eighties Allen Tate has achieved more recognition than he ever had in his lifetime. The prophecy of Ransom and the other original Agrarians, that cities like Nashville would make an important cultural contribution to the nation, has been fulfilled. Inner Charleston has risen from its earlier status as an urban museum to become a culture center, and inner Savannah has been rescued from dirt and decay. San Antonio, New Orleans, the Virginia Tidewater, and the Raleigh-Durham area have begun the work of cultural renewal that may lead them to surpass days of earlier greatness. Central to the changes in these cities is the fact that people in them believe that the growth of the arts is linked to the rebuilding of the life of the city.

Today in Atlanta I can see a play about the South by Tennessee Williams or Lillian Hellman and can hear discussions about how Williams's work has helped people to accept the fact that we need a more communal society in which the erotic side of life is not denied and repressed but is allowed its creative part in human existence. I have heard Williams himself discussing his work in Atlanta, following a performance of *The Night of the Iguana* that he pronounced to be a better production than the original New York version. I can talk to people in various walks of life who have read Wolfe and Faulkner and have accepted their visions of the tragic fall of the old southern culture and also their optimistic prophecies of the renewal of the South and the nation. I can talk to young people who have read and made a part of their lives the words of the great religious writer of our day, Flannery O'Connor. I can discuss with members of the black community of Atlanta how the work of Ralph Ellison and Langston Hughes has aided in the liberation of black people and how the great black leaders from Douglass to King have made the power of language a major force in their lives and works.

Now that southerners have been living for more than forty years in the restored South, it is possible to understand better the meaning of its new cultural centers. Before World War II, southern cities were either crumbling into the past, like Charleston and Richmond, or were caught up almost entirely in the pursuit of commerce and industry, like Dallas and Birmingham. In spite of the discovery by journalists of several "New Souths," there is really only one; it began almost as soon as Reconstruction ended and was named in 1886 by Henry W. Grady. This New South devoted itself largely to what W. E. B. DuBois called the "gospel of work and money," in order to catch up with the dominant region of America, the North—something many regions and nations were doing after 1870. By 1941, as shown in Cash's *The Mind of the South,* the South on the eve of World War II was nearly as modernized and industrialized as the North. The period of the New South had by this time passed, as new patterns of culture began to emerge. From 1940 to the present, cultural development has in fact become almost as im-

portant to the new southern cities as the maintenance of commercial and industrial progress.

The period of change from the New South to the restored South
is one of the great subjects of southern writers from 1930 to the
present. The best of these writers seek to go beyond the painful development of the New South and the idealized antebellum past, but
only in the past few years have we begun to take seriously their visions of southern cultural revival. When it became apparent, after
1970, that the nation was becoming largely a collection of ethnic
communities, many people realized that America's old unified culture—made up of three regional cultures, the North, South, and
West—had disappeared. Now we as a nation are going through one
of our greatest changes—that which accompanies the movement
from one unified culture to a new culture that must be based on the
great population shifts in the nation after 1970.

The old cultural writing cannot be resurrected because most of
the old cultural hierarchs have lost their credibility and our communities have suffered because of the death of our earlier unity. Yet
out of the psychic pain of cultural death comes the challenge to
find new creative energies in the human spirit. Many will deny the
fact of death and others will try to bring back the past, but those
who answer the challenge to create new cultural patterns will be the
new hierarchs. Whether famous or obscure, they will be natural
aristocrats of merit and virtue in the Jeffersonian sense, and they
will lead others to discover the wisdom to unlock the creative energy within themselves so that they may join other creative people
in building a true community. From the unified efforts of these
people will spring the new cities that will be the future centers of
cultural development.

The establishment of new cities in America will mark the beginning of the new American life that Emerson and Whitman foresaw.
Our old cities were largely extensions of Europe, and the time
when Americans will create their own cities now awaits us. In the
midst of the megalopolitan confusion and disorder that is the most
obvious fact of twentieth-century life, the seeds of rebirth already
exist, planted by thinkers, visionaries, and artists. As the visionaries
of the nineteenth century saw the seeds of twentieth-century cultural disintegration at a time when most people saw only social stability, so many of our great visionaries in this century see the signs
of new life that will in the twenty-first century become the basis of
the rebirth of cultures throughout the world. Now it is for us to discover those visions of rebirth and to celebrate them.

Notes

Introduction

1. Joel Garreau, *The Nine Nations of North America* (Boston: Houghton, Mifflin, 1981), 149.

2. Steve Oney, "A Southern Voice," *Atlanta Journal and Constitution Magazine*, September 16, 1979, 57.

3. Lewis Mumford, *The Pentagon of Power* (New York: Harcourt Brace Jovanovich, 1970), 417.

4. Charles Flato, *The Golden Book of the Civil War* (New York: Golden Press, 1961), 203; introduction by Bruce Catton. This book was adapted by Charles Flato from *The American Heritage Picture History of the Civil War*, by the American Heritage editors with a narrative by Bruce Catton.

5. George Core, "One View of the Castle: Richard Weaver and the Incarnate South," in *The Poetry of Community*, ed. Lewis P. Simpson (Atlanta: Georgia State University, 1972), 9.

6. Louis D. Rubin, Jr., *A Gallery of Southerners* (Baton Rouge: Louisiana State University Press, 1982), xvii.

7. Oney, "Southern Voice," 13.

8. Clifford Geertz, *Negara: The Theater State in Nineteenth-Century Bali* (Princeton: Princeton University Press, 1980), 14.

9. Arnold J. Toynbee, *A Study of History* (New York: Oxford University Press, 1953), 309.

10. George B. Tindall, *The Ethnic Southerners* (Baton Rouge: Louisiana State University Press, 1976), 42.

11. Rubin, *Gallery of Southerners*, xii.

12. Jack Temple Kirby, *Media-Made Dixie* (Baton Rouge: Louisiana State University Press, 1978), 159.

13. William C. Havard, "The Distinctive South: Fading or Reviving," in *Why the South Will Survive* (Athens: University of Georgia Press, 1981), 39.

14. Tindall, *Ethnic Southerners*, 4.

15. Theodore Roszak, *The Making of a Counter Culture* (Garden City, N.Y.: Doubleday, 1969), 47–48.

Chapter 1: The City and the Quest for Cultural Values

1. Pitirim A. Sorokin, *The Crisis of Our Age* (New York: E. P. Dutton, 1941), 13–29.

2. Robert Langbaum, *The Mysteries of Identity* (Chicago: University of Chicago Press, 1982), 144.

3. Ibid., 11.

4. Ibid., 5.

5. Sorokin, *Crisis*, 25, 26.

6. Quoted in Daniel G. Hoffman and Samuel Hynes, eds., *English Literary Criticism: Romantic and Victorian* (New York: Appleton-Century-Crofts, 1963), 245, 246.

7. Quoted ibid., 252.

8. Quoted ibid., 321.

9. James D. Wilson, *The Romantic Heroic Ideal* (Baton Rouge: Louisiana State University Press, 1982), 167.

10. Ibid., 194.

11. C. G. Jung, *The Undiscovered Self*, trans. R. F. C. Hall (New York: New American Library of World Literature, 1959), 117, 118.

12. Carl Bridenbaugh, *Myths and Realities: Societies of the Colonial South* (Baton Rouge: Louisiana State University Press, 1952), 116, 117.

13. Blaine A. Brownell and David R. Goldfield, *The City in Southern History* (Port Washington, N.Y.: Kennikat Press, 1977), 16.

14. Bridenbaugh, *Myths and Realities*, 6.

15. Noemie Emery, *Washington: A Biography* (New York: G. P. Putnam's Sons, 1976), 51.

16. Sorokin, *Crisis*, 17.

17. W. J. Cash, *The Mind of the South* (Garden City, N.Y.: Doubleday, 1954), 150.

18. George B. Tindall, *The Ethnic Southerners* (Baton Rouge: Louisiana State University Press, 1976), 42.

19. Robert Manson Myers, ed., *The Children of Pride* (New Haven: Yale University Press, 1972), 10.

20. Emery, *Washington*, 13, 15, 52.

21. Blaine A. Brownell, *The Urban Ethos in the South* (Baton Rouge: Louisiana State University Press, 1975), 212, 213.

22. Amaury de Riencourt, *Sex and Power in History* (New York: David McKay, 1974), 402.

23. Quoted in Larry Shealy, "The Southern Accent . . . We Ain't All Gomer Pyles," *Atlanta Journal and Constitution,* January 6, 1980, 1F, 10F.

24. R. W. Collingwood, "Oswald Spengler and the Theory of Historical Cycles," *Antiquity* 1 (1927): 323, 324.

25. Arnold J. Toynbee, "Cities in History," in *Cities of Destiny,* ed. Arnold J. Toynbee (New York: McGraw-Hill, 1967), 13.

26. Langbaum, *Mysteries,* 220.

27. Joseph Campbell, *The Masks of God: Creative Mythology* (New York: Viking Press, 1968), 678.

28. Ibid., 672.

29. Alan W. Watts, *The Two Hands of God* (New York: George Braziller, 1963), 1–46.

30. Marion Montgomery, "Solzhenitsyn as Southerner," in *Why the South Will Survive* (Athens: University of Georgia Press, 1981), 196.

Chapter 2: Ransom and Tate

1. Lewis A. Lawson, "A Band of Prophets: The Vanderbilt Agrarians after Fifty Years," *South Atlantic Review* 48 (May 1983): 114.

2. Lewis P. Simpson, "The Southern Republic of Letters and *I'll Take My Stand,*" in *A Band of Prophets: The Vanderbilt Agrarians after Fifty Years,* ed. William C. Havard and Walter Sullivan (Baton Rouge: Louisiana State University Press, 1982), 65.

3. Thomas Daniel Young, "Introduction," *John Crowe Ransom,* ed. Thomas Daniel Young (Baton Rouge: Louisiana State University Press, 1968), 18.

4. John Crowe Ransom et al., *I'll Take My Stand* (New York: Peter Smith, 1951), xv.

5. Ibid., xviii–xix.

6. Thomas Daniel Young, *Gentleman in a Dustcoat* (Baton Rouge: Louisiana State University Press, 1976), 266.

7. Louis D. Rubin, Jr., "John Ransom's Cruell Battle," in *John Crowe Ransom,* ed. Thomas Daniel Young (Baton Rouge: Louisiana State University Press, 1967), 165.

8. Quoted in Young, *Gentleman in a Dustcoat,* 256.

9. Rubin, "Cruell Battle," 166.

10. Ibid., 164.

11. John Crowe Ransom, *Poems and Essays* (New York: Vintage Books, 1955), 29.

12. Ibid., 10.

13. Graham Hough, "John Crowe Ransom: The Poet and the Critic," in *John Crowe Ransom,* ed. Thomas Daniel Young (Baton Rouge: Louisiana State University Press, 1967), 201.

14. Quoted in Young, *Gentleman in a Dustcoat,* 166.

15. Quoted ibid., 216.

16. Simpson, "Southern Republic of Letters," 89.

17. Young, *Gentleman in a Dustcoat,* 155.

18. Ibid., 146.

19. Simpson, "Southern Republic of Letters," 70.

20. Karl F. Knight, "Love as Symbol in the Poetry of Ransom," in *John Crowe Ransom,* ed. Thomas Daniel Young (Baton Rouge: Louisiana State University Press, 1967), 185.

21. Quoted in Lawson, "A Band of Prophets," 114.

22. Young, "Introduction," *John Crowe Ransom,* 21, 22.

23. Young, *Gentleman in a Dustcoat,* 434.

24. Thomas Daniel Young, *The Past in the Present* (Baton Rouge: Louisiana State University Press, 1981), 84.

25. Simpson, "Southern Republic of Letters," 90.

26. Lewis P. Simpson, *The Dispossessed Garden* (Athens: University of Georgia Press, 1975), 71.

27. Ibid., 90.

28. Ibid.

29. Robert Buffington, "Allen Tate: Society, Vocation, Communion," *Southern Review* 18 (January 1982): 64.

30. Simpson, "Southern Republic of Letters," 90.

31. Richard C. Moreland, "Community and Vision in Eudora Welty," *Southern Review* 18 (January 1982): 99.

32. Allen Tate, *Collected Essays* (Denver: Alan Swallow, 1968), 250–51.

33. Lewis P. Simpson, *The Man of Letters in New England and the South* (Baton Rouge: Louisiana State University Press, 1973), 249.

34. Young, *Past in the Present,* 63.

35. Buffington, "Allen Tate: Society, Vocation, Communion," 62.

36. Louis D. Rubin, Jr., *A Gallery of Southerners* (Baton Rouge: Louisiana State University Press, 1982), 111.

37. Tate, *Collected Essays,* 435.

38. Ibid., 471.

39. Ibid., 470.

40. Ibid., 313.

41. Ibid., 435, 471, 470, 429, 431.

42. Ibid.

43. Simpson, *Man of Letters,* 254.

44. Simpson, "Southern Republic of Letters," 91.

45. Andrew Lytle, "A Semi-Centennial," in *Why the South Will Survive* (Athens: University of Georgia Press, 1981), 224.

46. Young, *Past in the Present,* 26.

Chapter 3: William Faulkner

1. Robert Langbaum, *The Mysteries of Identity* (Chicago: University of Chicago Press, 1982), 211.

2. Louis D. Rubin, Jr., ed., *The Literary South* (New York: John Wiley and Sons, 1979), 461.

3. Robert E. Spiller, *The Cycle of American Literature* (New York: New American Library, 1957), 224.

4. Thomas Daniel Young, *The Past in the Present* (Baton Rouge: Louisiana State University Press, 1981), 25.

5. Eugene Genovese, *The Political Economy of Slavery* (New York: Vintage Books, 1967), 23.

6. Louis D. Rubin, Jr., *A Gallery of Southerners* (Baton Rouge: Louisiana State University Press, 1982), 18.

7. William Faulkner, *Mosquitoes* (New York: Liveright, 1955), 117.

8. David Minter, *William Faulkner* (Baltimore: Johns Hopkins University Press, 1980), 233.

9. Ibid., 81.

10. Ibid., 8.

11. William Bedford Clark, "Cleanth Brooks: Mr. Eliot's Christian Critic," *Southern Review* 18 (Winter 1982): 81.

12. William Faulkner, *The Sound and the Fury* and *As I Lay Dying* (New York: Random House, 1946), 21.

13. Ibid., 306, 307.

14. Ibid., 313.

15. Panthea Reid Broughton, *William Faulkner: The Abstract and the Actual* (Baton Rouge: Louisiana State University Press, 1974), 114.

16. Faulkner, *The Sound and the Fury* and *As I Lay Dying*, 9.

17. Cleanth Brooks, *William Faulkner: The Yoknapatawpha Country* (New Haven: Yale University Press, 1963), 329.

18. Allen Tate, *Collected Essays* (Denver: Alan Swallow. 1968), 386.

19. Minter, *William Faulkner*, 119.

20. Faulkner, *The Sound and the Fury* and *As I Lay Dying*, 448.

21. Robert D. Jacobs, "William Faulkner: The Passion and the Penance," in *Modern Southern Literature in Its Cultural Setting*, ed. Louis D. Rubin, Jr., and Robert D. Jacobs (Garden City, N.Y.: Doubleday, 1961), 161.

22. William Faulkner, *Light in August* (New York: Random House, 1950), 419.

23. Ibid., 430.

24. Ibid., 426.

25. William Faulkner, *Absalom, Absalom!* (New York: Random House, 1951), 178.

26. Ibid.

27. Ibid., 350.

28. Ibid.

29. Rubin, *Gallery*, 17.

30. Jacobs, "William Faulkner: The Passion and the Penance," 154.

31. Ibid., 165.

32. William Faulkner, "Delta Autumn," in *Go Down, Moses* (New York: Modern Library, 1970), 364.

33. Ralph Ellison, *Shadow and Act* (New York: New American Library, 1964), 271.

34. Thomas L. McHaney, "Literary Modernism: The South Goes Modern and Keeps on Going," in *Southern Literature in Transition*, ed. Philip Castile and William Osborne (Memphis: Memphis State University Press, 1983), 48.

35. Malcolm Cowley, *The Faulkner-Cowley File: Letters and Memories 1944–1962* (Harmondsworth, England: Penguin Books, 1966), 24.

Chapter 4: Conrad Aiken

1. C. Hugh Holman, *Three Modes of Modern Southern Fiction* (Athens: University of Georgia Press, 1966), 1–10.

2. *The Island Packet*, Hilton Head, S.C., May 4, 1978, 31.

3. Ibid.

4. Ellen Glasgow, *A Certain Measure* (New York: Harcourt, Brace, 1943), 204.

5. Christopher Lasch, *The Culture of Narcissism* (New York: Warner Books, 1979), 74.

6. Ibid.

7. Ellen Glasgow, *The Romantic Comedians* (Garden City, N.Y.: Harcourt, Brace, 1926), 3.

8. Conrad Aiken, *Collected Poems* (New York: Oxford University Press, 1953), 395.

9. Ibid., 287.

10. Ibid.

11. Arthur E. Waterman, "Conrad Aiken—Chronology," *Studies in the Literary Imagination* 13, no. 2 (Fall 1980): 1.

12. Aiken, *Collected Poems*, 755.

13. Ibid., 736.

14. Ibid., 757.

15. Frederick J. Hoffman, *Conrad Aiken* (New York: Twayne Publishers, 1962), 395.

16. Aiken, *Collected Poems*, 812.

17. Reuel Denney, *Conrad Aiken* (Minneapolis: University of Minnesota Press, 1964), 40.

18. Mary M. Rountree, "Conrad Aiken's Heroes: Portraits of the Artist as a Middle-Aged Failure," *Studies in the Literary Imagination* 13, no. 2 (Fall 1980): 83.

19. Ibid.

20. Conrad Aiken, *Ushant* (Cleveland and New York: World Publishing Co., 1962), 211.

21. Ibid., 293.

22. Ibid., 364.

23. Ibid., 220.

24. Ibid., 365.

25. E. P. Bollier, "Conrad Aiken's Ancestral Voices: A Reading of Four Poems," *Studies in the Literary Imagination* 13, no. 2 (Fall 1980): 69.

26. Ted R. Spivey, "Conrad Aiken, Resident of Savannah," *Southern Review* 7 (October 1972): 802.

27. Alexander A. Alexander, "228 Habersham Street," *Georgia Review* 13 (Fall 1968): 317–34. For Aiken's reaction to Alexander's article and related matters, see Ted R. Spivey, "Christ in Savannah: Conrad Aiken's Religious Vision," *Essays in Arts and Sciences* 12 (March 1983): 99–112.

28. Stanley Edgar Hyman, *The Armed Vision* (New York: Vintage Books, 1955), 315.

29. Arthur E. Waterman, "Conrad Aiken as Critic: The Consistent View," *Mississippi Quarterly* 17 (Spring 1971): 91–110.

30. Denney, *Conrad Aiken*, 6.

31. Douglas Robillard, "Conrad Aiken and Herman Melville," *Studies in the Literary Imagination* 13 (Fall 1980): 93.

32. Joseph Killorin, "Conrad Aiken's Use of Autobiography," *Studies in the Literary Imagination* 13 (Fall 1980): 28.

33. Conrad Aiken, "T. S. Eliot," *Life*, January 15, 1965, 93.

34. Conrad Aiken, *Thee* (New York: George Braziller, 1967), 14.

Chapter 5: Thomas Wolfe

1. Richard Chase, "Introduction," *You Can't Go Home Again*, by Thomas Wolfe (New York: Dell, 1960), 13.

2. C. Hugh Holman, "The Dark, Ruined Helen in His Blood: Thomas Wolfe and the South," in *South: Modern Southern Literature in Its Cultural Setting*, ed. Louis D. Rubin, Jr., and Robert D. Jacobs (Garden City, N.Y.: Doubleday, 1961), 178.

3. Ibid.

4. Concerning Wolfe's repeated phrase "Dark Helen," Floyd Watkins in *Thomas Wolfe's Characters* (Norman: University of Oklahoma Press, 1957) concludes: "Cosmopolitan and provincial Asheville proved to be a microcosm that provided subject matter and a standard of reference, throughout Wolfe's career. Truly, the land of his origins was the 'Dark Helen' of his blood" (184).

5. Thomas Wolfe, *The Web and the Rock* (New York: Dell, 1960), 276.

6. Ibid.

7. F. Scott Fitzgerald, *The Great Gatsby* (New York: Charles Scribner's Sons, 1953), 149.

8. Ibid.

9. Wolfe, *Web and the Rock*, 36.

10. Pamela Hansford Johnson, *The Art of Thomas Wolfe* (New York: Charles Scribner's Sons, 1943), 44.

11. Louis D. Rubin, Jr., "Southern Literature: The Historical Image," in

South: Modern Southern Literature in Its Cultural Setting, ed. Louis D. Rubin, Jr., and Robert D. Jacobs (Garden City: N.Y.: Doubleday, 1961), 41.

12. Chase, "Introduction," *You Can't Go Home Again,* 16.

13. Paschal Reeves, "Thomas Wolfe and the Family of Earth," in *The Poetry of Community,* ed. Lewis P. Simpson (Atlanta: School of Arts and Sciences, Georgia State University, 1972), 48.

14. Thomas Wolfe, *Look Homeward, Angel* (New York: Charles Scribner's Sons, 1929), 602.

15. Lewis P. Simpson, *The Brazen Face of History* (Baton Rouge: Louisiana State University Press, 1980), 4.

16. Robert Spiller, *The Cycle of American Literature* (New York: New American Library, 1957), 190.

17. Andrew Turnbull, *Thomas Wolfe* (New York: Charles Scribner's Sons, 1967), 34.

18. Chase, "Introduction," *You Can't Go Home Again,* 16.

19. Wolfe, *You Can't Go Home Again* (Garden City, N.Y.: Sun Dial Press, 1942), 424.

20. Chase, "Introduction," *You Can't Go Home Again,* 15.

21. Ibid., 5.

22. Ibid., 15.

23. Wolfe, *You Can't Go Home Again,* 401.

24. Ibid., 14.

25. Reeves, "Family of Earth," 53.

26. Ibid.

27. Johnson, *Art of Thomas Wolfe,* 26.

28. Ibid., 112.

29. Wolfe, *You Can't Go Home Again,* 743, 741.

30. Ibid., 741.

31. Norman Mailer, *Cannibals and Christians* (New York: Dial Press, 1966), 62.

32. Floyd Watkins, "Rhetoric in Southern Writing: Wolfe," *Georgia Review* 12 (Fall 1958): 82.

33. Louis D. Rubin, Jr., *The Literary South* (New York: John Wiley and Sons, 1979), 515.

34. Chase, "Introduction," *You Can't Go Home Again,* 20.

Chapter 6: Tennessee Williams

1. T. E. Kalem, "The Laureate of the Outcast," *Time,* March 7, 1983, 88.

2. *Atlanta Journal and Constitution,* February 26, 1983, 13A.

3. Joseph K. Davis, "Landscapes of the Dislocated Mind in Williams' *The Glass Menagerie,*" in *Tennessee Williams: A Tribute,* ed. Jac Tharpe (Jackson: University Press of Mississippi, 1977), 196.

4. Ibid.

5. Esther M. Jackson, "Tennessee Williams: Poetic Consciousness in Cri-

sis," in *Tennessee Williams: A Tribute,* ed. Jac Tharpe (Jackson: University Press of Mississippi, 1977), 68.

6. Tennessee Williams, *The Glass Menagerie,* in *The American Tradition in Literature,* ed. Sculley Bradley et al., 4th ed. (New York: Grosset and Dunlap, 1974), 1092.

7. Williams, *The Glass Menagerie,* 1093.

8. Ibid., 1094.

9. Lincoln Barnett, "Tennessee Williams," *Life,* February 16, 1948, 114.

10. Williams, *The Glass Menagerie,* 1108.

11. Ibid., 1110.

12. Kalem, "Laureate of the Outcast," 88.

13. Williams, *The Glass Menagerie,* 1110.

14. Leonard Quirino, "The Cards Indicate a Voyage on *A Streetcar Named Desire,*" in *Tennessee Williams: A Tribute,* ed. Jac Tharpe (Jackson: University Press of Mississippi, 1977), 86.

15. Tennessee Williams, *A Streetcar Named Desire* (New York: New American Library, 1951), 3.

16. Ibid.

17. Jacob H. Adler, "Tennessee Williams' South: The Culture and the Power," in *Tennessee Williams: A Tribute,* ed. Jac Tharpe (Jackson: University Press of Mississippi, 1977), 41.

18. Ibid., 31–37.

19. Williams, *A Streetcar Named Desire,* 13.

20. Ibid.

21. Ibid., 43.

22. Louis D. Rubin, Jr., ed., *The Literary South* (New York: John Wiley and Sons, 1979), 604.

23. Jacob H. Adler, "Tennessee Williams' South," 43.

24. Thomas J. Richardson, "The City of Day and the City of Night: New Orleans and the Exotic Unreality of Tennessee Williams," in *Tennessee Williams: A Tribute,* ed. Jac Tharpe (Jackson: University Press of Mississippi, 1977), 636, 634.

25. Victor A. Kramer, "Memories of Self-Indictment: The Solitude of Tennessee Williams," in *Tennessee Williams: A Tribute,* ed. Jac Tharpe (Jackson: University Press of Mississippi, 1977), 664.

26. Robert Jacobs, "The Humor of 'Tobacco Road'," in *The Comic Imagination in American Literature,* ed. Louis D. Rubin, Jr. (Washington: Voice of America Forum Series, 1974), 311.

Chapter 7: Ralph Ellison

1. Norman Mailer, "The Dynamic of American Letters," in *Norton Anthology of American Literature,* ed. Gottesman et al. (New York: W. W. Norton, 1979), 2: 2080.

2. Esther Merle Jackson, "The American Negro and the Image of the

Absurd," in *Ralph Ellison's Invisible Man,* ed. William Goyen (New York: American R. D. M. Corp., 1966), 38.

3. Ibid.

4. Thomas D. Jarrett, "Recent Fiction by Negroes," *College English* 16 (November 1954): 87.

5. Ralph Ellison, *Shadow and Act* (New York: New American Library, 1966), 25.

6. Ibid.

7. Ibid., 44.

8. Ibid., 124.

9. Ibid., 146.

10. Ibid., 26–27.

11. Ralph Ellison, *Invisible Man* (New York: Vintage Books, 1972), 345.

12. Ellison, *Shadow and Act,* 180.

13. Ibid., 181.

14. Ihab Hassan, *Radical Innocence: Studies in the Contemporary American Novel* (Princeton: Princeton University Press, 1961), 169.

15. Ibid., 177.

16. Ellison, *Invisible Man,* 109.

17. Ibid., 42.

18. Hassan, *Radical Innocence,* 172.

19. Ellison, *Invisible Man,* 562.

20. Joseph Campbell, *The Hero with a Thousand Faces* (New York: Meridian Books, 1956), 90–97.

21. Ellison, *Invisible Man,* 563.

22. Ibid., 564.

23. Ibid.

24. Ibid., 566.

25. Ibid., 566–67.

26. Ibid., 567.

27. Martin Esslin, *The Theatre of the Absurd* (Garden City, N.Y.: Anchor Books, 1961), 303.

28. Ibid., 316.

29. Ellison, *Invisible Man,* 566.

30. Ibid., 285.

31. Ibid., 286.

Chapter 8: Flannery O'Connor

1. Lewis P. Simpson, *The Brazen Face of History* (Baton Rouge: Louisiana State University Press, 1980), 246.

2. Ibid.

3. "Short Reviews," *Atlantic,* June 1979, 96.

4. Robert Fitzgerald, "Introduction," *Everything That Rises Must Con-*

verge, by Flannery O'Connor (New York: Farrar, Straus & Giroux, 1966), xv.

5. *Flannery O'Connor: The Habit of Being*, ed. Sally Fitzgerald (New York: Farrar, Straus & Giroux, 1979), 83.

6. Ibid.

7. Flannery O'Connor, *Wise Blood* (New York: New American Library, 1964), 90.

8. O'Connor, *Wise Blood*, 90.

9. Beth Dawkins Bassett, "Converging Lives," *Emory Magazine* 58, no. 4 (April 1982): 18.

10. Quoted ibid., 19.

11. Stanley Edgar Hyman, *Flannery O'Connor* (Minneapolis: University of Minnesota Press, 1966), 40.

12. Ibid., 46.

13. Flannery O'Connor, "A Good Man Is Hard To Find," in *A Good Man Is Hard To Find* (New York: Harcourt, Brace, 1955), 28–29.

14. Flannery O'Connor, "Revelation," in *Everything That Rises Must Converge* (New York: Farrar, Straus & Giroux, 1965), 217.

15. Flannery O'Connor, *The Violent Bear It Away* (New York: Farrar, Straus & Cudahy, 1960), 157.

16. Ibid., 242.

17. Ibid., 243.

18. See Ted R. Spivey, "Flannery O'Connor: Georgia's Theological Storyteller," in *The Humanities in the Contemporary South* (Atlanta: Georgia State College, 1968).

19. O'Connor, *The Lame Shall Enter First*, 188.

20. Ibid., 190.

21. Robert Drake, *Flannery O'Connor* (Grand Rapids, Mich.: William B. Erdmans, 1966), 19.

22. Sally Fitzgerald, "Introduction," *Flannery O'Connor: The Habit of Being*, xviii.

23. Drake, *Flannery O'Connor*, 21.

24. O'Connor, "A Good Man Is Hard To Find," 21.

25. Lewis P. Simpson, *The Brazen Face of History*, 263.

26. Frederick Asals, *Flannery O'Connor: The Imagination of Extremity* (Athens: University of Georgia Press, 1982), 255.

Chapter 9: Walker Percy

1. Lewis P. Simpson, *The Brazen Face of History* (Baton Rouge: Louisiana State University Press, 1980), 246.

2. Ibid., 249.

3. Ashley Brown, "An Interview with Walker Percy," *Shenandoah* 18 (Spring 1967): 7.

4. Ibid.

5. Robert Coles, *Walker Percy: An American Search* (Boston: Little, Brown, 1978). See particularly the chapters dealing with Percy's extensive reading.

6. Walker Percy, "Symbol as Need," in *The Message in the Bottle* (New York: Farrar, Straus & Giroux, 1979), 290.

7. Jay P. Telotte, "Walker Percy: A Pragmatic Approach," *Southern Studies* 18 (Summer 1979): 230.

8. Ibid.

9. Patricia Dixon Carroll Bowden, "'The It and the Doing': Sacramental Word and Deed in the Writings of Walker Percy" (Master's thesis, Georgia State University, 1980), 3.

10. Quoted by E. F. Schumaker in *A Guide for the Perplexed* (New York: Harper and Row, 1977), 129.

11. Walker Percy, "Questions They Never Asked Me: A Self-Interview," *Esquire*, December 1977, 193.

12. Walker Percy, "Southern Comfort," *Harper's*, January 1979, 82.

13. Walter Kaufmann, *Existentialism from Dostoevsky to Sartre* (New York: Meridian Books, 1956), 11.

14. F. H. Heinemann, *Existentialism and the Modern Predicament* (New York: Harper and Brothers, 1958), 13.

15. Quoted ibid., 204.

16. Percy, "Notes for a Novel about the End of the World," in *The Message in the Bottle* (New York: Farrar, Straus, & Giroux, 1979), 113.

17. Denis J. Fodor, *World War II: The Neutrals* (New York: Time-Life Books, 1982), 8.

18. Percy, "Notes for a Novel about the End of the World," 113.

19. Ibid., 118.

20. Walker Percy, *The Moviegoer* (New York: Alfred A. Knopf, 1961), 13–14.

21. Ibid., 146.

22. Janet Hobbs, "Binx Bolling and the Stages on Life's Way," in *The Art of Walker Percy*, ed. Panthea Reid Broughton (Baton Rouge: Louisiana State University Press, 1979), 48.

23. Walker Percy, *The Last Gentleman* (New York: Farrar, Straus & Giroux, 1966), 161.

24. Brown, "An Interview with Walker Percy," 7.

25. Percy, "The Mystery of Language," in *The Message in the Bottle* (New York: Farrar, Straus, & Giroux, 1979), 158.

26. Ibid.

27. Percy, "Culture: Autonomy of Scientific Method," in *The Message in the Bottle* (New York: Farrar, Straus, & Giroux), 242.

28. Walker Percy, *Love in the Ruins* (New York: Farrar, Straus & Giroux, 1971), 246.

29. Cleanth Brooks, "Walker Percy and Modern Gnosticism," in *The Art*

of Walker Percy, ed. Panthea R. Broughton (Louisiana State University Press, 1979), 269.

30. Simpson, *The Brazen Face of History,* 254.

31. Lewis A. Lawson, "The Fall of the House of Lamar," in *The Art of Walker Percy,* 243.

32. Walker Percy to Ted R. Spivey, October 29, 1979.

33. Ibid.

34. Walker Percy, *The Second Coming* (New York: Farrar, Straus & Giroux, 1980), 108.

35. Ibid., 360.

36. Walker Percy, "Southern Comfort," 83.

37. Ibid., 81.

38. Ibid., 79.

39. Ibid., 83.

Epilogue

1. Theodore H. White, *In Search of History* (New York: Harper and Row, 1978), 538.

2. C. G. Jung, *The Undiscovered Self* (New York: New American Library, 1959), 122–23.

3. Ibid., 123.

Index